D0024097

Latin American Studies from Zed Books

Zed Books publishes on international and Third World issues. In addition to our general lists on economics, development, the environment, gender and politics, we also publish area studies in the fields of African Studies, Asian and Pacific Studies, Latin American and Caribbean Studies, and Middle East Studies. Our Latin American titles include:

Frederique Apffel-Marglin with PRATEC (eds), *The Spirit of Regeneration: Andean Culture Confronting Western Notions of Development*

Susan Bassnett (ed.), *Knives and Angels: Women Writers in Latin America*

Cristovam Buarque, *The End of Economics? Ethics and the Disorder of Progress*

Raff Carmen and Miguel Sobrado (eds), *Capacity Building and the Poor: An Introduction to Latin American Approaches to Urban and Rural Development*

Jacques M. Chevalier and Daniel Buckles, *A Land Without Gods: Process Theory, Maldevelopment and the Mexican Nahuas*

Catherine Davies (ed.), *A Place in the Sun? Women Writers in Twentieth Century Cuba*

Gustavo Esteva and Madhu Suri Prakash, *Grassroots Post-Modernism: Remaking the Soil of Cultures*

Stefano Harney, *Nationalism and Identity: Culture and the Imagination in a Caribbean Diaspora*

Clare Hargreaves, *Snowfields: The War on Cocaine in the Andes*

Elizabeth Jelin (ed.), *Women and Social Change in Latin America*

Michael Kaufman and Alfonso Dilla (eds), *Community Power and Grassroots Democracy: The Transformation of Social Life*

Kees Koonings and Dirk Kruijt (eds), *Societies of Fear: The Legacy of Civil War, Violence and Terror in Latin America*

Peter Mayo, *Gramsci, Freire and Adult Education: Possibilities for Transformative Action*

Ronaldo Munck, *Latin America: The Transition to Democracy*

Rhoda E. Reddock, *Women, Labour and Politics in Trinidad and Tobago*

Oscar Ugarteche, *The False Dilemma: Is Globalization the Only Choice?*

Bill Weinberg, *War on the Land: Ecology and Politics in Central America*

For full details of this list and Zed's other subject and general catalogues, please write to: The Marketing Department, Zed Books, 7 Cynthia Street, London N1 9JF, UK or email: sales@zedbooks.demon.co.uk

Visit our website at: http://www.zedbooks.demon.co.uk

Miraculous Metamorphoses

The Neoliberalization of Latin American Populism

EDITED BY JOLLE DEMMERS,
ALEX E. FERNÁNDEZ JILBERTO AND
BARBARA HOGENBOOM

Zed Books

LONDON • NEW YORK

Miraculous Metamorphoses: The Neoliberalization of Latin American Populism was first published by Zed Books Ltd, 7 Cynthia Street, London N1 9JF, UK and Room 400, 175 Fifth Avenue, New York, NY 10010, USA in 2001.

Distributed in the USA exclusively by Palgrave, a division of St Martin's Press, LLC, 175 Fifth Avenue, New York, NY 10010, USA.

Cover designed by Andrew Corbett
Set in Monotype Garamond by Ewan Smith, London
Printed and bound in Malaysia

A catalogue record for this book is available from the British Library

Library of Congress Cataloging-in-Publication-Data has been applied for

ISBN 1 85649 886 7 cased
ISBN 1 85649 887 5 limp

Contents

Tables and Figures

Tables

Figures

About the Contributors

KEES BIEKART is a fellow of the Amsterdam-based Transnational Institute (TNI), where he has coordinated research programmes on Central America and democratization. His most recent publications include *Compassion and Calculation: The Business of Private Foreign Aid* (London: Pluto 1996) and *The Politics of Civil Society Building: European Private Aid Agencies and Democratic Transitions in Central America* (Utrecht: International Books 1998).

JEAN CARRIÈRE, MA (McGill), PhD (London School of Economics), works at the Centre for Latin American Research and Documentation (CEDLA), in Amsterdam. His research focuses on the connection between neoliberalism and ecologically sustainable development in Latin America.

JOLLE DEMMERS studied Political Science and International Relations at the University of Amsterdam and conducted her PhD research at Utrecht University. She currently works at the Department of Cultural Anthropology and the Centre for Conflict Studies at the same university. She is the author of *Friends and Bitter Enemies: Politics and Neoliberal Reform in Yucatán, Mexico* (Amsterdam: Thela Thesis, 1998).

ALEX E. FERNÁNDEZ JILBERTO is senior lecturer in International Relations at the University of Amsterdam. He has published various articles and books on the political economy of Latin America and Third World countries in general. His most recent publications include (with André Mommen) *Regionalization and Globalization in the Modern World Economy: Perspectives on the Third World and Transitional Economies* (London: Routledge 1998) and 'The Political Economy of Open Regionalism in Latin America' (edited with Barbara Hogenboom), *International Journal of Political Economy*, vol. 26, no. 3 (New York: M.E. Sharpe, 1997).

BARBARA HOGENBOOM is a fellow of the Wiardi Beckman Foundation in Amsterdam. She has published on transnational politics, financial liberalization, and regionalization and neoliberal restructuring in Latin America. She is author of *Mexico and the NAFTA Environment Debate: The Transnational Politics of Economic Integration* (Utrecht: International Books, 1998), for which she received the Award for the Best Dutch Political Science Dissertation of the year 1998.

KARLA LEMANSKI-VALENTE is currently working as an independent consultant and continuing her studies on international trade and commerce at the University of California, Los Angeles. She received her MA from the University of Amsterdam, and has a law degree from Brazil.

GIUSEPPE SOLFRINI is a political anthropologist (University of Bologna) and PhD candidate at the Department of International Relations of the University of Amsterdam. He was a research fellow at the Instituto de Estudios Peruano in Lima.

MIGUEL TEUBAL is professor of economics at the University of Buenos Aires and researcher at the National Council of Scientific and Technological Research (CONICET) in the Center for Advanced Studies at the same university. He has published articles and books on the political economy of food, agriculture and poverty in Latin America and Argentina. Recent work includes *Globalización y expansión agroindustrial. Superación de la pobreza en América Latina?* (Buenos Aires: Ediciones Corregidor, 1995); *Teoria, estructuras y procesos económicos*, a collection of essays in honor of Dr Julio H. G. Olivera and *Globalización: efectos sobre las sociedades rurales de América Latina*. He has also contributed chapters to the recent books edited by Alex E. Fernández Jilberto and André Mommen.

Preface

A ghost is haunting Latin America. During the transition from the twentieth to the twenty-first century, this pronouncement of Venezuela's populist president Hugo Chávez resonated throughout the region. By using what sounds a lot like the famous first sentence from the first Communist Manifesto to describe the current Latin American situation, Chávez was warning the world of the anger of the millions of *latinos* who are tired of their poverty and the corrupt governments of their countries. It seems that the unexpected successful neoliberalization of Latin American populism is now facing the more problematic results of its own ambiguities.

During the last two decades of the twentieth century, Latin America experienced a process of deep economic, social, political and institutional restructuring, the extent of which can only be compared to the regional impact of the international crisis of the 1930s. The programmes of stabilization and structural adjustment brought an end to Latin America's capitalist structures, which were based on the state regulation of the economy that had dominated in the post-war era. The model of import substitution industrialization that prevailed in Latin America during this phase was presented by populist governments as a third way between capitalism and socialism. The substitution of this model was implemented by violent military dictatorships, in particular in the Southern Cone. They disarmed the populist Utopia with blood and fire, and more or less gradually imposed neoliberal policies. When in the final stages of these dictatorships the transition to democracy was debated, one of the major dilemmas for populist parties was whether democratization would have to remain limited to the replacement of the authoritarian political regime, or whether it also implicated the replacement of the neoliberal economic policies.

The outcome of the democratization processes of the 1980s in Latin America was a continuity of neoliberal policy. While the political regime transformed, and populist parties regained strength, strong presidentialism – a regional characteristic that was only intensified in the authoritarian period – remained as well. Even in countries that had not suffered under military dictatorships, this mix of neoliberalism and presidentialism occurred. The end of socialism in Eastern Europe, and the Latin American debates on globalization and 'open regionalism', enforced the neoliberalization of its populist parties. The Argentinian 'Menemism', the Concertación para la Democracia of Chile, the Cardoso regime in Brazil, the *caudillismo* of Fujimori in Peru, the PRI in Mexico, to name a few, are all representative of the new regional political disposition. This neoliberal populism considers it essential to reconcile the state and the economy with transnational capital in order to take part in globalization. In addition, this strategy is perceived as a means to ensure populists their political legitimacy, by preventing the economic inefficiencies of prior state interventionism, even though a weakened state may be unable to develop the economic sectors in which there is no direct corporate interest. Latin America's neoliberal populists have thus implemented radical and aggressive programmes of privatization, deregulation and economic opening to the world market, while abandoning the system of fixed exchange rates pegging the local currency to the dollar. Based on these programmes, during the 1990s Latin America temporarily achieved some 'economic miracles', while simultaneously economic inequalities, poverty and the informalization of the economy increased.

The success of the populists' new economic policy, and their hopes of accelerating growth through regionalization (NAFTA and Mercosur), however, received serious warnings with the Mexican peso crisis in 1994–95 and Brazil's currency crisis in 1999. Infected by the financial crises in East Asia, the devaluation of the Brazilian *real* profoundly destabilized the whole of Mercosur. This has reopened the debate on dollarization (substitution of national currencies by the US dollar) of the Latin American economy, especially in Argentina, Mexico, Peru and Ecuador. Moreover, the debate on the potential of neoliberal policy has been reopened too. Latin America as a whole has passed through a problematic 'pause' in the inflow of international capital since the beginning of the problems in Asia, as foreign investors have seriously reconsidered the risks and benefits of investing in the region. Evidently, part of the miracles of the early 1990s were based on the speculative bubble that was a result of the Washington Consensus (macroeconomic stability and sound money as the main ingredients for growth), rather than on a stable foundation for growth. Whether Latin America's populist parties will be the ones that will learn the lessons from the disillusions of neoliberal restructuring, and will continue to be the major political force in the region, remains to be seen.

Like all books, this one has its own history. It started from the fascination of our co-authors and ourselves with the transformation of Latin American populism and its electoral success. The fact that, apart from many differences in the current history of the various countries of the region, there are several important similarities in the political and policy changes that have occurred over the past two and a half decades cried out for a critical regional analysis. Building on previous 'transnational' research projects on issues such as liberalization in developing countries and the linkages between regionalization and globalization, we found a group of Latin America experts willing to write about the political, economic and social dimensions of the neoliberalization of Latin American populism. These researchers come from different countries, different intellectual generations and different academic positions in institutions in Latin America and Europe. From their diverse perspectives, they share a critical vision towards the social implications of the neoliberal policies of Latin America's new democracies. Without the authors' profound knowledge of the region and their intellectual dedication to understanding its current transformation processes this book would not have been possible.

Jolle Demmers, Alex E. Fernández Jilberto
and Barbara Hogenboom

Abbreviations

AD	Democratic Alliance (Chile)
AP	Popular Action (Peru)
APRA	Revolutionary American Popular Alliance (Peru)
ARENA	National Republican Alliance (El Salvador)
ARI	Left Revolutionary Alliance (Peru)
ARS	Socialist Revolutionary Action (Chile)
BI	Left Wing Bloc (Chile)
BIS	Bank of International Settlements
BPR	Revolutionary Popular Bloc (El Salvador)
CARICOM	Economic Community of the Caribbean
CD	Democratic Current (Mexico)
CGE	General Economic Federation (Argentina)
CGT	General Confederation of Labour (Argentina)
CNI	Confederation of Indigenous Nationalities of Ecuador
CONICET	National Council of Scientific and Technical Research
CTCh	Chilean Workers' Centre
CUC	Committee of Workers' Unity (Guatemala)
CUT	United Workers Central (Chile)
DC	Christian Democratic Party (Chile)
ECLAC	Economic Commission for Latin America and the Caribbean (UN)
EGP	Guerrilla Army of the Poor (Guatemala)
ERP	People's Revolutionary Army (El Salvador)
FAPU	United Popular Action Front (El Salvador)
FAR	Rebellious Armed Forces (Guatemala)
FDNG	Guatemalan National Democratic Front
FMLM	Farabundo Martí National Liberation Front
FNL	National Liberation Front (Chile)
FOCEP	Worker, Peasant, Student and Popular Front (Peru)
FP	Popular Front (Chile)

FPL	Popular Liberation Forces (El Salvador)
FRAP	Popular Action Front (Chile)
FREDEMO	Democratic Front (Peru)
FSLN	Sandinista National Liberation Front (Nicaragua)
FT	Workers' Front (Chile)
FTAA	Free Trade Agreement of the Americas
GATT	General Agreement on Tariffs and Trade
GDP	gross domestic product
IAPI	Argentine Institute of Trade Promotion
IC	Communist Left (Chile)
IDB	International Development Bank
IEPES	Institute of Political, Economic and Social Studies (Mexico)
ILO	International Labour Organization
IMF	International Monetary Fund
IS	Socialist Left (Peru)
ISI	import substitution industrialization
IU	United Left (Peru)
MCCA	Central American Common Market
MDI	Democratic Movement of the Left (Peru)
Mercosur	Mercado Común del Sur (Common Market of the South)
MIR	Movement of the Revolutionary Left (Chile)
MPR	United Popular Movement (Nicaragua)
MRS	Socialist Recovering Movement (Chile)
MRS	Renovated Sandinista Movement (Nicaragua)
NAFTA	North American Free Trade Agreement
NAP	New Public Action (Chile)
OLAS	Latin American Organization for Solidarity
ORPA	Organization of the People in Arms (Guatemala)
OS	Socialist Order (Chile)
PAN	National Action Party (Mexico)
PARM	Authentic Party of the Mexican Revolution
PCCh	Communist Party of Chile
PCP	Peruvian Communist Party
PD	Democratic Party (El Salvador)
PDP	Popular Democratic Party (Chile)
PECE	Pact for Stability and Economic Growth (Mexico)
PGT	Guatemalan Workers' Party
PLN	National Liberation Party (Costa Rica)
PNR	Revolutionary National Party (Mexico)
PPC	Popular Christian Party (Peru)
PPS	Socialist Popular Party (Mexico)

PR	Radical Party (Chile)
PRD	Party of the Democratic Revolution (Mexico)
PRI	Institutional Revolutionary Party (Mexico)
PRONASOL	National Solidarity Programme (Mexico)
PRTC	Central American Revolutionary Workers' Party
PSCh	Socialist Party of Chile
PSE	Economic Solidarity Pact (Mexico)
PSOE	Spanish Socialist Workers Party
PSP	Socialist Popular Party (Chile)
PST	Socialist Workers' Party (Chile)
PSU	Unified Socialist Party (Chile)
PVP	Popular Vanguard Party (Costa Rica)
PUM	Unified Mariateguist Party (Peru)
SI	Second International
SL	Shining Path (Peru)
SNA	National Society of Agriculture (Chile)
SOFOFA	Society for the Promotion of Industry (Chile)
SPD	Social Democratic Party (West Germany)
TF	Third Front (Chile)
TNI	Transnational Institute
UCR	Radical Civic Union (Argentina)
UCRI	Intransigent Radical Civic Union (Argentina)
UDR	Democratic Rural Union (Brazil)
UNCTAD	United Nations Conference on Trade and Development
UP	Popular Unity (Chile)
UPP	Union for Peru
URNG	Guatemalan National Revolutionary Party

ONE

The Transformation of Latin American Populism: Regional and Global Dimensions

JOLLE DEMMERS, ALEX E. FERNÁNDEZ JILBERTO
AND BARBARA HOGENBOOM

Over the past two decades, Latin American populist parties have changed beyond recognition. Latin American populism was long synonymous with Keynesian policies of import substitution and redistribution. From the early 1980s onwards, however, populist parties and their leaders have adopted neoliberal notions and policies. This transition is remarkable for two reasons. First, notwithstanding the long and troublesome process many populist parties in Latin America have been through, populism and neoliberalism got along rather well. While they are often perceived as natural antagonists, their cross-breeding was more than a 'marriage of convenience'. Second, despite 'un-popular' policies and major ideological twists, a large share of Latin America's populist parties regained or continued to be in power.

Scholars of Latin American politics did not foresee this successful trans-formation. Populism, as it emerged and gained influence from the 1940s onwards, was generally identified with a 'socialist' political agenda, and populist parties were expected to lose much of their support in the neoliberal era. The fact that Latin American populism changed from 'classic' into 'neoliberal' shows that previous theories and analyses were partly misconceived. Therefore, a re-examination of the nature of populism in Latin America is needed. How can we account for the 'neoliberalization' of Latin American populism? How did populist parties 'survive' the shift to neoliberalism of the 1980s and 1990s?

This book will explore the transformation of populism in Latin America. It aims to study both the theoretical and empirical dimension of this change. Bringing together a large variety of case-studies, ranging from Mexico, Central America to the Cono Sur, this volume is among the first coherent con-tributions to this field of study. As with any concept, the notion of Latin American (neo)populism stands a risk of simplifying the divergent national cases. Fortunately, the chapters on the changes in eleven Latin American countries serve as a hedge against this risk, and provide ample information on the *couleur local* of neopopulism. Although primarily focused on Latin America, this introductory chapter aims to place the process of Latin America's 'neoliberalization' within an international context. In the following pages, the 'Latin American case' will be repeatedly linked to developments and processes elsewhere. Both the rise of 'classic populism' and the emergence of 'neo-populism' in Latin America were closely linked to international developments in the economic, political and ideological domains. In both transformation processes, a severe economic and financial crisis played a key role, functioning as the turning point in a pendulum motion. Not only had the cause of the crisis of the 1980s major global components, but the subsequent transforma-tion of Latin American populism was conditioned by changing international circumstances. As a result, Latin America's neoliberal transformation process bears a certain resemblance to global trends.

In this introductory chapter we will address the following issues. First, we will look into the historical and doctrinal roots of Latin American populism and its links with the socialist international. Next, we will assess the shift to neoliberalism and the emergence of neopopulist regimes. Finally, we will discuss the current Latin American situation from a global perspective.

The Doctrinal and Historical Roots of Latin American Populism

DEFINING POPULISM: ECONOMIC AND POLITICAL NOTIONS The term populism is defined in various ways. Much of the discussion – and confusion – surrounding populism stems from the discrepancy between (a) scholars who see populism primarily as an *economic* model, closely linked to import substitution and Keynesianism (e.g. Dornbusch and Edwards 1991; Kaufman and Stalling 1991), and (b) authors who apply a *political* notion of populism (e.g. Weyland 1996). It is important to distinguish between these notions, since they influence the recent discussion on the 'survival of populism' and 'neopopulism' in neoliberal times. This section will first briefly discuss the economic and political notions of populism. We will then look into Latin America's 'populist past', that is, the period of 'classic populism' (1930s–1960s) and 'late populism' (1970s–1980s). In the next section we will look into the neoliberal transformation of the 1980s and 1990s and the impact of these changes on populism and populist parties.

Both liberal economists (Sachs 1989; Dornbusch and Edwards 1991) and scholars drawing on dependency theory (e.g. Cardoso and Faletto 1979) primarily associate populism with economics. Populism is closely related to the early stage of import substitution industrialization (ISI), when economic growth allowed Latin American political leaders to attract a large following by enacting mass-incorporating, moderately distributive policies. Dornbusch and Edwards (1991: 9), for instance, see this *redistributive objective* as the central part of the populist paradigm. They understand populism as '*an approach to economics* that emphasises growth and income redistribution and de-emphasises the risks of inflation and deficit finance, external constraints, and the reaction of economic agents to aggressive nonmarket policies' (emphasis added). Taking a strong anti-populist stand the authors claim that populist policies do ultimately fail, always most hurting those groups that they were supposed to protect. They distinguish four phases of populist economics, the final phase often being the total collapse and destruction of the economy and, consequently, the implementation of orthodox stabilization programmes under a *new* government.

Kaufman and Stalling (1991: 16) apply a somewhat less strict 'economic' interpretation of populism. They define it as involving a set of *economic policies* designed to achieve specific *political goals*. Those political goals are '(1) mobilising support within organised labour and lower-middle-class groups; (2) obtaining complementary backing from domestically oriented businesses; and (3) politically isolating the rural oligarchy, foreign enterprises, and large-scale domestic industrial elites'. The economic policies to attain these goals include, but were not limited to: (1) budget deficits to stimulate domestic demand; (2) nominal wage increases plus price controls to effect income distribution; (3) exchange-rate control or appreciation to cut inflation and to raise wages and profits in non-traded-goods sectors.

Drake (1982: 218) defines populism in much broader (and more political) terms. In this definition three elements are stressed:

> (1) populism uses political mobilization, recurrent rhetoric and symbols designed to inspire the people; (2) it draws on a heterogeneous coalition aimed primarily at the working class, but including and led by significant sectors from the middle and upper strata; and (3) populism has connoted a reformats set of policies tailored to promote development without explosive class conflict. (P)rograms normally respond to the problems of underdevelopment by expanding state activism to incorporate the workers in a process of accelerated industrialisation through ameliorative redistributive measures.

Weyland (1996: 4–5) takes this idea a step further. Where Drake still relates populism to an expansion of state activism, Weyland strips populism of any specific socioeconomic characteristics. Weyland clearly applies a *political* notion of populism. He defines populism as:

> a political strategy with three characteristics: a personal leader appeals to the heterogeneous mass of followers, many of whom have been excluded from the mainstream of development, yet are now available for mobilisation; the leader reaches the followers in a seemingly direct, quasi-personal manner that largely bypasses established intermediary organisations, such as parties and interest associations; if the leader builds new organisations or revives earlier

populist organisations, they remain personal vehicles with low levels of in-
stitutionalisation.

Weyland states that populism varies, depending on its primary mass constituency. Populist leaders try to strategically attract those social sectors that they
consider most suited for populist mobilization. In this sense, populism is first
and foremost a political strategy: socioeconomic characteristics can be added
to this political concept in order to distinguish different types of populism.

We thus see that populism is understood and defined in rather diverse
terms, ranging from 'economic policy' to 'political strategy'. In the following
section on neoliberal transformation we will again address the diverse views
on populism and discuss their explanatory power. First, however, we look
into Latin America's 'populist experience'.

LATIN AMERICAN POPULISM The disruptions of international trade by
the First World War and the shock of the Great Depression of 1929 paved
the way for the formation of influential new development doctrines in Latin
America. In the aftermath of these shocks, discontent with *laisser-faire*
economics and with exclusionary political systems swept the region. The
oligarchic, export-oriented regimes, which had laid the base for national state
formation during the early nineteenth century, and had created the *estado
oligárquico* (supported by the mining and *latifundista* oligarchy), faced a fourfold
crisis of growth, distribution, participation and legitimization. This gave room
to the rise of populist regimes, emphasizing inward-oriented strategies for
development, industrialization, state welfare, worker mobilization and mass
support for the government. The 'classic' populist regimes that emerged
after the Depression were known for both their anti-oligarchy and anti-
communist tendencies and were represented by administrations such as that
of Lázaro Cárdenas in Mexico (1934–40), Juan Domingo Perón in Argentina
(1946–55 and 1973–74), Getulio Vargas in Brazil (1930–45 and 1951–54), José
Maria Velasco Ibarra in Ecuador (1944–47), the APRA of Victor Haya de la
Torre in Peru (founded in 1924) and Victor Paz Estenssoro in Bolivia (1952–
56; 1960–64).

From the 1930s to the 1960s, 'classic' populism was the predominant
arrangement in Latin America. An important characteristic of the classic
populist regimes was their shared ideal of a strong and interventionist state.
Economically, this was reflected in the support for a model of development
based on import subtitution industrialization. Latin American populist regimes
adopted Keynesian economic policies, resulting in state capitalist promotion
and urban welfare. Economic populism was characterized by state control
(nationalization) of the export sector, particularly prime commodities, with
the objective of strengthening capital accumulation. In addition, state intervention was aimed at the redistribution of income in order to improve
domestic consumption (particularly in the urban areas) and to diminish social

inequalities through the provision of free education and social health services.

Politically, mass incorporation, redistribution and elite leadership were important elements of populism. Because of their policy of industrialization, populist parties could easily mobilize and incorporate previously marginal lower-class groups, particularly urban workers. Rhetorical references to 'The People' and 'The Nation' served to avoid alienating other social sectors, such as peasants. Apart from 'state centrality', strong charismatic leadership and a political culture of personalism were important elements of classic populism. 'More than the alleged "irrationality of the masses" what was behind the emergence of populist leadership – identified by the excluded as their "father" and saviour – was still the dominant logic of personalism' (Alvarez et al. 1998: 10). Populist regimes relied on elite leadership and coalitions, especially from industrialists, the middle class and intellectuals.

During the 1960s, populism waned in many Latin American countries. The relatively easy stage of import substitution, that is, the substitution of manufactured consumer goods from abroad, was exhausted. As economic resources tightened, demands for incorporation and redistribution from various groups (migrants, peasants) increased. The high level of inflation and economic decline laid bare the internal contradictions of the populist model of accumulation. In several countries, the tension between capital accumulation on the one hand, and redistribution policies on the other, led to the unravelling of populist coalitions. The *estado populista* was criticized from various sides. Rightist groups derided populists as demagogues who spurred excessive mass expectations and inflations. Simultaneously, more radical social movements – heavily influenced by the Cuban Revolution of 1959 – denounced populists as 'charlatans who duped the workers into settling for reform instead of revolution' (Drake 1991: 39).

During the 1970s and 1980s, various Latin American countries experimented with different forms of populism. Presidents such as Luis Echeverría in Mexico (1970–76) and Alan García in Peru (1985–90) tried to overcome economic decline by the continuation of import substitution and the provision of benefits to a wide range of social groups. Likewise, Raúl Alfonsín (Argentina: 1983–89) and José Sarney in Brazil (1985–90) refused to solve the economic crisis by imposing costs on important sectors. However, they failed to fight the causes of inflation, such as large fiscal deficits, which were deepened by the drain on public resources caused by service on the huge external debt. High inflation, price explosions and economic decline soon wrecked the Latin American economies and undermined support for these 'late' populist governments.

During the 1980s and 1990s most Latin American countries made the shift to a neoliberal model of development. Import substitution and state interventionist programmes long associated with populist governments made way for neoliberal economic formulas. The shift to neoliberalism was by no means an exclusively Latin American affair. In the West, the rise of the New

Right, of 'Thatcherism' and 'Reaganomics' and the conservative and liberal critique on the post-war Keynesian social democracy laid the base for the neoliberal critique on import substitution. Before we discuss Latin America's neoliberal transformation, which took place in the context of this global shift of paradigm, we will first look into the history of the international political embeddedness and isolation of Latin American populist parties.

Latin America and the Socialist International

Populist parties have often been characterized as the Latin American version of social democracy, to a certain extent rightly so. This characterization, however, should not conceal the fundamental differences between the two, for the reason of which the label 'social democratic' does not seem to fit Latin American populist parties very well. Historically, socialism emerged in Europe as an answer to industrial capitalism and aimed to mobilize the industrial proletariat. While sharing views on the importance of income distribution and a strong state with European social democrats, Latin America's populist parties developed prior to the process of industrialization, and aimed to be the motor of this process. Nevertheless, for populist parties the most natural allies outside the region seemed to be social democratic parties in Europe. As the other chapters focus on the national political roles of Latin American populist parties, we will here consider their rather complicated international relations a little further since they help to better understand the nature and development of populism in Latin America.

The lack of a 'natural' constituency of workers plays a central role in the distinct political development of Latin American populism. The major Latin American populist parties (e.g. Venezuela's Acción Democrática, Peru's APRA, Mexico's PRI and Chile's Partido Socialista) have never been authentic social democratic parties. Rather than referring to socialism, their identity was built on references to The People and/or The Nation. Their political linkages with the state apparatus have traditionally been stronger than those with labour unions. Popular support has been primarily obtained through *caudillismo* (strong charismatic leadership) and clientelism.

To a certain extent, these contrasts with key European views of citizenship and democracy are also the result of Latin America's political culture, of which some elements may be traced back to the indigenous background and to the colonization of the region (cf. Demmers 1998). At the national level, *caudillismo* is manifested in the tendency of governing populist parties to give preference to the presidency and the executive power, which is often combined with authoritarian forms of domination. Meanwhile, large bureaucracies serve as the primary links of the clientelist relations between populist parties in power and their constituencies. In addition, these bureaucracies are a clientelist mechanism in themselves, for a long time functioning as the major employer of the middle class.

The different nature of Latin American populism and European Social Democracy only partly explains the difficulty of establishing feasible relations. The discrepancy of the slogan 'Proletarians of all Countries become United' and the practice of international solidarity has a long history. After the internationalism of the early European socialist movement, with its institutionalization it became increasingly focused on internal (national) affairs. Both the First International (1864–76) and the Second International (1889–1914) hardly touched upon the non-Western world, which was perceived as an issue of second order that would have to wait for the victory of socialism in the West (Van Doorn 1999: 486). Contrary to the idea of solidarity, a strong current within the Second International justified colonial rule and suppression of independence movements in the name of civilization. The Latin American answer to this lack of genuine solidarity came in the interbellum period. Influenced by the Russian revolution, the overall majority of Latin America's populist parties entered the Communist International, which had taken a fierce anti-imperialist position (Lowy 1984: 282). The understanding between Latin American populists and communists on this point, and the fact that the first distanced themselves from European socialist parties, reinforced the weakness of worldwide socialist relations.

After the Second World War, in the era of decolonization, the Socialist International's interest in linking up with counterparts in the Third World increased. The rapidly fading colonial relations of European countries diminished the ambiguity of the social democrats' international position, which had stemmed from the tension between nationalist colonial interests and internationalist socialist orientation. Simultaneously, however, the Pax Americana and the Cold War became new sources of discord and tension. From the Latin American perspective, the SI had too much of an Atlantist and anti-Soviet orientation.[1] Europe's perception of the USA as its ally and benefactor clashed with the *latino* perception of the USA as enemy and exploiter. The fact that the SI did not react to the US invasion in Guatemala in 1954 proved to Latin Americans that European social democrats still did not support their anti-imperialist struggles. In this context, the SI decided to set up a secretariat for Latin America. Although the SI attempted to attract more Latin American interest for this regional secretariat by not requesting alliance to the SI itself, by demanding an anti-communist declaration at a time of deepening Latin American anti-imperialism (Salvador Allende's presidential candidacy in 1958 and the Cuban revolution in 1959), the project was bound to fail.

On other levels, however, mutual acknowledgement of Latin American populist parties and European social democratic parties was enhanced by growing similarity in the course of political and economic developments. In both regions, these parties had obtained mass support and government experience. Furthermore, in both regions they aimed to pursue a distinct course in between US capitalism and Soviet communism. Supported by international Keynesianism, the 'third ways' of import substitution industrialization (Latin America) and a mixed economy (Europe) were put into practice, initially with great economic and political success.

During the 1970s the relation between Latin American and Western social democracy finally improved. Various political changes motivated another attitude of European social democrats. First, Europeans were concerned over the proliferation of military dictatorship in Latin America. With Augusto Pinochet's coup against the government of Salvador Allende in 1973 in Chile as the internationally most visible case, European social democrats aimed to support democratic parties in Latin America. Second, next to solidarity there was also a dose of political self-interest involved. Latin American nationalism had created considerable international tensions through its major influence in formulating the demands of Third World countries in fora of the United Nations (including UNCTAD), in particular with the call for a New International Economic Order. Third, the collapse of Portuguese colonialism in Africa, the arrival of Soviet and Cuban military specialists on this continent, and the election of Fidel Castro as president of the Organization of Non-Allied Countries in 1979 all together contributed to a growing sense within the USA and Europe that the Third World was becoming ungovernable (Evers 1993: 46). As the second and third motivations demonstrate, the SI partly intended to influence the role of Latin America in the group of Third World countries in favour of European and US interests.

The enhanced European interest in Latin America was not only political; economic motives played some role as well. It was no coincidence that the first contacts of the SI with Latin America in the 1970s were with Mexico and Venezuela, the largest oil exporting countries of the continent. In 1974 oil prices reached a historical height and diversification of oil-resources was deemed of utmost importance to Europe. Of a more long-term interest was the continuation and extension of trade. During the 1970s (and even more the 1980s), European trade with Latin America weakened as a result of the international economic crisis, whereas US trade with and investment in the region were further strengthened. Part of the SI 'offensive' in Latin America can thus be explained as an attempt to bring about change in the historical US domination over the continent. Taken together, Europe's social democracy had ample political and economic reasons for its wish to become the 'third power' in Latin America.

Social democrats from West Germany, Sweden, Spain and Portugal worked most actively on reviving relations with Latin America. German Chancellor Willy Brandt internationally pleaded for an alternative between authoritarianism and communism in Latin America, and his SPD started to support political and human rights organizations fighting for the restoration of democracy. This support revived the idea that the social democracy would favour new democratic perspectives for those countries suffering from US hegemony. The Swedish position was more progressive and less linked to the interests of European capitalism. Prime Minister Olof Palme's visit to Cuba in 1975 and the Palme doctrine, which aimed at cooperation between developed and developing small states in the Cold War era, were important factors in a changing attitude of Europe towards the Western Hemisphere (Petras 1980). The European dismissal of the US role in the crisis and civil war in Central America marked this changing attitude. The democratization processes in Spain and Portugal allowed the Spanish PSOE and the Portuguese Partido Socialista to recapture a position of intermediary between Latin America and the SI. Their anti-communist and Atlantist accents functioned as a counter-weight to the more radical Swedish and German positions (Alcantara Sez 1993: 104). SI meetings between European and Latin American parties demonstrated that the mutual rediscovery was not without tensions.[2]

The impact of the overture of Latin American populists and European social democrats in the late 1970s was severely limited by the major global shifts taking off in that same period. For both sides, cooperation had raised expectations of the economic viability of international Keynesianism, although in Europe the first steps had already been taken towards combining Keynesian policy with an opening towards international capital. The debt crisis that started in Mexico in 1982 ended the hopes of a restoration of Keynesian policy. Politically, during the 1980s Europe played a relevant role in the evolution of Central American conflict resolution, and the democratization processes in the Southern Cone (Biekart 1999). With respect to socioeconomic development, conversely, the new Europe–Latin America relations were of little substance. The European and Latin American reactions to the crisis and the rising star of international neoliberalism were very distinct, inhibiting fruitful debate and exchange. European social democratic parties, on the one hand, initially resisted the new paradigm and only in the (late) 1990s achieved an ideological and policy renewal that translated into renewed political domination. In Latin America, however, a more rapid process of ideological readaptation of the major populist parties took place. We will now turn to the general features of this regional process.

Latin America's Neoliberal Transformation

The debt crisis and the severe economic crisis of the early 1980s were generally seen as the fatal blow to populism. Scholars, both liberal economists and those drawing on dependency theory, did not expect populism and neoliberalism to coexist: neoliberal austerity was generally seen as incompatible with populist interventionist and redistributive objectives. On both economic and political grounds, populism and neoliberalism were seen as mutually exclusive.

Generally, the 'exhaustion' of ISI was put on a par with the 'exhaustion' of populism. Technically, the economic crisis could be attributed to causes other than strictly the 'failure of ISI policies': both excessive international lending to the region in the 1970s and the catalyst effect of rising interest rates on the international capital market gave an impulse to the economic crisis of the 1980s. Nevertheless, in the context of the global rise of neoliberal thinking, the Keynesian model of import substitution was internally and externally held responsible for the economic decline of the 1980s and adjudged bankrupt. Under pressure from both international lending institutions and private creditors, Latin American governments were left with little alternative than to abandon the development model that had been at the basis of populism's popularity. The main ingredients of the economic restructuring policy of the 1980s included privatization of the state sector, an end to numerous price controls, subsidies, indirect state support mechanisms and protectionist measures, and a significant lowering of barriers for trade. These measures brought about enormous economic changes and, for the first few years, enormous social costs.

The neoliberal reforms of the 1980s and 1990s involved profound ideo-logical and political implications, too. First, the proclaimed reconciliation of the state and the economy with transnational capital implied a significant ideological shift. At the time of the primacy of extensive capital accumulation, the notion of imperialism had been key to the understanding that the creation of a national economic space – by transforming national borders into economic frontiers – was indispensable to allow for capital reproduction and later on intensive capital accumulation. This thinking contrasts with neoliberal thinking, which perceives liberalization of capital flows as the only option for more investment and economic growth. In need of foreign investment, and in the context of the globalization of capital markets and decreasing official funding to the region, Latin American parties had to abandon their anti-imperialist position. This ideological reversal may be described as a complete change of world view. It was generally believed that populist parties would not be able to make such an 'ideological shift'.

Second, neoliberal restructuring radically changed the model of state–society relations in Latin America. In the era of 'classic' populism, government policies facilitated rapid industrialization as well as income distribution, which mostly benefited the urban popular sector. The stability of the political regime was considered to depend directly on the continuity of this distribution. State companies indirectly supported and subsidized the development of the private industrial sector, while generating public resources for social policy (such as health care and education). The privatization of the parastatal sector thus had a profound political impact as it brought an end to this type of state–society relations.

Similarly, the political role of populist parties changed considerably. At the time of classic populism, the electoral strength of populist parties was for a large part based on their successful channelling of social demands to the state. Central elements of the populist political model, then, were the state as the centre of social and political conflict, and – either authoritarian or democratic – charismatic leadership. In the neoliberal era, the state transferred its functions of economic agent and of regulator of social inequality towards the market, thereby undermining much of the historical political tasks of populist parties.

As stated above, at the beginning of the 1990s, populism was rendered obsolete. Nevertheless, as the decade unfolded, it turned out that various populist parties had managed to 'survive' the neoliberal transformation. Basically, the 'neoliberalization' of populist parties followed three distinct courses. In countries such as Chile and Argentina, the neoliberal restructuring process initiated by military dictatorships of the 1970s and 1980s was adopted by populist parties in the 1990s (e.g. Chile's Socialist Party). In other countries, internal shifts within the ruling (populist) party resulted in the weakening of the Keynesian faction, and the rise of a neoliberal, technocratic rulership (e.g. the PRI in Mexico). In other cases, populist parties lost terrain to a new type of neoliberal populist leadership, personified by President Alberto Fujimori in Peru. How can the survival of populist parties in neoliberal times be explained? First of all, a distinction has to be made between 'classic' populism and 'neoliberal populism' or 'neopopulism'. Much of the socio-economic characteristics associated with populism (state intervention, Keynesian policies) have been pushed aside by the 'neoliberal populist' parties of the 1990s. What has remained is, apart from the parties themselves, a continued need for mass support, and a stress on (charismatic) personal leadership.

Important socioeconomic and political transformations of the 1980s and 1990s can account for the re-emerging of populism in many Latin American countries. These included the emergence of new democracies, urbanization, economic crisis and neoliberal restructuring. The socioeconomic modernization and economic differentiation of the postwar era, and the economic crisis of the 1980s had weakened traditional corporatist control and concentrated large numbers of people in urban centres. As democracy emerged, this mass of politically uncommitted people gained full access to the ballot-box. At the same time, in many countries the heritage of military dictatorship or one-party rule created a situation in which interest associations, political opposition and organizational networks remained weak. In addition, partly as a result of the economic crisis and neoliberal restructuring, Latin America's informal sector increased rapidly, sometimes involving half of the population. In sum, a growing mass of politically and organizationally uncommitted people appeared in the region. It was these groups that the neopopulist leaders of the 1980s and 1990s appealed to.

Neopopulists thus differed substantially from 'classic' populists in that they appealed directly to the huge informal sector and unorganized urban and rural poor, instead of the 'traditional' populist sectors such as urban workers and the provincial lower middle classes. In addition, neopopulists such as Carlos Menem, Fernando Collor de Mello and Alberto Fujimori adapted populism to the severe economic constraints of the late 1980s and 1990s. They showed, together with the Salinas administration in Mexico, that neoliberal policies did not preclude continued populist policies. 'They used political populism to impose economic liberalism, and in turn used economic liberalism to strengthen their populist leadership' (Weyland 1996: 9). Having pragmatically stripped populism of its unfashionable Keynesian economic characteristics, neopopulists continued to rely on populist political strong-points such as the political cultural arrangement of personal leadership and the (electoral) mobilization of the 'informal masses'. Contrary to what many scholars had predicted, former populist parties such as Chile's Socialist Party, the PRI in Mexico and the APRA in Peru managed to 'adapt' themselves to neoliberal formulas. In fact, it turned out that populist (or, rather 'neoliberal populist') parties actually managed to profit from neoliberal policies.

How can we account for this 'marriage of neopopulism and neoliberalism'? Weyland (1996) points out a number of inherent affinities of neopopulism and neoliberalism. First, neopopulists and neoliberals converge in their adversarial relationship to much of organized society. Both neoliberals in their deep-seated individualism and neopopulist leaders with their quasi-direct links to their followers dislike autonomous collective organization, which threatens to undermine universalist market rules and to disturb the leaders' unmediated connection to the masses. Furthermore, neoliberalist and neopopulist strategies of applying power coincide in relying on a strong top-down approach and on strengthening the apex of the state in order to affect profound economic reform and to boost the position of the personal leader, respectively. While trying to reduce state involvement in the economy, neoliberals apply the concentrated power of top state agencies, above all the presidency and the finance ministry, to break the resistance of groups that have benefited from state intervention and highly imperfect competition. A third affinity mentioned by Weyland is the claim that neoliberal policies, by ending hyperinflation and enacting targeted anti-poverty programmes, tend to benefit the poorer sectors, which neopopulists court. This, however, seems highly questionable. It is exactly on the issue of redistribution that populist and neoliberal views diverge. It is seriously debatable whether the poor in Latin America have benefited from the neoliberal anti-poverty programmes. We can easily turn the argument upside down by stressing another inherent affinity of neoliberalism and neopopulism, that is, the extreme poverty of many people in the informal sector – caused by neoliberal restructuring – which allows neopopulist leaders to buy large numbers of supporters with limited resources. Nevertheless, the argument that indeed Latin American neopopulism and neoliberalism show important inherent similarities remains unchanged.

Above we have seen how current coexistence of populism and neoliberalism in many Latin American countries contradicts established approaches that identify populism with non-liberal economic policies. By applying a political understanding of populism, and by making the distinction between 'classic' and 'neoliberal' populism, we are able to assess recent developments in Latin American politics.

Which Way Ahead?

The country studies in this book provide a rich and thorough account of the changing nature of Latin American populism in the era of neoliberalism. As the authors show, this is an ongoing process with major internal contradictions and unresolved matters that may, in time, turn out to be the seeds of new change. In addition, their analyses of national political processes demonstrate the effective flexibility of populist parties and leaders to politically survive a major economic crisis and a profound shift of ideology, development model and economic policy. There is, therefore, little reason to believe that the majority of neopopulists ruling Latin America today will be unable to remain in power when faced with problems that are either generated or insufficiently tackled by neoliberal policies. The following brief analysis of the main external obstacles to growth in Latin America at the beginning of the twenty-first century serves as a reminder of the unresolved matters that might require new policy restructuring or even another shift of paradigm. In addition, we will contemplate on the relevance of current third way thinking among social democrats for Latin American populist parties.

After Latin America's 'lost decade', when economic growth was very limited and GDP per capita even fell slightly, neoliberal restructuring contributed to a period of economic progress. Average growth of GDP between 1991 and 1998 accounted for 3.4 per cent, whereas inflation rates were brought down from an average 1,680 per cent in 1990 to 12 per cent in 1997 (United Nations 1998: 128, 137). Policies of trade and financial liberalization have, however, not provided for the anticipated basis of *stable* economic growth. Financial integration has made Latin American economies more vulnerable to speculative attacks and financial instability in the rest of the world. Trade integration has been less global and profitable than planned, and worldwide regionalization processes hamper Latin America's access to the main economic centres. Apart from these economic threats, social inequality (like ecological damage) has only worsened as a result of neoliberal restructuring and disappointing economic results.

The volatility of international capital flows stands out as the major concern for economic instability in Latin America. The experience of the 1980s' debt crisis did not protect Latin American countries from new financial crises such as the peso crisis in 1994/95 and the fall of the Brazilian *real* in 1999. Despite profound reforms after the debt crisis, various sources of vulnerability in fact returned. While government budget deficits and current account shortages were rising again, domestic savings decreased and (until Brazil's crisis) foreign capital inflow increased considerably. Ironically, while neoliberal restructuring was presented as the only possible way out of the debt crisis, the new policies incorporated new sources of financial instability. In particular policies of opening national financial sectors, including stock markets, to foreign investors have rendered the economy more dependent on the partly irrational behaviour of global capital. While net foreign direct investment in Latin America has become a source of steadily growing capital inflow, short-term capital flows (short-term borrowing and domestic outflows) as well as medium- and long-term foreign private credit fluctuate tremendously.

The series of international financial crises of the late 1990s have clearly shown the risks of rapid financial integration for developing countries. The peso crisis, at that time referred to as the first financial crisis of the twenty-first century, was followed by the Asia crisis of 1997–98, Russia's default in 1998 and the collapse of the Brazilian *real* in early 1999. These crises all had different immediate causes, but also point at general problems with the globalization of capital markets. Comparing the Mexican and Asian crises, Griffith-Jones (1999: 6) concludes that the broad areas of similarity are: 'the international economic environment and the emerging markets countries' access to international capital, the surge of capital inflows to affected countries, and the sudden and deep nature of the market panic and capital reversals'. Both at the national (governments and central banks) and the international (IMF, World Bank, Bank of International Settlements) levels, institutional regulation, surveillance and funding to prevent or limit financial crises have turned out to be no longer able to deal with the massive flows of short-term capital.

As a result of globalization cross-border effects of financial crises have become more far-reaching. The Asia crisis, for instance, was transmitted to Latin America via trade[3], financial contagion[4], and subsequently policy adjust-ments (higher interest rates and budget cuts) that might even have given occasion to a downward spiral of shrinking demand and investment (Vos 1998). Similarly, the recession of Brazil (Latin America's largest economy) has had considerable effects on the other countries of Mercosur and the rest of Latin America. While national currencies were not directly affected, growth figures tumbled and might take considerable time to recover.

The political response of Latin American neopopulists to the risks of financial globalization vary. While a proper institutional and regulatory framework at the international level is generally perceived to be crucial, views of the role of the national government differ. Some proposals for reform stress the significance of state sovereignty combined with regional financial and monetary cooperation.[5] Although the terminology has been completely abandoned, fear of imperialist domination appears to remain topical. An opposite reaction concerns renewed proposals for dollarization,[6] in particular by President Menem of Argentina who, after the collapse of the Brazilian *real*, also repeated his idea of a single currency (i.e. the US dollar) for Mercosur. It is, however, most unlikely that the United States and the Mercosur countries will agree to this form of deep regionalization in the near future.

With respect to Latin American production and trade, regionalization dominates. From the late 1980s onward, Latin American countries embarked on a course of 'open regionalization', that is regional integration without elements of exclusion or discrimination against outsiders (CEPAL 1994). Efforts were made to reanimate the Central American Common Market (MCCA), the Andean Group and the Economic Community of the Caribbean (CARICOM). Mercosur was created by Argentina, Brazil, Paraguay and Uruguay, later on joined by Chile and Bolivia, and rapidly became the most successful integration process in the region. These initiatives formalized and significantly added to economic regionalization in Latin America. Between 1985 and 1997, exports to other Latin American countries increased from 13.8 to 21.8 per cent of the region's total exports (United Nations 1998: 140).

Although primarily intended as a strategy against economic bloc formation in general, open regionalization initiatives clearly aims at better access to the US market. Improved relations with Europe and East Asia are also strived for, but processes of economic and political integration in these regions inhibit easy access for Latin American countries and trade blocs. As a consequence, since the 1980s Latin American trade has become increasingly directed towards the USA. The percentage of exports to the USA increased from 40.0 to 45.1 between 1985 and 1997, while exports to Europe decreased from 22.0 per cent to 13.4 per cent (United Nations 1998: 140). The negotiation of the NAFTA agreement between the USA, Canada and Mexico raised hopes among other Latin American countries for rapid entry to the US market. However, President Clinton's plans for a hemispheric trade area have been faced with a deadlock between left and right in the US Congress, which almost prevented ratification of NAFTA too. Although officially a start has been made with the negotiation process for the Free Trade Agreement of the Americas (FTAA), which should lead to a free trade area by the year 2005, it is questionable whether, when and how US free trade, protectionist and progressive forces are able to agree on regional integration.

So far, neoliberal restructuring has not been very accurate in dealing with the 'old' Latin American need for diversifying exports (products and markets) and substituting imports. Diversification of exports that did take place was primarily into natural resource-based manufactures, with the exception of Mexico. While imports of consumer and capital goods increased during most of the 1990s (due to liberalization, economic growth and the relative decline in the prices of imported products), domestic demand dropped. Moreover, trade liberalization and macroeconomic reforms did not provide the expected stimulus for exports. According to the United Nations Economic Commission for Latin America and the Caribbean, the region has reached a turning point in terms of their export promotion policies (ECLAC 1995).

In short, whereas Latin America has become more vulnerable for financial turmoil, trade liberalization and regionalization have only been of limited economic benefit, and may continue to be so as long as the USA remains paralysed on the issue. The absence of better access to the industrialized countries' markets and the mixed prospects of the Asian markets may limit Latin America's growth potential and thereby its access to long-term invest-ment. If this dark scenario materializes, Latin American countries will become more dependent on the volatile markets of short-term capital. In the near future, Latin American populism will probably have to reconsider its ideo-logical and programmatic approach, and rethink the role of the state in enhancing sustained economic growth. As before, the nature of this shift depends heavily on dominant views within international organizations and major industrialized countries.

Starting in the countries of Reaganomics and Thatcherism with the New Democrats and New Labour, over the past few years some social democratic parties in Europe have become involved in a thorough discussion on ideological and programmatic modernization. Let us here briefly consider the third way debate, not so much to compare the development of Latin American populism with European social democracy, but rather to assess the possibilities of renewed cooperation between the two and the chance of this recent debate contributing to an international shift of paradigm. Like classic social democracy, third way thinking cannot be easily translated to Latin American populism. As described above, the social democratic label never fitted Latin American populist parties well, while the adaptation to neoliberalism proceeded earlier and further in Latin America than in Europe.

According to Anthony Giddens (1998: 26), the third way should be considered 'an attempt to transcend both old-style social democracy and neoliberalism'. The idea of matching social democratic values with liberal notions and practices involves the final replacement of old-style socialist thought and discourse with pragmatic thinking about the state and the market. The common denominator of the various national third way debates is the centrality of the question of how to deal with globalization. So far, it has rather been a debate on (national) third ways than on *the* third way. In addition, its main concepts are far from uncontested, as the discussions within parties and the non-involvement of several countries, such as France, demonstrate.

At face value, the third way debate in Europe could be the starting point of a rapprochement with the 'new' populists in Latin America. The import-ance of the issue of globalization, the search for 'liberalism with a human face', and even the media-type of party politics that are increasingly based on symbolism and the leader's image (a neopopulist tendency in European politics) are all shared by Latin American neopopulist parties and European 'third way parties' alike and might be a starting point for transnational cooperation. In reality, however, attention to and concern for Latin America, as for Asia and Africa, have been shrinking among European social democrats. Although it is not necessarily a zero-sum game, since the end of the Cold War Western Europe has directed a considerable share of its external attention and effort to its Eastern neighbours. With Latin America doing both politically and economically better than in the early 1980s, the sense of compassion is to some extent replaced by a fear of competition. The recent history of troublesome attempts for economic cooperation with the European Union (dominated by social democrats) by Mexico and Mercosur show that in the age of globalization competitive forces easily undo sentiments of solidarity.

Does this imply that Latin America has little to expect if third way thinking, by maturing and sinking in, eventually brings about a global paradigm shift? Not necessarily. Notwithstanding the fact that much of the third way debate deals with globalization from an economic point of view in which emerging markets are adversaries rather than allies, third way politicians and thinkers have voiced strong criticism of neoliberal global integration. Particularly with respect to international regulation of global capital markets, a third way approach could make quite a difference from the 'market-is-always-right' ideology. Giddens (1998), for instance, incorporates proposals for a Tobin tax (international tax on currency transactions) and cosmopolitan democracy into his agenda for the third way. A third way era, then, could theoretically support Latin American efforts for stable economic growth.

Summing up, economic liberalization has not yet delivered the expected progress in Latin America, and may in fact not do so at all. Latin American countries seem to be caught between financial globalization and economic regionalization. In addition, despite the domination of social democratic parties in Europe and the fact that their ideological and programmatic reorientation bears significant similarities with the neoliberalization of Latin American populist parties, a strengthening of their political relations is unlikely in the short run. The difficult dilemmas facing Latin America may be illustrated by some pressing questions. Will the success of neoliberal policy for the export sectors trickle down to the rest of the economy and eventually result in growing national or regional markets? Do the restructured states have the capacity to absorb future financial shocks, which are expected to be more frequent and fierce? Will a lack of stable economic progress become a threat to political stability and the domination of Latin American populism? How can development be achieved now that the neoliberal era has proved to result in financial instability and limited prospects for sustained economic growth? Will it be economically and politically possible for Latin American countries to sustain the current trajectory of openness? If not, how will populist parties reform? And for long-term stability, are these parties capable of enhancing income distribution and genuine environmental protection? The analyses of the contemporary history of Latin American populism made in this book will, we hope, contribute not only to the understanding of current changes, but also to the thinking about these questions and a more rewarding course of development of Latin America.

Seven Views on Neoliberalism and Populism in Latin America

This book contains seven case studies on neoliberalism and populism in Latin America. Chapter 2 presents the perhaps most 'classic' and widely known case of Latin American populism: Peronism. Miguel Teubal studies Argentina's difficult transition from ISI to the open economy and looks into the factors that determined the remarkable metamorphosis of Peronism, and its transition to *menemismo*. The questions that are posed in this first chapter are relevant to several other cases in the book (such as that of Mexico), especially the questions of *how* and *why* the transition from ISI to the open market strategies of the 1990s took place under the auspices of one and the same political movement. In Chapter 3, another, but similar, metamorphosis is studied: that of the 'ideological neoliberalization' of the Socialist Party in Chile. The party moved from a Marxist to a liberal identity and contributed considerably to the success of Chile's economic restructuring. In the fourth chapter Karla Lemanski-Valente analyses the political and economic transformation processes that Brazil has gone through since the mid-1980s. Issues such as the Brazilian decision-making culture, presidentialism, leadership, and the main economic reform programme (the *Real* Plan) are discussed. In a book on neoliberalism and (neo)populism in Latin America the Peruvian case (and 'Fuji-populism') cannot be missing. Chapter 5, therefore, examines the drastic neoliberalization of the Peruvian economy. The rise of the neopopulist leader *par excellence*, Fujimori, is viewed in the light of the crisis of the Peruvian left. Starting off with the violent popular protests of early 1999, Chapter 6 examines the impact of neoliberal adjustment in Ecuador. The chapter touches upon the contradictions of the Andean variant of populism, which have made it impossible for any coherent response to the neoliberal agenda to emerge. Consequently, we leave the Cono Sur behind and move to Mexico. The Mexican case shows another example of *trasformismo*: that of the transition from revolutionary nationalism to 'social' liberalism within Mexico's PRI. Again, neoliberal reforms are linked to the rise of presidentialism and personalist rule, especially the 'Salinas cult'. Finally, Chapter 8 deals with Central America. Kees Biekart shows how – paradoxically – progressive revultionary parties became key allies of leading advocates of neoliberal restructuring in Central America. To explain this paradox, Biekart explores the development of the Central American left over the past three decades, in which it oscillated between reformism and revolution, and finally was caught up by the imperatives of liberal democracy.

Notes

1. Latin American populist parties were anti-communist in the sense that in the national political arena communist parties were their primary competitors. In their international position, however, anti-US sentiments dominated.

2. Meetings took place in Caracas (1976), Vancouver (1978) and Santo Domingo (1980). In Vancouver, the Swedish social democrats clashed with the German SPD, as the Swedes attempted to limit the SPD's influence in Latin America. In Santo Domingo the first regional conference of the SI for Latin America and the Caribbean took place, with representatives of political extremes, including liberal parties and socialist liberation movements. The resolutions of this last conference were the most radical, and contrary to European social democratic thinking: the implantation of socialism in Latin America was declared a historical objective of the SI (Petras 1980).

3. The trade effect involves more international competition, decreasing exports to Asia, lower worldwide growth and lower prizes of commodities, in particular raw materials. While the export volume expanded nearly 8 per cent in 1998, the export value fell (ECLAC 1995).

4. At first, short-term capital left the region and the cost of external financing increased, but later on also banks shifted credits out of Latin America, back to industrialized countries.

5. This view was also taken by a task force of the Executive Committee on Economic and Social Affairs of the United Nations (1999), headed by ECLAC's executive secretary. Contrasting proposals of the Group of Seven, the task force stressed the need for preservation of autonomy for developing countries with regard to capital account matters, and the design of a network of regional and subregional organizations to support monetary and financial management.

6. Adopting the dollar should contribute to investors' confidence and financial stability, but would involve strict budgetary controls and joint bank supervision with the USA. American countries would not be able to build up part of their reserves in euros, thereby hurting their financial, economic as well as political relations with Europe.

References

Alba, Victor (1953) *Le Mouvement ouvrier en Amérique Latine*, Paris: Editions Ouvrier.

Alcantara Sez, Manuel (1993) 'Spanish social democracy and Latin America', in M. Vellinga, *Social Democracy in Latin America: Prospects for Change*, Boulder, CO: Westview Press.

Alvarez, Sonia, Evelina Dagnino and Arturo Escobar (1998) *Cultures of Politics, Politics of Cultures: Re-visioning Latin American Social Movements*, Boulder, CO: Westview Press.

Biekart, Kees (1999) *The Politics of Civil Society Building: European Aid Agencies and Democratic Transitions in Central America*, Utrecht: International Books.

Camacho, D. and R. Menjivar (1989) *Los Movimientos Populares en América Latina*, Mexico: Siglo XXI.

Cardoso, F. E. and E. Faletto (1969) *Dependencia y Desarrollo en América Latina*, Mexico: Ciudad de Mexico.

— (1979) *Dependency and Development in Latin America*, Berkeley: University of California Press.

Castañeda, J. G. (1995) *La Utopia Desarmada*, Barcelona: Ariel.

CEPAL (1994) *El regionalismo abierto en América Latina y el Caribe: La transformación económica al servicio de la transformación productiva con equidad*, Santiago: CEPAL.

— (1999) *Panorama de la Inserción Internacional de América Latina*, Santiago: CEPAL.

Cox, Carlos (1973) *El Marxismo Latinoamericano de Mariategui*, Buenos Aires: Editorial Crisis.

Debray, R. (1975) *La Critique des armes*, Paris: Seuil.

Demmers, Jolle (1998) *Friends and Bitter Enemies: Politics and Neoliberal Reform in Yucatán, Mexico*. Amsterdam: Thela Thesis.

Di Tella, T. (1989) *Hacia una Estratégia de la Social-democracia en Argentina*, Buenos Aires: Editorial Puntosur.

Dornbusch, Rudiger and Sebastian Edwards (1991) *The Macroeconomics of Populism in Latin America*, Chicago: University of Chicago Press.

Drake, Paul W. (1982) 'Conclusion: requiem for populism?', in M. L. Coniff (ed.), *Latin American Populism in Comparative Perspective*, Alburquerque: University of New Mexico Press.

— (1991) 'Comment', in R. Dornbusch and S. Edwards, *The Macroeconomics of Populism in Latin America*, Chicago: University of Chicago Press.

ECLAC (1995) *Latin America and the Caribbean: Policies to Improve Linkages with the Global Economy*, Santiago: ECLAC.

Erickson, K. P. (1977) *The Brazilian Corporative State and Working-class Politics*, Berkeley: University of California Press.

Evers, Tilman (1993) 'European social democracy in Latin America: the early history with emphasis on the role of Germany', in M. Vellinga, *Social Democracy in Latin America: Prospects for Change*, Boulder, CO: Westview Press.

Executive Committee on Economic and Social Affairs of the Untited Nations (1999) *Towards a New International Financial Architecture*, report released on 22 January.

Fernández Jilberto, A. E. and K. Biekart (1991) 'Europa y la socialdemocratización de America Latina', *Afers Internacionals* 20: 5–26.

Giddens, Anthony (1998) *The Third Way: The Renewal of Social Democracy*, Cambridge: Polity Press.

Griffith-Jones, Stephany (1999) 'Capital Flows: How to Curb Their Volatility', paper presented to conference of the Wiardi Beckman Foundation, 20 March.

Ianni, Octavio (1975) *La Formación del Estado Populista en América Latina*, Mexico: serie popular, ERA.

Jaguaribe, Helio (1989) *A Proposta Social-democrata*, Rio de Janeiro: Jos Olympio Editora.

Kaufman, Robert and Barbara Stallings (1991) 'The political economy of Latin American populism', in R. Dornbusch and S. Edwards, *The Macroeconomics of Populism in Latin America*, Chicago: University of Chicago Press.

Lowy, Michael (1980) *Le Marxisme de l'Amérique Latine*, Paris: Maspero.

— (1984) 'Trayectoria de internacional socialista en la América Latina,' in Sofía Méndez, *La Crisis Internacional y la América Latina*, Mexico: Fondo de Cultura Económica.

Mariategui, J. C. (1964) *Siete Ensayos de Interpretación de la Realidad Peruana*, Santiago: Editorial Universitaria.

OECD, (1986) *Development Cooperation Report*, Paris: OECD.

Petras, James (1980) 'La social-démocratie en Amérique Latine', *Le Monde Diplomatique*, 8–11 June, pp. 15–17.

Sachs, Jeffrey (1989) 'Social conflict and populist policies in Latin America', Cambridge, MA: NBER Working Paper no. 2897.

Smith, W. and R. Korzeniewicz (1997) *Politics, Social Change, and Economic Restructuring in Latin America*, Miami: North South Center Press.

Touraine, Alain (1986) *América Latina: Política y Sociedad*, Madrid: Espasa.

United Nations (1998) *World Economic and Social Survey 1998: Trends and Policies in the World Economy*, Washington, DC: UN Department of Social and Economic Affairs.

Van Doorn, J. A. A. (1999) 'De sociaal-democratie en het koloniale vraagstuk', *Socialisme & Democratie*, 59 (11): 483–92.

Vellinga, M. (1993) *Social Democracy in Latin America: Prospects for Change*, Boulder, CO: Westview Press.

Vos, Rob (1998) 'De crisis in Azië en Latijns-Amerika. En nu de zondvloed?', *Internationale Spectator*, November, pp. 571–5.

Weyland, Kurt (1996) 'Neopopulism and Neoliberalism in Latin America: Unexpected Affinities', *Studies In Comparative International Development*, Fall 1996, 31 (3).

TWO

From Import Substitution Industrialization to the 'Open' Economy in Argentina: The Role of Peronism

MIGUEL TEUBAL

In a sense, ISI policies and strategies were to the Third World what Fordism, Keynesianism and the policies leading to the welfare state were to the First World. In the era of globalization, an age in which transnational corporations and financial and speculative activities have acquired a prominence hitherto unheard of, pressures to de-industrialize and to apply structural adjustment programmes – to privatize, deregulate and 'open up' to the world economy – have replaced previous ISI policies and strategies. In the First World neoliberalism confronts the welfare state and Keynesian–Fordist policies and strategies. In the Third World, in particular in countries that had attained a certain degree of industrialization, neoliberal policies included a series of measures tending to disarticulate ISI policies as well as the local versions of the welfare state. The present liberalization spree constitutes in many respects the opposite image of what ISI used to be. Whereas in the past a certain form of government interventionism used to acquire a consensus, it is now looked upon with awe. The current world crisis, however, seems to evoke many of the same pressures to regulate the world economy that occurred during the 1930s regarding the nation-state.

Under the scrutiny of neoliberalism, import substitution industrialization (ISI) has recently been criticized for being anathema to the open market economy. Although much has been said concerning its failures, the impact of ISI on Latin American economies and societies has seldom been critically compared with that of the 'open economy'. ISI strategies prevailed in a certain epoch of Third World history that is more or less comparable to the 'golden age' of capitalism in the First World. This 'golden age' spanned the 1945–70 period. While in Argentina import substitution industrialization began prior to this period (notably in the 1930s) it became prominent after 1945 and up to the mid-1970s.

What was the nature of these ISI strategies as applied to a country such as Argentina? How and in response to what external and internal factors did they emerge? What impact did they have? What are the specificities of the 'Argentine' case? How does ISI compare with market economy policies applied since the mid-1970s to the present? What was the role of Peronism in ISI and in open market strategies? Why and how did the transformation come about from the support of traditional ISI strategies to a support of an extreme neoliberal programme? In other words, what were the factors that determined this strange *metamorphosis* of Peronism, and its transition to Menemism? These are some of the questions that will be approached in this chapter.

While in the 1930s, as a response to the world crisis, government interventionism under the auspices of conservative governments led to ISI strategies, historically ISI has been associated with Peronist administrations (1946–55; 1973–74). Under the *desarrollista* (developmentalist) governments (Arturo Frondizi 1958–62 and the military government of the Revolución Argentina, 1966–73) ISI was also pursued. However, Peronism (under Isabel Perón in 1974–76 and more recently under the *menemismo* of Carlos Menem (since 1989) is also one of the main artificers of neoliberalism in Argentina. Neoliberal programmes were also carried out by the military government of the Proceso (1976–83), and the Raúl Alfonsín administration (1983–89). Although these latter governments applied important adjustments, the more extreme structural adjustment programmes were implemented during the Menem administration.

One of the main questions considered in this chapter is how and why this transition from ISI to the open market strategies of the 1990s took place under the auspices of the same political movement. Although it is interesting to study the role that international factors or contexts have played in this transition, it is equally important to consider the extent to which the local socioeconomic context and the broad nature of the political parties or movements involved were instrumental to these developments.

Although some industrialization had been carried out prior to the world crisis of the 1930s, notably during the First World War, when essential imports were restricted and ways for producing them locally were induced, the main institutions of ISI began as a consequence of the effects of the Depression of the 1930s. They were actively enhanced during the first Peronist government of 1946–55. In the 1960s ISI was continued, although its redistributive aspects were increasingly eclipsed by the more *desarrollista* perspective. In the period ending in 1976, economic policies were intensely debated and competing projects set forth: the 'nationalistic' economic policies were increasingly confronted with the more 'liberal' ones. The two paradigmatic *desarrollista* regimes, that of Frondizi (1958–62) and that of the Revolución Argentina (1966–73), contrasted with that of the second Peronist or Justicialista administration under Cámpora and Perón (1973–74). Up to the elections of 1973 Peronism was in the opposition, and in fact was proscribed from presenting itself in elections. Finally, in 1973 this movement was once again democratically elected to government: in the first two years of the new administration, a nationalistic ISI was pursued once again. With the military coup of 1976 most of the tenets of ISI were set aside, and a new overture to transnational corporations and financial interests began. ISI was definitely banned from the books under the Menem administration.

In this chapter we consider the origins and nature of ISI policies in Argentina, and the role played by Peronism in their implementation. In the first part, we consider ISI as a consequence of policies coping with the impact of two world wars and the crisis of the 1930s. Next, we consider the ISI policies of the first Peronist administration followed by those applied in 1955–76, a period also marked by Peronism: first as an opposition force – from the fall of the first *peronista* government in 1955 to its ascent to power once again in 1973 – and then as part of government up to the death of Perón in 1974. Finally, we consider the adjustments applied in the mid-1970s and the role of Menem and *menemismo* in the structural adjustment programmes implemented in the 1990s. We conclude with reflections on ISI and the open economy as 'regimes of accumulation' and the continuing presence of Peronism in the recent political history of Argentina.

The focus of this chapter is not on Peronism but on the transition from ISI to the 'open economy'. Within this context the metamorphosis of Peronism or, as it is considered by many, the transition from *peronismo* to *menemismo* is one of the more notable processes. The role of the 'national bourgeoisie' and the alliances – implicit or explicit – sustained with the labour movement, or with the different factions that sustained ISI policies, are taken into account. Furthermore, comparisons are made with the adjustments implemented during the period from the 1970s to the present.

Development and Crisis of the Agro-export Economy

Two world wars and the Great Depression of the 1930s marked the crisis of the agro-export economy throughout Latin America. They were also instrumental in inducing the adoption of ISI policies in many countries, including Argentina. The traditional primary goods export economies in which primary commodity exports were the dynamic locus of growth apparently came to an end. The crisis brought forth enormous falls in the value and volume of Latin American exports, together with a closure of the region's traditional export markets. It induced governments throughout Latin America to rethink their development strategies. At the beginning of this period a new 'model' of development or 'regime of accumulation' was set in motion.

The Argentine economy had grown substantially in the period extending from the 1870s to the 1930s. This was largely due to the ever-increasing expansion and exports of agricultural and livestock products provided by the fertile lands of the Pampean region. Supported by foreign capital investments and financing, railways, port facilities and other basic infrastructures were constructed. Massive immigration provided the necessary labour force in this 'new and empty land', turning it into a 'land of recent settlement'. Some infant industries related to the growing agro-export economy and the enhancement of agricultural exportables were established in the late nineteenth century – sugar and flour mills, meatpacking, forestry – as well as mechanical industries associated with the extension of the railways and other basic infrastructures.

In the early years of the twentieth century, Argentina was certainly a land of promise for vast segments of the population. Social mobility was quite high, and income per capita estimated to be on a par with countries such as Germany, Holland and Belgium, and even higher than that of Austria, Spain and Italy (although somewhat lower than that of the USA, Canada and Australia).

According to some estimates Argentina's growth in 1860–1930 was one of the highest in the world: GDP grew at an average annual rate of 6.3 per cent in the period 1900–04 until 1910–1914, and 3.5 per cent in 1910–14 until 1925–29 (Díaz Alejandro 1975: 20). Rapid growth of total GDP was accompanied by large population increases largely due to massive immigration. In the same periods, the population increased by 4.3 per cent and 2.8 per cent per annum respectively. Immigration was in comparative terms more massive than in the USA. While the total population increased from 1.7 million in 1865–69 to 7.2 million in 1910–14 and to 10.9 million in 1925–29, between 1857 and 1930 net immigration amounted to 3.5 million. In 1914, 30 per cent of the population was foreign, and in the city of Buenos Aires more than 50 per cent came from outside Argentina.

Some additional measures of the rapid growth of the Argentine economy include the expansion of the railway system from an average of 503 kilometres in 1856–59 to more than 38,000 kilometres in 1925–29. Foreign investments were mostly directed to the railways, port facilities and other basic infrastructures. Land incorporated into agricultural production increased from about half a million hectares in 1872 to 25.18 million hectares in 1925–29. These processes were followed by substantial increases in the volumes and values of exports and imports. Exports began their rapid increase in the 1840s, and wool exports overshot the traditional exports of leather, jerked meat and grease products. Subsequently, in the 1880–1900 period cereal exports increased from almost nil to several million tons per annum. By the late 1920s, cereal exports represented more than half of total exports followed by beef, other meat products and fruit, cotton, wood and sugar (Díaz Alejandro 1975: 18, 321). In Figure 2.1 we represent the growth of income per capita from 1875 to 1995. As can be observed, during the development of the agro-export economy (1880–1930) growth was very rapid, interrupted only by the First World War and the Great Depression of the 1930s.

It needs to be mentioned, however, that this growth was not the result of industrialization, but was based on the expansion and exports of agricultural

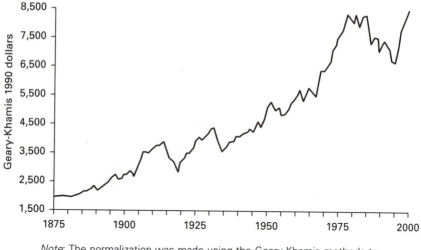

Note: The normalization was made using the Geary-Khamis methods to obtain a series of 1990 constant dollars.

FIGURE 2.1 GDP per capita in Argentina, 1875–1995 (*Source*: Lemarchand 1996; Cortés Conde 1995; Maddison 1995)

and livestock commodities to the world economy, mainly to the British market. This growth (and development) without industrialization can be attributed to the large differential Ricardian rents provided by the fertile lands of the Pampas. Even nowadays many observers are baffled by the fact that Argentina was not a characteristically 'underdeveloped' country of the Third World, equivalent to the colonies in Africa or Asia, or Latin America at the time, basically because it was in comparative terms quite rich. Hobsbawm has observed that Third World countries emerging in the postcolonial era were mostly poor 'with the rarest exceptions, notably Argentina, which though rich, never recovered from the decline and fall of the British Empire, which had given it prosperity as a food exporter until 1929' (Hobsbawm 1995: 357).

The fact that Argentina was considered as a land of promise also had to do with the opportunities for small business that provided for a high degree of social mobility. There were also opportunities for social mobility via education, a factor that has traditionally characterized Argentina. According to Germani (1955: 224), the period extending from the last 20 years of the nineteenth century to the first quarter of the twentieth century was characterized by a very high degree of social mobility. Popular classes became middle-class via the liberal professions or by some dependent category of employment. And immigrants ascended socially through autonomous activity in commerce, industry or agriculture.

In 1928–29 just prior to the great Depression, Argentina was an important foreign trader in the world economy. Furthermore, with 26 inhabitants per motor vehicle, she had more vehicles per capita than the US despite the fact that she did not have the required highway or road network. The rate of illiteracy had been reduced substantially from 77 percent in 1869 to 36 percent in 1914 and to about 24 percent in 1929. In 1929 Buenos Aires was one of the great cultural centres of the Spanish speaking world; with a series of journals and publishers she was frequently the first to publish the works of important cultural personalities ... Another indicator of welfare acquired was the rate of mortality: in 1929 it amounted to 13.1 per 1000 inhabitants, which was not very far from that of Canada (11.4 per thousand). (Díaz Alejandro 1975: 66)

While the growth of Argentina's GDP was substantial, the growth of income per capita was not as notorious. This resulted from the massive inflow of immigrants, which provided for a quasi-elastic supply of labour to the productive processes. The social and power structure that was consolidated had much to do with the nature of this development process as income distribution became quite regressive. As Cortés Conde puts it: 'surely [up to 1910] wealth had not been distributed equally. Nevertheless, despite notorious inequalities the exploitation of the labour force and the doubtless misery of the mass peasantry were isolated cases that did not heavily influence the life of the country' (Cortés Conde 1969: 219, my translation).

Massive immigration provided cheap labour and contributed to reducing costs of production. The agro-export economy offered important opportunities to the land-owning class, which had been consolidated in the late nineteenth century when the remaining indigenous populations were almost totally exterminated during the so-called desert campaigns. A homestead movement, equivalent to that of the USA, Canada or Australia, or other lands of recent settlement, did not take place in Argentina. Land was rapidly concentrated in the hands of a few. Nevertheless, in some regions a farm and (settlers) colonization movement was developed when tracts of land were rented or sold to immigrant labour. This elicited important conflicts and in 1912 an important tenant movement known as El grito de Alcorta marked the beginnings of the Federación Agraria Argentina (Argentine Federation of Agriculture). In the census of 1937, a large proportion of farm operators were still tenants who did not own the land. Thus the structure of Argentine agriculture included, on the one hand, a land-owning class with considerable economic and political power, the so-called *oligarquía terrateniente*, who formed part of the establishment and directly controlled succeeding governments, at least up to 1916 and after the coup of 1930 up to the first Peronist administration. But then there were the settlers of the colonies, tenants and farm labourers who provided most of farm labour and became eventually the farmers or *chararreros* of the Pampas. Compared to, for example, Mexico, Bolivia or Brazil, the traditional peasantry was relatively small, and was mostly localized in some areas of the interior: in Tucuman (sugar cane farmers), Chaco (cotton) or Misiones (yerba maté).

In the late nineteenth century a highly urbanized society emerged in Argentina, with 37 per cent of the total population living in localities of more then 2,000 inhabitants in 1895. By 1914 the rate of urbanization had increased to 53 per cent, and by 1847 to 62 per cent (Germani 1955: 67). In 1914, the city of Buenos Aires (including its suburbs) had a total population of almost 2 million, representing more than one-fourth of the total population. This urbanization, however, was not based solely on industrialization but was the result of other processes as well. For instance, many immigrants could not find a place in agriculture due to the prevailing land tenure situation. Commerce and service industries in urban areas offered alternative sources of employment. In 1914, at the peak of the great expansion of Argentina's agro-export economy, 31 per cent of the economically active population were employed in primary activities, a similar proportion in secondary activities, and almost 38 per cent (about 2.7 million inhabitants) in tertiary activities (commerce, services and domestic services) (Germani 1955: 129). The secondary activities consisted of several craft activities, small workshops, and *trabajadores a domicilio por cuenta propia* (self-employed workers) as well as factory labourers. Small business in industry prevailed to a large extent: in 1914 47,779 plants employed 410,000 persons, an average of 8.4 persons per establishment. The number of these plants increased to 90,440 in 1947, employing 1,332,339 persons, an average of 14.7 persons per establishment. A similar situation prevailed in the service industries.

In urban areas industry was relatively scarce. Yet even at an early date, important anarchist and socialist political and trade union movements emerged related to the railway workers, the local industrial proletariat and those working in commerce. However, an industrial bourgeoisie that could confront the traditional oligarchy did not exist, at least not in this period. This was to emerge later under the impetus of ISI.

Finally, a factor that is important for an understanding of the origins of ISI needs to be pointed out. While Argentina was not a formal colony, its economy was largely dependent on the British Empire. Exports were oriented mostly to Great Britain, and imports of coal and petroleum were provided by British companies. Much has been said concerning the vulnerability of the Argentine economy being extremely export-oriented at the time, and dependent on international prices and policies adopted by the British government and foreign capital. As we shall see, the need to industrialize was visualized as a means to reduce this extreme vulnerability and dependency of the Argentine economy.

Argentina's history since 1853 is the history of British economic penetration, voluntary in its beginnings, forced in the end. This economic penetration was based mainly on the property and exploitation of the railway system, conceived for the export of beef, cereals and other raw materials for the consumption of British consumers. Then there were capital investments in the meat-packing industry, banks, insurance companies and important trading companies. Britain was almost an exclusive purchaser of Argentina's meat exportables, a factor that made livestock production dependent upon the preferences of the British consumer. The British market was a provider of petroleum and coal and of large-scale imports of manufactured goods (Sclabrini Ortiz in Cafiero 1961: 272). All these factors marked the foreign trade and investments dependency and vulnerability of the Argentine economy. In this context Prebisch began to think over his theories on the relations between the centre and the periphery and their effects on deteriorating terms of trade. Landowners, commercial traders and financiers operating from the port of Buenos Aires and foreign capital firms constituted the privileged sectors. Their high incomes tended to influence the composition of imports (of consumer luxury and intermediary goods). Cyclical fluctuations and crises had an impact on incomes and unemployment levels. Generally, these crises were absorbed by rural and urban workers, the middle classes and some infant industry associated with the processing of domestic raw materials.

Even before the 1930s Alejandro Bunge had argued for the need of a new model of development in Argentina, one that 'without abandoning her foreign trade or existing international connections, could offer industry the possibility of acting as the principal motor of a new process of growth' (Villanueva 1975: 59). According to Whitaker few civilians heeded this warning at the time. The armed forces, however, were more receptive. This was understandable, for they believed that industrialization was essential for national defence and would require technical skills (Whitaker 1975:20). Hence the importance the military assigned to certain basic industries: YPF (the petroleum company founded in 1922); YCF (the company producing coal); certain steel industries during the later Peronist administration; and the military industry itself.

The Crisis of the 1930s and the Beginnings of ISI

The year 1930 is an important landmark in Argentine history. The military coup of 6 September inaugurated a series of military interventions and governments that were to stay in power well into the following decades. The coup of 1930 overthrew the middle-class government of Yrigoyen that had governed Argentina since 1916, restoring a new oligarchic government. With this, the so-called 'infamous decade' began, in which fraudulent elections became rampant, civil rights were trampled upon and many of the democratic and cultural advances that had been attained suffered a serious setback. In the following decades, few democratically elected governments concluded their term in office without military intervention. As a matter of fact, prior to 1984 the only government that did so was the first *peronista* administration of the 1946–52 period.

The crash of the 1930s brought about a substantial fall in the value of Argentina's exports (due to falling prices and the closure of traditional markets). Although some industrialization oriented to the domestic market had been developed during the First World War, when the flow of essential imports was interrupted and ways of producing them locally were induced, the main institutions of ISI were established in the 1930s. So, in fact, the institutions dated from before the Peronist government of 1946–55. Nevertheless, ISI became paradigmatic of the first Peronist government.

The main impact of the Great Depression in Europe and the United States was a fall in international demand for Argentina's exports and a drastic fall in agricultural prices on world markets. This situation coincided with agricultural protectionism and the formation of preferential blocks that discriminated against Argentina's exports. In the 1920s, increased protectionism prevailed in the countries of the centre. The 1928 presidential election in the USA was followed by a protectionist wave leading to the Smoot-Hawley tariff of 1930, in 1931 Great Britain imposed certain importation preferences, and in 1932 the preferences of the Ottawa Conference were quite discriminatory for Latin American and, in particular, Argentine exports. Trade barriers erected by the USA and Europe against agricultural products and raw materials placed these Latin American countries at 'the vanguard of their foreign trade decadence ... National self sufficiency was imposed on these countries in large measure due to the official policies of the US and European Nations' (Phelps cited by Díaz Alejandro 1975: 149).

For instance, this was reflected in the price trends affecting wheat, corn and linseed – Argentina's three basic export commodities, which at the time represented over 90 per cent of the Pampas' crop production and about 56 per cent of its exports. It was estimated that the prices of these crops fell an average of 43 per cent in the period 1929–33. The collapse of Argentina's traditional export markets had a tremendous impact on the domestic economy. Thus the initial effect of the Great Depression resulted in a seriously deteriorating balance of trade situation that led to a 40 per cent devaluation of the peso in 1931–32 and the establishment of exchange controls. Despite the drastic effects caused by the world crisis on the domestic economy, up to 1933 the government adopted a *laisser-faire* and, in a certain sense, a *laisser-passer* attitude based on the assumption that the crisis was of a temporary nature. Nevertheless, a recovery programme for the temporary relief of the situation was adopted in 1933, a year in which the economy reached rock-bottom levels. Subsequently, the measures and institutions created reflected beginnings of a very different policy orientation. These new institutions and controls aimed to defend the dominant (mostly agricultural and livestock) interests and the stability of the economy as a whole. With this, the beginnings of what were to become important elements of an ISI strategy were set in motion.

As Whitaker has put it:

Ironically, measures such as quotas and exchange controls, which were designed to protect only the landlords, had the unintentional effect of providing a modicum of protection to manufacturers, while failing to bring relief to the many little people in the lower reaches of the agricultural-pastoral sector. It was also ironic that such relief as these little people – mainly small farmers, tenants, and peons – did receive came from the growing industrial sector through its increasing demand for factory workers and foodstuffs. (Whitaker 1975: 4)

A series of agricultural regulatory boards similar to those of Canada and Australia were established. These were to regulate the prices and incomes of the agricultural sector; in essence, however, they aimed to defend the dominant interests of agriculture. In addition, complementary protectionist measures were adopted. The need to attain an external balance in the balance of payments led to exchange controls and import duties that tended to favour not only agricultural interests but industrial interests as well. These measures helped to raise profit rates in the new import substituting manufacturing and rural activities (Díaz Alejandro 1975: 102).

These measures, designed to cope with the impact of the Great Depression, complemented already existing ISI related industries and policies. For instance, the creation of YPF, the state petroleum entity, was to a large extent proposed by the nationalist military establishment. Emphasis on strategic industries (petroleum, coal, steel) had been already mentioned in military circles as essential to reduce foreign dependency of the economy.

Since the bulk of government revenue was based on export and import duties, the falling external demand and hence government revenue brought about an increase in the government deficit. The government tried to cope with this situation by floating titles on the market. While the initial response to the crisis was oriented towards balancing the budget and paying the foreign debt even at the expense of a domestic contraction, new instruments of policy were created and used. Raúl Prebisch at the time worked in the research department of the Banco de la Nación Argentina. New sources of public revenues were established when the income tax was instituted. He also was keen on establishing the need to create a central bank. In 1933, Prebisch had read four articles Keynes had published in *The Times* of London (13–16 March 1933). He became convinced of the need to develop an expansive policy and elaborated a Plan de expansión económica, which was adopted in November 1933. This was a Keynesian plan of economic expansion that was to control foreign trade with a very selective foreign exchange policy. Furthermore, the overall contraction of domestic economic activities had led to an increase in the number of unemployed. The only way to overcome this situation was though a state programme of public works that was to contribute to a redistribution of purchasing power among a large quantity of workers, increasing overall market demand, and contributing to an absorption of the unemployed in private industry (Fernández López 1996: 25). Solving the problem of unemployment thus became an important policy issue.

It is not difficult to visualize why this was so. The crisis had an immense impact on wages and earnings, and generated a high level of unemployment. The balance of trade deficits became problems that had to be tackled effectively, as did large-scale unemployment. ISI was to solve both problems: new industries had to substitute imports and hence contribute to restoring the balance of trade difficulties, and they had to provide employment. The crisis had already reduced employment opportunities in agriculture, as massive domestic migrations substituted for previous external immigration. A new working class was in the making and urban industry was soon to become the main source of employment and income for the economy as a whole.

Background to the Rise of Peronism

The 'infamous decade' of the 1930s and the Second World War brought about new conflicts and political and economic processes. Industrialization increasingly oriented to the domestic market was to a large extent based on the increase in the number of small and medium-sized businesses. The composition of industry changed as the products actually manufactured were concentrated to a large extent in metal products and textiles. Foreign capital investments in industry were increasingly non-British, enhancing the conflicts between rival foreign capital interests (Villanueva 1975: 72–3) Furthermore, the Second World War created a natural protection for domestic industry, and induced it to find new markets not only domestically but in other Latin American countries as well. These were industries that required a certain degree of protection on behalf of the state, specially after the war, considering that they were too weak to lobby in favour of their own interests or to have a significant representation in the traditional party system (Murmis and Portantiero 1971: 115). Domestic migration to the cities not only increased urbanization, but also increased the importance and composition of the working classes. With agriculture stagnating as a source of employment and income (in particular for the small tenants and agricultural labourers), industry became increasingly the more attractive and often the only source of income and employment.

On the foreign policy front new conflicts emerged. The treaties with Great Britain, in particular the Roca–Runciman treaty of 1931, were considered extremely onerous for Argentine interests. Attempts were made in the early 1930s to replace Great Britain as a market for Argentina's exports, in consonance with the ever-increasing role played by the USA in the world economy and as an important source of Argentina's imports. Nevertheless, the attempts failed, probably due to the fact that 'satisfying Argentina's needs had repercussions for the entire United States farm program. While failure to conclude a treaty with Argentina would not undermine the [US] administration's trade policy, further pressure in support of Argentine interests might destroy the coalition that Roosevelt depended upon to support his farm program' (Tulchin 1975: 103, 106–7). For these and other reasons, by the end of the 1930s antipathy to Argentina's imperial connections was widespread.

During the Second World War the conflicts between the Axis and the Democracies influenced both Argentina's role in the world economy and its domestic policies. The issue of neutrality *vis-à-vis* the Axis constituted a source of conflict in particular with the US government. While domestically the watershed between the pro-Allied and the pro-Axis cut through several governments, an overall consensus was maintained with regards to the need to maintain a certain neutrality. This was sustained not only by the pro-Axis, but also by the British diplomacy as well: it was considered that this was necessary to maintain Argentina's role as a provider of food and raw materials to the Allies (Escudé 1983).

> Neutrality, then, was a nationalistic policy. It and the concept of nationalism from which it was derived, the mechanism of State control over exports and foreign exchange upon which it was based, and the technicians who carried it out were essentially the same under pro-Allied democrats like Ortiz and his Foreign Minister José María Cantilo, or pro-Axis leaders with fascistic proclivities, like Castillo or Ruiz-Guiñazú. It should not be cause for surprise then, that the military leaders who took power in 1943 followed a nationalistic line in foreign policy. Their policy was not something alien to the Argentine spirit, invented by the military mind. Colonel Juan Domingo Perón the emerging leader of the 1943 military junta, therefore followed the lead of a foreign policy which had been evolving throughout the 1930s. What was to become the Third Position ... an expression of strong Argentine nationalism, was thus in many ways a response to the failure of Great Britain and the United States to strengthen their commercial relations with Argentina during a period of profound economic crisis. (Tulchin 1975: 109)

Needless to say, these factors were to influence domestic events, in particular those concerning the labour movement and the legitimacy of the Peronist regime.

The ISI process of the 1930s had not been redistributive or reformist in any sense. Though important trade unions under anarchist, syndicalist or socialist auspices had been active prior to the 1930s – La Fraternidad of the railway workers, that of the printers, and state workers – they, as well as the new trade union movement of the textile and metallurgical, chemical industry and tobacco workers, were relatively excluded from reaping the fruits of industrial development. Once the war began, the traditional trade union movement, dominated by the communists and socialists, was reluctant to strike or present claims lest its actions might stifle the supplies provided to the Allies as part of the war effort. A series of protracted grievances were accumulated and not addressed. The assumption that the Peronist movement was to be based exclusively on the new trade unionists, provided by traditional agrarian workers that had migrated to the cities, had shown to be insufficient

(Murmis and Portantiero 1971). In the early 1940s, the trade union movement of Argentina was already one of the strongest in Latin America. Its support to the impending Peronist movement was quite crucial, being the basis of a certain autonomy not found at the time in other populist movements such as the *vargista* movement in Brazil (ibid.). '[T]he adherence of the workers to populism at its moment of construction could be legitimately perceived as the most adequate election, given the alternatives provided by reality, for this political alliance served as a solution to an industrialization process that had been carried out under the control of a traditional elite, without any working-class participation or social interventionism of any sort' (Murmis and Portantiero 1971: 124, my translation).

ISI under Peronism (1946–55)

The coup of 1943 was carried out by a group of army officers (the GOU) with strong nationalist and pro-Axis tendencies, and Colonel Perón was one of their main ideologues. Perón soon became minister of defence and secretary of labour and social security. In the latter capacity he was particularly active, legitimizing trade unions and solving labour conflicts, in most cases in favour of labour. Labour began to be recognized and institutionalized to an extent unheard of previously. In the view of Perón and his military colleagues, apart from the military, labour was to become one of the main pillars of the new political regime. As of yet a domestic 'national bourgeoisie' was too weak to have any political significance. Only in the 1950s, during the second term of the Peronist administration, was the Confederación General Económica (CGE) created, representing a vast segment of mostly small and medium-sized businesses of the interior. The CGE acquired considerable influence.

Consequently, various trade unions and trade unionists of varied political tendencies transferred their support to Perón and became the backbone of the impending Peronist government. When Perón was imprisoned in 1945, the labour movement moved for his liberation, which took place on 17 October 1945. Subsequently the trade union movement was to be one of the main supports of the developing *peronista* movement. After the Peronist government won the elections in 1946, ISI policies were continued, including pro-labour and social welfare measures unknown up to then.

Perón and the *peronista* movement developed a strong nationalist and industrialist policy, intending to attain a certain economic independence. To do so, important reform and redistributive measures had to be adopted. As was frequently mentioned during the Peronist government, the main objectives of that movement were to attain economic independence, social justice and political sovereignty. It is in this context that the institutions of ISI developed in the 1930s, and were soon transformed and made instrumental to the needs of the developing Peronist administration.

The Peronist state became an important instrument of policy. The prevailing political, economic and social conditions were such as to permit the state to acquire an economic role that it had not had previously. The series of institutions created in the 1930s, directed to cope with the impending world Depression, were transformed, a transformation that meant the development of a new state. Now those same instruments, plus several others created under the Peronist administration, were to make ISI part of a conscious effort of development policy. The Central Bank was nationalized, the IAPI (see below) was created, and a series of nationalizations of public services took place. Planning became part of government policy. And apart from the benefits to the trade union movement, social policy, to a large extent given impulse by Eva Perón, also acquired new dimensions.

In 1944, a decree established special promotional measures in favour of industrialization. Industries that used the country's raw materials and destined their production to the domestic market and those producing essential goods were marked as being of 'national interest', as were the industries that were of interest to national defence. Import tariffs for these industries were raised, and in some specific cases special quotas or prohibitions for competing or similar production were specified. Moreover, tariffs on machinery were reduced and special credits and subsidies were established for the activity to be promoted (Apiazu 1988: 2).

Among the new institutions were the Consejo Nacional de Postguerra (National Council for the Postwar period), a planning board that developed a series of diagnosis concerning the socioeconomic situation, and the Instituto Argentino para la Promoción del Intercambio (Argentine Institute of Trade Promotion, IAPI), which was allowed a monopoly of foreign trade, retaining part of the agriculture surplus, to provide for the purchase of inputs for industrial development, and to redistribute income in favour of industry. In addition, the financial system was reformed and the Central Bank nationalized. With these institutions the First Five Year Plan of 1947 was to be financed. Industrialization based on the domestic market thus became one of the central objectives of economic policy. An economic policy based on the domestic market directed by the state, which was also to plan investments on the basis of the future needs of society, was presumably the means whereby income was to be redistributed towards small and medium-sized business, and in favour of the working classes. Thus an implicit or explicit alliance between the new and more dynamic sectors of the industrial bourgeoisie and organized labour, guaranteed by the state, defined the essence of the new populist government (Girbal-Blancha 1998: 3). Needless to say, the new government represented an important change. It reflected an important change in the traditional power structure, which had been incapable of solving many important socioeconomic problems related to the dependency of the Argentine economy.

The Peronist state thus acquired a crucial role. It was to help consolidate

the autonomy of the nation – that is, to attain a greater economic independence, an objective solemnly proclaimed in 1947. This was illustrated
by a series of nationalizations, including those of railways, gas, telephones,
electricity and shipping. Funds accumulated during the war and in large
measure blockaded by the inconvertibility of the pound sterling were used
to finance part of these nationalizations. The foreign debt was reimbursed.
In addition, income distribution was substantially enhanced: wages were
increased, labour laws were set on the books, trade unions were legitimized,
and social welfare measures related to health, pension funds and education
were significantly enhanced and made the law of the land in the reformed
Constitution of 1949. All these measures had an enormous impact on income
distribution, and hence on the dynamics of ISI based on the domestic market.
Industrial development was largely based on the production of wage goods,
oriented to the demands of lower-income strata – for example, textiles, light
metallurgical products and household goods. Cheap credit oriented towards
industries meeting the demands of wage-earners was also intensified. Other
industries would produce luxury goods, consumed by upper-income groups.

Before the Peronist government was installed after the 1946 elections, a
series of labour laws and welfare measures had already been legislated by the
secretary of labour of the military government under the auspices of Perón:
mechanisms for the effective implementation of collective bargaining; a series
of norms regulating important severance payments; collective bargaining
agreements and paid vacations; and the extension of the retirement and
pension funds system to employees and workers of industry and commerce.
As Tulio Halperin Donghi puts it: 'all these innovations were presented as
a reparation that the nation presented to its working classes, they were
therefore invited to look upon themselves as a legitimate part of the nation'
(Halperin Donghi 1972: 37, my translation).

The Peronist ISI project was nevertheless financed in large measure by the
surpluses provided by agriculture, this being simultaneously the main source
of Argentina's exports. In 1943, a government decree reduced tenants' rents
by 20 per cent, and tenants' contracts were extended and executions suspended. There was also talk of land reform, and Agrario Nacional, created
in 1940, realized some expropriations of land and began a certain colonization
(settlements). However, this proclaimed agrarian reform in favour of 'those
that work the land' was not fully implemented. The reforms introduced did
not bring about a substantial change in the power structure: to a large extent
the power of the landowning elite was not broken. Consequently, investments
tended to be reduced. Both freezing rents and the menace of a land reform
that nevertheless was not fully implemented led to the stagnation of agricultural production and hence exports. The government tried to maintain a
certain balance between the interests of landowners, tenants and exporters
for political reasons: it was deemed necessary that tensions within agriculture
were reduced. Furthermore, wage increases for agricultural labourers, the

Estatuto del Peón of 1944 regulating labour conditions of agricultural workers, and the corresponding statute regulating dairy tenants (Estatuto del Tambero-Mediero) of 1946, were measures favouring agricultural labourers and tenants, which implied increased costs for landowners. In accordance with overall ISI policies, considerable support was given to agrarian cooperatives, credit and otherwise, that had traditionally been very important in Argentine agriculture.

Up to 1950, the IAPI paid relatively low prices for agricultural produce. Low prices plus controls on tenant payments and increases in rural wages were resisted by landowners, and this was reflected in a reduction of the area sown. These low prices were in part compensated by cheap credit provided by the official banking system, yet they were apparently insufficient to stem the trend towards lower investments. According to some observers, in the first years of his administration Perón sacrificed the rural sector, eliminating all stimuli that would increase agricultural production, at a time when increased domestic consumption had also reduced export availability. Economic policy lacked a deliberate investment policy in infrastructures and in basic industries, a fact that made the economy extremely vulnerable (Halperin Donghi 1972: 72).

The situation became critical in 1951–52, when a severe drought affected the Pampean region. In addition, low international prices had a bearing on the overall situation affecting Argentine agriculture. International prices of Argentina's agricultural export commodities fell in 1949–50, due to bumper harvests in Europe, Canada and the USA.

Thus, due to the fact that the vulnerability of the economy had not been addressed sufficiently, the economic programme began to experience difficulties. It was in this context that the government began to reverse its course on several public policy issues. Agriculture was given new incentives through a number of changes of IAPI policies: in contrast to previous years, subsidies were now transferred to agriculture. This led to increases in agricultural production. Prices were increased, and the efficiency and productivity of agriculture were again considered as essential. Measures were taken to influence the foreign exchange rate, allowing the purchase of agriculture machinery abroad. Farmers were given special credits and agricultural products were purchased at higher than international prices. These measures were taken to intensify agricultural production. In 1953, Perón claimed that the crisis situation was under control, mainly due to the reactivation of agricultural production, more rapid and efficient mechanization, the organization of agrarian unions and the support given to cooperative organizations, which made up 45 per cent of total agricultural production (Girbal-Blancha 1998: 73).

New liberal practices were introduced elsewhere in the economy as well. As a reaction to the crisis, the overall trend of transferring agricultural surpluses to industry and a strengthening of real domestic wages was halted. Some observers notice that these were the beginnings of the adjustments that many years later Menem was to apply forcefully during his administration. As we shall see, there is some truth in this idea, but there are also many differences.

In 1953, a stabilization programme was implemented. During a meeting of the Congreso de la Productividad, the official Confederación General del Trabajo (CGT) and the newly formed entrepreneurial CGE, it was agreed that essential new investments were to be made and that the goal of increasing productivity should be sustained. However, machinery that was to be purchased had to be paid for with foreign exchange. This implied the need for new sources of foreign financing, something that, apparently, had been forcefully rejected in 1947 when the economic independence of Argentina was proclaimed (Halperin Donghi 1972: 79). The Argentine government started to look for new sources of finance and as a result the foreign debt increased once again. In 1953, a new law on foreign investments guaranteed foreign investors their profit remittances. In 1954, these measures were followed by changes in the policy on petroleum investments, and again new concessions were made to foreign companies. All these measures formed part of policies that seriously reversed the course the regime had taken earlier. In one area, however, the Peronist government did not falter: social welfare and labour and trade union benefits that had been legislated, and that had been written into the Constitution of 1949, were not changed. As Halperin Donghi (1972: 79) observes:

> confronted with the alternative of liberalising but inducing greater investments so as to increase ISI, or simply reducing the benefits that had been given to the labouring classes, government opted for a limited liberalisation, that did not affect the distribution of income. ISI was arrested, and some liberalisation was begun. But though it was not accompanied by the redistributive measures of the first years, neither were there the drastic cuts in income and wages (both direct and indirect) that labour was to receive later on.

After the First Peronist Government: ISI under *Desarrollismo*

In 1955, a military coup overthrew the Peronist government. The government of General Eduardo Lonardi that assumed power had a somewhat conciliatory attitude towards Peronism and, in particular, towards the Peronist-dominated trade unions. But his overtures led to his replacement by Eugenio Aramburu. This government of the 'Revolución Libertadora' was to last only a few years. In 1958, elections were called and Arturo Frondizi, who had detached himself from the UCR and had created a new party, the Unión Cívica Radical Intransigente (UCRI), came to power with the support of Perón and the *peronista* movement that had been proscribed from presenting itself in elections. In exile, Perón signed a Pact with Frondizi, in which a series of policies in favour of labour would be continued in exchange for the support given to his election. This pact lasted only a couple of years; after that Frondizi followed a policy of persecution of labour and the labour movement. Alvaro Alsogaray, who has become one of the symbols of neoliberalism in Argentina, was named minister of the economy in 1962 in an attempt to stave off the impending military coup. Nevertheless, Frondizi was overthrown by the military in 1962 and Arturo Illia was elected in 1963 with only 24 per cent of the vote. The constitutional government of Illia was overthrown in 1966, and a new military regime took over. The military regime of the Revolución Argentina was to last up to 1973 when the Peronists finally came to power once again, only to be overthrown in 1976.

This period (1960s to mid-1970s) marked a new stage in the political and socioeconomic development of Argentina, extending throughout the 1960s and up to the mid-1970s. The political terrain was dominated to a large extent by the opposition of Peronism, in particular the Peronist trade union movement, to successive governments as well as by the attempts of the *antiperonistas* to do away with all vestiges of Peronism in Argentine society. After this period of La Resistencia, during the first years of the Revolución Libertadora, the Peronist movement not only survived, despite serious attempts to prohibit everything that had to do with it, but tended to dominate politics as well. The trade union movement became highly heterogeneous, and one of its important factions, dominating some of the more important trade unions, developed a *neoperonista* outlook, considering that Peronism had to dispose of Perón, and acquire an autonomy which would permit it to negotiate with other factions in order to survive. This marked the beginnings of the so-called 'trade union bureaucracy', a group that played an important political role in the Argentine society of the 1960s.

The above described political situation led to a succession of civilian and military governments. Military interventionism came about when the advances of Peronism and labour appeared to be a threat to the more dominant factions of bourgeois society. In effect, Peronism was questioned by other factions and sectors of society, as well. Peronism and antiperonism and the different brands of Peronism vied in a context in which numerous alliances were sought and broken. While conflicting views reflected important ideological undercurrents underlying the complex political scenario, one could describe this period as one in which different bourgeois factions vied for their say in economic and social policy. On the one hand, we can identify the more 'nationalist' alliance based on an explicit or implicit pact of labour with certain bourgeois factions generally interested in furthering ISI and the domestic market. On the other hand, the 'liberal' alliance between the traditional agrarian interests, associated with certain transnational interests and with foreign capital, vied continuously for their say in policy decisions, tending towards a greater liberalization of the economy and monetarism (Teubal 1993). ISI policies were continued but, under the aegis of *desarrollismo*, foreign capital was now considered essential for its development. *Desarrollismo* also favoured planning of different sorts, for example the indicative planning of the French type, for which a series of institutions were created in Argentina, and state enterprises in charge of infrastructure services remained in State hands, while important servicing was frequently contracted abroad or to local business groups. In 1958, several decrees promoting specific sectors were legislated: the steel, petrochemical and paper industries were earmarked as of special interest, as were certain geographic regions of the interior – for example, the Patagonia, the North West, and the Province of Corrientes were singled out. These decrees were also related to the new regulations on foreign investments.

Another consideration involving the political scenario of the 1960s and 1970s was the impact and revalorization of Peronism among certain middle classes, mainly youth organizations, and amidst the emerging guerrilla movements. Already in the 1960s Peronism was increasingly seen as a revolutionary movement forming part of the wave of revolutionary politics prevalent in the 1960s. This idea permitted Perón to approach new youth organizations and movements. Perón himself began to see his movement as part of a Third World movement, this being, according to some authors, a reinterpretation of the Third Position that he had assumed in the 1940s (see Ben Plotkin 1993: 56). Perón started to cite Mao, Nasser, Castro, and even De Gaulle and to associate his own movement with other movements of the Third World, representing alternatives to both capitalism and communism. In many circles Peronism, to a large extent induced by Perón's comments in interviews or writings, was looked upon as a revolutionary movement. The series of guerrilla movements that ascribed to Peronism during the late 1960s were not disqualified by Perón. Moreover, Perón's return to Argentina was looked upon as the prelude to revolution. When Hector Campora was elected President in 1973 with the support of the left (the assorted *formaciones especiales* (guerrillas) active at the time) one of the slogans used in the campaign was 'Cámpora al gobierno, Perón al Poder' (Campora in government, Perón in power). It was thought that Perón's assuming power would signify a revolution. Nowadays, with the benefit of hindsight, the strong reformist policies of the second Peronist government, which came to power for a short period in 1973–74, was, compared with what was to come about next, highly reformist, but still quite revolutionary indeed in terms of its economic policy.

Under the auspices of *desarrollismo* (or developmentalism) ISI policies were continued in this period. Development was considered crucial for the modernization of society, and development was to be induced by industrialization. One of the characteristics of *desarrollismo* was its emphasis on the role of foreign capital. The two governments most representative of *desarrollismo* were that of Frondizi in 1958–62, and that of the military regime of the so-called Revolución Argentina of the 1966–73 period. Needless to say, the redistributive aspects of ISI based on a social pact between labour and the national bourgeoisie, characteristic of Peronism, were not sustained by these governments. Foreign capital was given prominence under the *desarrollista* administrations of Frondizi and Juan Carlos Onganía. They were invited to invest in petroleum, the automobile industry, petrochemicals, etc. Under the *desarrollista* perspective of Rogelio Frigerio, one of the main ideologues of this political ideology, what was important for Argentine society was the development of 'productive forces', and that this could be done with the concourse of foreign capital. Thus foreign capital and foreign investments became key elements of the *desarrollista* perspective.

Throughout this period the trade union movement consolidated its power and continued to be one of the most powerful and organized of Latin America. Trade unionists had an important say in the politics and economics of succeeding governments. While along the economic cycle different social sectors were favoured by economic policies, as had occurred during previous regimes, ISI also periodically had to confront foreign trade vulnerability: the import of inputs and intermediary and capital goods tended to increase more rapidly than agricultural exports, which remained the main source of Argentina's exports. Periodically, balance of trade and payments crises led to stabilization programmes, whereby the peso was devalued transferring income to agriculture, reducing wages in industry and in urban areas, and hence stifling demand and industrial growth. Stop-go policies were related to these succeeding phases of economic policy (Ferrer 1969).

While imports reduced when global domestic demand fell, unemployment increased. An external balance was usually sought through domestic 'adjustments'. The ensuing inflation that a devaluation tended to create was caused by the *puja sectorial* of the diverse bourgeois factions, mainly agriculture versus industry, but also by the resistance of labour to wage reductions. This situation created economic instability. Some scholars observed the development of a political and economic cycle: these cycles were nevertheless accompanied by military coups, which interrupted civilian governments. That of 1966 was the first 'authoritarian bureaucratic government' (O'Donnell) and lasted until 1973. Subsequently, that of 1976 inaugurated a new regime of accumulation in a much more forceful way.

The ISI policies of the 1960s were quite different from those of the 1940s and 1950s. Oscar Braun termed this stage 'dependent monopolistic capitalism' (Braun 1973: 12–13). Planners and intellectuals proclaimed the need to pass on to the more 'difficult' stage of import substitution, that is, the substitution of intermediary and capital goods imports with industries, producing goods with a greater degree of complex technologies. This process of import substitution required the establishment of 'heavy industry', which was to guarantee a certain degree of autonomy to the economy as a whole. New import substituting industries plus the exports of non-traditional manufactured goods were some of the main components of these strategies. All this required an important degree of government interventionism: some industries were established with government participation, incentives or other measures provided by government. Earlier, unbalances of ISI were 'treated' via an intensification of the ISI, that is, by extending substitution of imports to capital and intermediary goods industries. A new non-traditional export strategy was also proclaimed necessary, but was not fully implemented.

Nevertheless, while a structuralist approach to ISI emphasized industrialization *per se*, the *dependentista* perspective brought out other features related to the dynamics of capitalist society. An economy can be to a large extent 'self-centred', to use Samir Amin's expression, but still highly dependent. Braun summarized succinctly many of the features of dependency: a primary export economy; the concentration of exports in a group of a few products or markets; lack of technology; the foreign control of a substantial part of business; and the dependence on foreign debt for the balancing of balance of payments (Braun 1973: 13–14). In the 1960s, GNP grew by 4.2 per cent per annum while industrial growth amounted to 4.3 per cent in 1960–64 and 5.1 per cent in 1965–69. The growth of GNP was one of the highest of Argentine history (see Figure 2.1). New industries were established, and Argentina was definitely considered to be a semi-industrialized country (see Díaz Alejandro 1975). Industry producing mainly food, textiles and metallurgical products (including the automobile industry) absorbed 71 per cent of total industrial employment. Paper, heavy chemicals and petrochemicals advanced substantially in this period, but not necessarily as a source of employment. Electricity and petroleum and other sources of energy were sources for substantial new investments.

Literacy rates continued to increase as education continued to extend, in particular university education. The economy apparently responded to the demands of an increasingly middle- and working-class society and to increased investments in science and technology. This was the heyday of higher education and new sources of investments in science and technology. Foreign capital also had a say in this process as investments were oriented to petroleum, automobile, petrochemical and other industries. Next, the national bourgeoisie consolidated its power, presumably supported by a vast array of medium and small-sized businesses.

During the mid-1970s, however, some changes occurred. The renewed Peronist administration of Campora (1973–74), and Perón, up to his death in 1974, attempted a return to a more traditional Peronist policy. During this first stage of the new Peronist regime economic policy was led by José Ber Gelbard (the representative of the CGE, the organization of the national bourgeoisie in Argentina). Under the organization of the CGE, the Argentine national bourgeoisie had become an important factor. The appointment of José Ber Gelbard as minister of economy only contributed to this. The CGE represented the interests of small and medium-sized business oriented towards the domestic market and traditionally often clashed with the Unión Industrial Argentina. One of the main instruments of the new Peronist government was the celebration of a social pact between the CGE and the CGT whereby wages were to be increased and prices controlled. Furthermore, other measures contributing to ISI were agreed upon as well.

An important aspect of this government's policy – apart from its income policy – was the declared intention of adopting a new exports strategy, which led to breaking the blockade that the USA had imposed on Cuba and establishing new relations with Russia and the Eastern Bloc. This new relationship with Cuba and the new overture to Russia and Eastern Europe were in some respects continued by the succeeding military regime of the *proceso*. This programme was one of the last attempts to establish a national popular programme in Argentina. It was criticized from several quarters. The traditional agricultural interests boycotted the policies, in particular the attempts to establish a land tax. Furthermore, foreign capital opposed the role the national bourgeoisie was acquiring. In addition, trade unionists criticized the programme once the political situation began foundering. Subsequent Argentine governments erased all traces of a bond between the national bourgeoisie and the trade unions.

Towards a New Regime of Accumulation: Structural Adjustments and the Role of Peronism[1]

Two highlights were important in paving the way for the establishment of a new regime of accumulation in Argentina: the military coup of 1976 and the so-called 'economic coup' of 1989. The military coup of 1976 was undoubtedly an important landmark; a ferocious new 'bureaucratic authoritarian State' (O'Donnell) was established, presumably for the purpose of 'doing away with subversion' and saving 'Western Christian Civilization from the perils of Communism'. A series of measures were adopted – some operating on the labour front, others aimed at financial and capital markets – that changed substantially the workings of the economy. The 'economic coup' of 1989 was a prelude to hyperinflation, which also served to create the need for new 'disciplinary' measures imposed on a large part of civil society via the Convertibility Plan of 1991. This plan was part of the extreme structural adjustment programme implemented during the Menem administration. Up to then the adjustments applied by the military and by the Alfonsín administration had been mostly short-term and did not consider some of the more 'structural reforms' that were presumed necessary to restructure the economy in order to make it much more 'market-friendly'. Nevertheless, these policies signified not only the end of ISI strategies in Argentina, but also the beginnings of a new 'regime of accumulation' in Argentina.

Freezing wage increases and reducing wages in the public sector for the purpose of dampening fiscal deficits were among the first measures adopted by the military government of the Proceso de Reorganización Nacional (national reorganization process) in April 1976. This was the recommended pattern for the private sector as well. Real wages fell substantially (a result also of price liberalization and a reduction in government expenditures). In the first three months of the new military regime real wages fell by an estimated 40 per cent in relation to the levels attained in the first half of the decade (Marshall 1995: Table 3). Furthermore, the share of wages in GNP fell from about 49.3 per cent in 1975 (an average 45.9 per cent for the 1970–74 period) to 32.8 per cent in 1976 (and on average about 32.3 per cent of GNP in the 1976–80 period) (Schvarzer 1983: 130). These trends continued throughout the 1980s and 1990s. While in the first years of the Alfonsín administration and during the implementation of the Austral Plan (in 1985) there were small increases in real wages, at no time did these attain their pre-1976 levels. Real wages during the Convertibility Plan of the Menem administration continued to fell systematically. Thus real wages appear throughout the period as the main 'adjustment variable' of the policies adopted. All real wage estimates show decreases in the past decades. For the economy as a whole from an index of 150.8 in 1975 (1980=100) to 103.7 in 1985, and 74.4 in 1995 (data produced by FIDE as reported in *Cash*, economic supplement of *Página 12*, 2 July 1995).

Why did real wages fall? In the first place this was due to the impact of adjustment policies on labour markets, which induced real wages to fall, unemployment to increase and employment to become more precarious. Under the military regime trade union activity was prohibited, and labour leaders were persecuted or 'disappeared'. It has been estimated that about 40 per cent of the *desaparecidos* were wage-earners, including many factory shop-floor labour leaders. With the return to democracy, trade union activity was reinstated. But this did not impede the adoption of a series of measures tending towards the 'flexibilization' and 'precarization' of labour markets. These measures, particularly under the Menem administration, combined with a process of deindustrialization (increasing unemployment or changing the occupational structure) that induced large real wage falls. The military government also eliminated a series of regulations and subsidies, presumably for the purpose of increasing the 'efficiency' of the economy. Tariffs were reduced from an average 90 per cent *ad valorem* rate to a 50 per cent rate and interest rates were liberalized: the financial reforms of 1977–79 led to real interest rate increases. They also increased due to uncertainty and high banking transaction costs.

A new system for managing the foreign exchange rate – a preannounced exchange rate – was devised by Martínez de Hoz, the minister of the economy of the military regime. It was presumably to induce domestic inflation to converge to international inflation rates, and to guarantee foreign investors that local real interest rates were to be maintained at a higher than international interest rate levels, thus maintaining the profitability of money market operations and speculative investments in local money markets. These measures – opening up to the world economy, maintaining higher than international domestic interest rates, establishing an overvalued exchange rate – all contributed to deindustrialization and to disarticulation in that they were biased against medium and small business and labouring classes.

> [F]inancial speculation was exacerbated by the financial reform of 1979: profits channelled to the financial sector tended to remain within the financial circuit. Capital owners speculated domestically and abroad, made little investment in manufacturing activities at home, and their profit expectations were increasingly based on ever shorter time spans. To the rapid growth of speculation should be added the impact of the 'opening up' of the Argentine economy. The final outcome was the partial dismantling of the manufacturing sector and the substantial increase in idle capacity. (Marshall 1992: 14)

Thus deindustrialization was to a large extent deliberate. The economic establishment was interested in eliminating the possibility of there being a return to the 'national–popular' alliance of previous years that had been the main sustenance of ISI strategies. Not only were trade unions and trade union activity prohibited, but the CGE was also dissolved and several of its main leaders were persecuted (see Seoane 1998). These measures increased the importance of financial interests and particularly the activities of large local and international conglomerates (the so called *grupos económicos* analysed by Apiazu, Basualdo and Khavisse 1986). It was in this period that foreign debt increased from about $7 billion in 1976 to more then $43 billion in 1983, its main beneficiaries being these large economic conglomerates. The new economic power structure that emerged during the military dictatorship of the *proceso* years was the main beneficiary of this large foreign debt, which in 1982 was 'nationalized', that is, transferred to the state (see Basualdo 1987). Nevertheless, the large devaluation of 1981, the ensuing crisis that this caused, and the Malvinas (Falklands) war defeat were important events that arrested temporarily the development of this new neoconservative project. Foreign debt continued throughout the 1980s and 1990s under the administration of successive governments. Under Menem it increased from $62 billion in 1990 to $118 billion in 1997. A large part of this foreign debt financed capital flight, which is reflected in external deposits abroad of Argentineans officially estimated at about $75 billion in 1997 (see Mayo 1999).

The Alfonsín administration was beset by the problem of 'governability'. If democracy was to be defended – there were many forces interested in a return to a military dictatorship – 'governability' was to be maintained at all costs, even if this required a policy of non-confrontation with the military and economic establishments. On the economic front this implied following the dictates of the IMF and World bank. These policies were followed mostly under the minister of the economy Juan Sourrouille, after Bernardo Grinspun, his predecessor, had failed in his attempt to negotiate foreign debt servicing directly with creditor banks.

Thus, while the radical administration was initially committed to increasing real wages and reducing income inequality, the policies implemented during this administration ended in a prolonged economic stagnation and increased the marginalization of an important part of the workforce. Alfonsín's adjustments were severe due to the nationalization of the foreign debt carried out in the last years of the military government. Roll-overs of this foreign debt servicing and a plan to implement equity for debt swaps were elaborated. Nevertheless, his privatization programme was opposed by the Peronists in Congress, which controlled the Senate.

Furthermore, excessive popular participation was also considered unhealthy for 'democracy'. Despite these considerations the Alfonsín administration was beset by a series of military uprisings and pressures by the economic establishment. On the other hand he had to cope with 13 general strikes waged against his overall economic programme by the CGT. While his policies followed the recommendations of the 'Washington Consensus', he was unable to cope with the economic coup of 1989 and the ensuing hyperinflationary spurt and social chaos of that year, which obliged him to resign five months prior to the conclusion of his term in office.

The election campaign in early 1989 was carried out in the midst of an increasingly unstable economic situation marked by an inflation that rapidly transformed into hyperinflation. Monthly inflation rates had been 14 per cent in 1988; they escalated to a monthly rate of almost 200 per cent in July 1989, a consequence of the wholesale capital flight induced by the economic establishment. Capital flight to the dollar increased exchange rates and devaluation expectations exponentially. They were to punish Alfonsín for not having fully serviced Argentina's foreign debt in the last years of his administration, but also gave notice to Menem, at the time the Peronist presidential candidate, that the establishment would not permit a policy that did not follow the tenets of the 'Washington Consensus'. Thus in 1989 hyperinflation substantially disorganized the economy and society: it paralysed production, reduced real wages drastically and increased misery and social discontent.

Menem campaigned on a typically Peronist programme – he promised that he would implement a *salariazo* (large wages increase) and promote a *revolución productiva* (a productive revolution). Yet after winning the elections in May of that year he immediately changed course. He surprised friends and foes by setting aside his 'populist' convictions and programme and initiating a severe structural adjustment programme as part of a 'shock therapy' strategy. Menem's first minister of the economy was a director of Bunge and Born, the large Argentine conglomerate. Menem wanted to let the establishment know that he was not going to carry out a traditional Peronist programme. Despite several attempts to apply orthodoxy to monetary and economic matters in these first years of his rule, his government was not able to control the inflationary spurts of the 1989–91 period.

Only after Domingo Cavallo (a neoliberal minister who assumed office in 1991) established a Convertibility Plan was the Menem administration successful in bringing down inflation. A new fully convertible peso was established, of which the price was fixed on a 1 to 1 ratio to the dollar, and price indexing was prohibited by law (except when applied to certain public rates after the main public services had been privatized). All money creation not backed by foreign exchange reserves of the Central Bank – that is, by the inflow of foreign capital from abroad – was prohibited. The new convertibility regime, established by a law of Congress, aimed to eliminate all government discretionality with regard to monetary and foreign exchange policies. Its effect was equivalent to putting Argentina on a Gold Standard scheme limiting the functions of the Central Bank to that of an exchange broker (*caja de conversión*). Few countries at the time operated under such a convertibility regime. Apart from Argentina these schemes existed only in Gibraltar, Bermudas, Hong Kong, Estonia and Lithuania (Gerchunoff and Torre 1996: 745).

Cavallo hoped not only to bring down inflation by eliminating devaluation expectations drastically, but also to establish a new and enduring monetary and foreign exchange regime. This then permitted the implementation of drastic structural reform measures, including a wholesale privatization programme, a drastic open doors policy *vis-à-vis* foreign trade and investments and severe deregulatory measures, in particular concerning the flexibilization of labour markets.

The severity of Menem's programme was due in large measures to political considerations. Menem wanted to convince the national and international establishment that he was not going to apply a typically Peronist economic strategy (that is, nationalistic and popular), despite his electoral promises. According to Gerchunoff and Torre 'another reason that influenced the context in which structural reforms were initiated had to do with the classical problem of credibility'. A way to confront the political and economic crisis of the time was by 'resorting to those same policies that he [Menem] and the Peronist movement had always repudiated'. The uncertainty hyperinflation had created had much to do with this. But also the remembrance of the chaotic situation that had been prevalent under the previous Peronist administration, that is, in the 1973–76 period (Gerchunoff and Torre 1996: 735).

Thus once in power Menem immediately switched course and began the implementation of this extreme neoliberal programme, to be applied 'without parachutes or anesthesia' (these were his words), that is, without considering the possible rise of any opposition, or the social costs. All prior industrial, regional and export promotional regimes were suspended and the privileges national industries had had in providing for state purchases were eliminated. Government finances were controlled by a a reduction of inflation; taxes (mostly indirect on consumption) were increased, affecting mostly the middle classes. A surplus of public finances was necessary to finance the external sector, which included an important share of foreign debt servicing. The international financial establishment was delighted by the fact that Argentina entered the Brady Plan and began to reimburse its foreign debt services on a regular base. This was possible due to the income the state derived from its privatization programme, and, to some extent, to the overall economic expansion induced by increased consumption and the inflow of capital funds from abroad.

The privatization of the public sector was swift and exhaustive: in under three years more then thirty state public enterprises, the bulk of the state enterprises system, were privatized. Observers were elated by the swiftness and thoroughness with which the Argentine government proceeded to carry out this privatization programme. Privatization reached such diverse areas as: telephones and communications, airline companies, petrochemicals, petroleum, about 10,000 kilometres of highways, railways and other transport systems, natural gas distribution, electricity, water, iron and steel industries, coal, a series of firms in the defence area, hydroelectric dams, and other industries and services such as television channels, hotels, ports, silos and other port facilities, and horse-racing stadiums. Up to late 1993 these privatizations earned the government more than $15 billion (although net worth transferal was much greater. About $5.8 billion corresponded to the capitalization of public debt (domestic and foreign) (Apiazu 1994).

This privatization programme, however, excluded the institutionalization of regulatory boards, which in the First World are part and parcel of most privatization programmes. Deregulation followed similar procedures. Government finances were controlled; taxes, mostly indirect taxes such as VAT, were increased, affecting mostly the middle classes; and a surplus of public finances was sought to finance the external foreign debt servicing.

The Convertibility Plan was complemented by a drastic open doors policy and deregulatory measures, many of which were implemented by decree. By the end of 1990 almost all quantitative restrictions of imports were eliminated (except those concerning the automobile industry in relation to the Mercosur countries). A similar situation affected tariffs. In March 1991 a new tariff structure was set: raw materials were to have a nil tariff rate, inputs 11 per cent and final manufactured goods 22 per cent. The average tariff fell by 10 per cent. On the labour front the flexibility of labour and successive laws contributing to the precarization of labour markets ensued. Apart from foreign trade, the financial system and foreign investments procedures were also liberalized. Other regimes were deregulated as well. Apart from the sale of public services and state enterprises, the social security system was partially privatized and deregulated. Likewise, measures and institutions related to the agricultural sector were liberalized. As a matter of fact, the Agricultural Boards that had been created in the 1930s were now eliminated (Junta Nacional de Carnes, de Granos, del Azúcar, de la Yerba Mate, etc). But probably much more than other deregulatory measures the overall flex-ibilization of labour markets constituted a distinctive feature of the new regime of accumulation, and can be put on the par with measures such as the privatization of the bulk of state enterprises.

The reason why these adjustment programmes were implemented so rapidly was mainly political. As mentioned above, the Menem administration was elected on a typically Peronist platform, which included a series of government 'interventionist' measures. It was the type of programme that tended to be lenient with trade unions, and to develop nationalistic and pro-domestic market economic policies, based on the alliance of a 'national bourgeoisie' with the working and middle classes. However, Menem opted for the application of a 'shock therapy' treatment that was the total reverse of what had been promised. As Kohli mentions, and this could be confirmed in the case of Argentina:

> implicit in this prescription is the realization that reforms necessarily engender political opposition. The 'solution', in turn, is to take the society by surprise; if reforms are implemented, all at once, no one in the society will know what hit them and, meanwhile, economic rationality will have triumphed. This logic, however distasteful to those who value democracy, is at least internally consistent. It recognizes that the liberalization package is not something society demands but 'needs'; it is the 'bitter medicine' prescribed by 'economic doctors' that local rules must administer for a society's own good. (Kohli 1993: 682)

Nevertheless, the neoliberal strategy of the Menem administration would not have been as 'successful' as it apparently was (at least up to 1995, when the beginnings of the present crisis and massive unemployment began to be noted) were it not for the stability and economic expansion obtained in the wake of the Convertibility Plan. The initial 'success' of the Convertibility Plan was basic for the legitimization of Menem's severe structural adjustment programme. Probably, this programme would not have been successful without the 'stability' of the Convertibility Plan and the initial expansion and a certain welfare attained in the first years of its implementation.

The case of Argentina (at least up to the recent 'tequila effect'[2]) has been frequently portrayed in international fora as a showcase worth considering together with that of Chile and (pre-Chiapas) Mexico. The ex-minister of the economy, Domingo Cavallo, was seen as a wizard, and was well received in international fora. It is not difficult to see why this was so: since the application of the so-called Convertibility Plan in April 1991 inflation was brought down drastically. Consumer prices fell from about a 2,314 per cent increase in 1989 in the midst of hyperinflation to less than 4.2 per cent in 1994 and to 0.2 per cent in 1996, and the economy was reactivated somewhat. GNP increased throughout the 1992–94 period: 10.5 per cent in 1991, 10.3 per cent in 1992, 6.3 per cent in 1993, 8.5 per cent in 1995 (although there is some question concerning the trustworthiness of government statistics). The 'climate for foreign investments' was considerably improved due to the wholesale privatization programme. Foreign capital inflows increased substantially. In 1991, net capital inflows amounted to $3.2 billion, in 1992 they reached $11 billion and in 1993 they amounted to $10.7 billion. These inflows contributed to counterbalancing balance of trade deficits, but were mainly based on speculative capital. International credits and the foreign debt also increased. Nevertheless, the 'tequila effect' dampened part of this 'climate' and showed that much of the inflow of capital was of a speculative financial nature ready to leave on a minute's notice, as occurred in 1995, showing the vulnerability of this 'model'. Overall economic expansion levelled off in 1994, when international interest rates were increased and reached crisis proportions in 1995 when in the wake of the 'tequila crisis' GNP is estimated to have fallen by 4.6 per cent. Nevertheless, GNP continued to grow. In a country hit hard by the 'hyperinflation syndrome', which influences all walks of life, 'stability' was something highly valued indeed, and this permitted Menem to be elected once again in 1995.

The programme, however, elicited important 'social costs', which the government tended to minimize or characterize as 'inevitable'. First, unemployment in its varied forms increased, reaching record levels in 1995 when 'open unemployment' was registered at 18.6 per cent of the labour force. Urban unemployment had been relatively low in previous decades in Argentina, but in recent years it has increased drastically. In 1974 it amounted to 3.4 per cent of the workforce, increasing to 4.4 per cent in 1976. In 1985 unemployment amounted to 5.9 per cent, in 1990 to 6.3 per cent. Subsequently it rose substantially to 9.3 per cent in 1993, 12.2 per cent in October 1994, and a peak of 18.6 per cent in May 1995 (see Marshall 1995). Underemployment is also high and other forms of unemployment are widespread (see Sanchez 1995). Second, real wages and incomes of lower-income groups fell. When inflation was controlled, wages initially were increased in relation to the falls sustained previously. Subsequently nominal wages were frozen while prices continued to increase; thus despite price increases being relatively low real wages continued to fall throughout the period in which the Convertibility Plan was in effect. Despite real wage falls, especially in the non-industrial sector, wage costs in industry increased somewhat (Mayo 1999). Third, income distribution became more regressive despite economic expansion. In 1974, the richest 10 per cent income groups absorbed 28.2 per cent of national income; the lower 30 per cent received 11.3 per cent, and the poorest 10 per cent only 2.3 per cent of national income. In May 1997 the richest 10 per cent absorbed 37.1 per cent of total income; the poorest 30 per cent only 8.2 per cent, and the poorest 10 per cent only 1.6 per cent of national income. Our latest sources show that in August 1998 37.3 per cent of total income was absorbed by the highest 10 per cent income groups while only 8.1 per cent was received by the lowest 30 per cent income receivers (INDEC, as reported in various press sources). Forth, hunger and poverty remained widespread and intensified, largely due to the deplorable situation of the retired and pensioners. In 1974 7.7 per cent of households and 8.5 per cent of total population were defined as poor. A peak in poverty rates was reached in 1989 when, in the midst of hyperinflation, 48 per cent of households were estimated to be poor. In 1995,

18 per cent of households were defined as poor (see estimates reported in *Cash*, economic supplement of *Página 12*, 5 November 1995). This trend continued in recent years, with peaks of 20 and 19 per cent in October 1996 and 1997 respectively (*Clarín*, 4 June 1998: 32 on the basis of data of ECLA and INDEC). The need to 'adjust public expenditures' placed the burden of the adjustment process on wage-earners, the informal sector and much of the middle classes including medium and small sized businesses. Health, education and other services catering to basic needs of the population were drastically affected by the implemented cuts and increased costs of educational and health services (see Teubal 1992a, 1994b). According to a recent press release based on a report of the Ministry of Labour 1,357,995 persons in Argentina live in a critical situation. Of the 1,752,253 persons unemployed (13.39 per cent of economically active population) 795,000 are unemployed poor and 562,000 rural with unsatisfied basic needs (*Clarín*, 7 July 1998: 18).

Up to the 1995 presidential election in which Menem was re-elected with almost 50 per cent of the national vote, the main antidote to criticism was the matter of the stability attained after the hyperinflationary spurts of the 1989–91 period. This was a decisive factor when it came down to counteracting two points of critique: corruption charges, which could be related to the enormous concentration of power in the hands of the economic establishment and their political allies, and to the large-scale infringement and lack of transparency in democratic procedures; and the issue of poverty, misery and the (according to government sources) 'inevitable' social costs of the adjustments: the violation of minimal social and economic rights for the population. When reference is made to the question of poverty, and therefore regressive income distribution in Argentina, one should consider not only the impact of structural adjustment on wages and employment, but also its impact on access to food, health and other basic needs, which constitute part of the social wages as perceived in Argentine society (see Teubal 1992a, 1992b).

The restructuring of the economy, and the consequent concentration of economic power in certain industrial and service sectors, made unemployment and underemployment structurally endemic. The disarticulation of the economy is reflected in that in, for example, the food sector, the advance of supermarkets did away with a large part of the small business catering to the distribution of food. The same thing is happening to the food industry. Both these sectors are important components of the overall economy, and important to employment creation as well.

After 1995, the Menem project began to falter and his popularity reached an all-time low in 1998. The economic and social situation and the lack of an overall prospect for the future seem to influence this trend. Domingo Cavallo was replaced by Roque Fernández as minister of the economy in August 1996, but this implied reinforcing the economic orthodoxy in the management of the economy. To overcome the 'tequila effect', new loans were sought abroad, and a 'reinforcement' of the banking system was stipulated, meaning a greater concentration of the system with larger and international banks absorbing the smaller ones. This was the so-called 'solidity' of the banking system: making it fit to cope with capital flight and the lack of confidence of the depositors. While in January 1995 there were 205 banks in Argentina, of which 33 were publicly owned. By November 1998 this number had been reduced to 127, with only 17 publicly owned banks remaining. International banking rapidly took over. In 1994, prior to the 'tequila effect', foreign banks represented only 15 per cent of the total assets of the banking system. By December 1997, they already controlled 40 per cent, and at the end of 1998 52.6 per cent. This percentage represents a much higher share of foreign banking than that existing in other countries. In Chile, for instance, foreign banking represents 15 per cent of assets, in Brazil 14 per cent, Canada, 8.5 per cent, Korea 4.5 per cent and Italy 3.9 per cent (*Cronista Commercial,* 27 November 1998: 8).

Privatization rendered enormous profits to the new companies given that rates were kept high and indexed to the dollar, and in some cases were even increased. While the national telephone company was sold for a total of about $1,966 million, only part of which was paid cash, by 1998 the two newly privatized telephone companies had accumulated profits to the tune of $4,775.8 million. Profits of YPF were also very high, reaching an accumulated total of $4,222 million by 1998. All privatized firms had positive profit rates except Aerolíneas Argentinas (*Cash,* economic supplement of *Página 12,* 20 December 1998).

The transnationalization of the Argentine economy was also one of the main features, and maybe end results, of the new model of development introduced. Over the past eight years transnational groups have bought 426 firms for a total of $29.110 million. The bulk of these purchases were made only recently. In 1997, sales to foreign firms amounted to $10,976 million, and $10,020 million in 1998. With these acquisitions foreign companies control 53.2 per cent of the largest thousand companies of Argentina, representing 30 per cent of GDP (*Cash,* economic supplement of *Página 12,* 20 December 1998).

The large uncertainty and lack of confidence prevailing in more recent years were compounded to a large extent by the overall workings of the macroeconomy and by a lack of government response in the form of anti-cyclical measures. While exports increased from almost $12 billion in 1991 to $15.8 billion in 1995 and to a maximum of $23.8 billion in 1996, imports increased much more; they amounted to $8.2 billion in 1991, jumping to $21.6 billion in 1994 and to $23.7 billion in 1996. Following previous trends imports in the expansion phase tend to increase more than exports due to the high elasticity of imports to GNP levels, but the problem was compounded in the 1990s due to existence of the foreign debt. Balance of trade deficits were important in 1992, 1993 and 1994; in the latter year they amounted to a deficit of $5.7 billion. Nevertheless, the deficit in current account in that year amounted to $9.9 billion, a large share of which was for the servicing of foreign debt. In 1995 and 1994 due to the fall in income imports did not continue to increase as much and the balance of trade deficit was nil. But in 1997 the balance of trade deficit was very large ($4.9 billion), requiring more adjustments and more foreign debt sourcing. In 1998, some $17 billion were needed to finance the Argentine current account deficit, including foreign debt servicing and foreign investment profit remittances.

The government confronted this situation by increasing foreign debt and applying a strict financial adjustment, aggravating an already tense situation. As mentioned previously, foreign debt was increased from about $61.8 billion in 1990 to $117 billion in 1997. The privatization spree provided only a total of $26 billion, of which $12.8 billion were in cash, a factor that denotes a somewhat deceptive situation for Argentine finances (Mayo 1999: 13). According to government sources deposits of Argentineans abroad amount to $75 billion, while dollar deposits in the local banking system amount to $33 billion. But these are not funds applied to the payment of foreign debt servicing.

Final Remarks

At present we are living through a highly unstable situation, which the 'tequila', 'Thailand' 'Jakarta' and 'Russian' effects have only tended to compound. If Brazil had gone down – 30 per cent of Argentina's exports are to this main partner of Mercosur – the situation would surely have worsened. Furthermore, according to surveys about 70 per cent of the population of Greater Buenos Aires feel insecure economically speaking, 81 per cent consider the overall economic situation 'bad', and the majority feel that this situation will remain the same or get worse in the near future. Apart from this, 45 per cent of the population feel it is 'somewhat' or 'very' probable that they will lose their present employment in the next twelve months, while only 9 per cent feel that 'within the next six months there will be more employment opportunities then at present' (*Clarín* reporting on several surveys done recently, 13 November 1998).

Lester Thurow, the 'star economist' of MIT, is somewhat pessimistic concerning Argentina's future prospects. 'Today Argentina is growing at 8 per cent, and the paradox is that tomorrow you may have a great crisis … The foreign trade deficit should be closely monitored since it cannot be sustained for very long, because it can detonate a crisis very rapidly … Investors leave a country very rapidly without making too many considerations. One should consider ways for limiting the imports of consumer goods. One needs the imports of capital goods to be able to grow, but it would be logical to try to restrict consumer imports, for example, by increasing tariffs.' The interviewer then asks: 'Nowadays applying import restrictions or increasing tariffs sounds to "unfashionable" protectionism, doesn't it?' Thurow responds:

Maybe. But you cannot have the luxury of importing value added in consumer goods. Another thing you can do is to select certain local sectors, producers of consumer goods, and stimulate them, via the tax system, to thus substitute imports. When there is a large disequilibrium in the balance of payments, imports should be almost exclusively oriented towards capital goods so as to increase the repayment capacity in the long run, through more exports. Even so there may be a problem of the transition: one can never know if one will be able to solve the problems of the external sector without a crisis. It is a problem all of Latin America has ... As yet none of the countries in the region has assured itself a sustained growth for decades without suffering a crisis. (*Cash*, economic supplement of *Página 12*, 14 June 1998, my translation)

And so Lester Thurow brings us back to import substitution industrialization once again. Could it be that we are ending an era and that a 'new protectionism' is in the making (see Lang and Hines 1993)? Of course, this does not mean 'going back' to ISI, but implies looking forward to new alternatives. A look at the past is none the less useful in clarifying issues and situations. As we have shown in this chapter ISI was important in a certain episode of Argentine recent history, but acquired different characteristics under the various political regimes. ISI does not refer exclusively to government intervention: it implies a certain type of government intervention that promotes a certain 'regime of accumulation', which has as one of its main tenets the need to actively industrialize the country. The locus of ISI strategies is that all of them accept industrialization, and everything that comes with it, as a policy objective. This is what distinguishes the policies applied from the 1930s to the mid-1970s. After this, industrialization was dropped from the agenda. Even during the 1930s and the 1960s and in the second half of both the Peronist administrations (1953–55, though not necessarily in 1975 to early 1976) despite some liberalization, industrialization remained an objective of policy. In contrast, under the 'open economy' (1970s–1990s) industrialization was dropped as an important objective of policy. As a matter of fact, deindustrialization became an important objective. It became an important strategy to reduce the power of labour and block all possibilities for a social pact between labour and the 'national bourgeoisie'.

The 'initial' ISI was of the 'easy type', that is, the substitution of imported consumer goods that could be produced locally. In the more 'difficult' stage of ISI an effort was made to produce intermediary and capital goods locally. This was looked upon as a means of coping with external vulnerability and dependency. The second component of ISI is closely connected to the role of the domestic market. When, due to the world crisis of the 1930s, primary exports were no longer the main source of domestic accumulation the domestic market increasingly was seen as an object of accumulation. Industrialization is therefore oriented basically to the domestic market. As we have shown in this chapter, in the 1930s industrialization became one of the spin-offs of the measures adopted at the time to cope with the crisis; the same could be said with regards to the World War periods. Under the Peronist regimes, however, ISI became a conscious objective of policy and the domestic wages goods market was given precedence. Furthermore, ISI was continued under *desarrollismo* and the domestic market continued to be important in inducing the accumulation process. The difference between the Peronist and the *desarrollista* domestic markets was that during the first regime wage goods were promoted, whereas under *desarrollismo* the (purchasing power) of higher income levels and the middle classes were seen as the dominant sectors of the domestic market. Therefore, intermediary or 'luxury' goods requiring a more complex technology were established.

ISI was limited by the external sector, which periodically induced balance of payments crises that usually were confronted by stop-go policies or stabilization programmes of the sort applied notably in the 1960s. Nevertheless, other means for either deepening ISI towards intermediary and capital goods or orienting industrialization towards exports were looked upon as ways for structurally solving the balance of payments difficulties. Another means to strengthen ISI was to break the strait-jacket of the domestic market and develop a regional integration industrialization approach whereby industry could be established but would be associated with a much larger regional market. These were the various means sought to maximize ISI internationally (Teubal 1961, 1968).

A new exports strategy was in the making in the early 1970s, but for political reasons it was not pursued further. Argentina at the time had the chance to develop a wholesale exports strategy, but the opportunity was lost. This was probably due to the complex political situation prevailing at the time, and the fear that this strategy would enlarge the power of the 'national bourgeoisie'. In particular, its alliance with the working class was seen as a threat to the traditional establishment. The military coup of 1976 thus put an end to ISI. A period in which financial and speculative activities became prominent was begun. The external sector continued to limit economic expansion, and an important element in this limitation was the foreign debt accumulated throughout this period, which absorbed a large share of exports.

Now, who were the social actors or sectors promoting ISI? And who were the main antagonists of ISI? As we have seen above, during the first Peronist government the national bourgeoisie, with its strong bonds with trade unions, played an important role. In the 1950s the CGE emerged as an important social actor of the Peronist administration that, up to then, was supported by the military and the trade unionists. Under the second Peronist regime of the 1970s, the CGE was prominent for a short period. For instance, José Ber Gelbard (the chief of the CGE) was Perón's minister *par excellence* (Soares 1998). Under *desarrollismo*, foreign capital was an important antagonist of ISI. Compared to the post-1970s period, it seems that in the case of Argentina foreign capital is mostly associated with finance and speculative activities have become prominent.

Under ISI labour had an important say in policy and wages were more or less kept in line with productivity increases, or even rose in relation to these. Thus income distribution did not necessarily worsen under ISI. In periods of expansion income distribution improved and only in moments of crisis did it tend to worsen (Beccaria 1993). To a large extent this implied a greater articulation of the economy. Under the open economy, real wages were systematically lowered in relation to productivity increases, and this constituted one of the main elements of this regime of accumulation. This is reflected by the almost systematic fall in real wages in the period from the mid-1970s onwards. Even during the 1990s when growth was substantial, and stability was attained, real wages continued to fall and unemployment increased reaching record levels. The extreme structural adjustments and the ensuing restructuring that created redundancies in the state sector, which was privatized, and in the private sector itself was part and parcel of this process. Mass exclusion of vast social sectors was one of the end results of this 'inevitable' restructuring. Access to food, health, education, housing and other basic services also deteriorated substantially.

It remains to be seen whether Argentina has embarked on a widespread accumulation process. Deindustrialization has not necessarily led to a new industrial exports strategy except with regards to some agro-industrial activities, and mostly in relation to Brazil. Given the present turmoil in world finances it is therefore difficult to visualize any stable strategy for Argentina's future within the context of a neoliberal project.

Notes

1. For an analysis of structural adjustments in Argentina upon which this section is based see Teubal (forthcoming).

2. In 1995, capital flight and the dramatic devaluation of the Mexican peso led to a severe financial crisis and to a major bail-out by the Clinton administration.

References

Altmann, Werner (1979) *El Proyecto Nacional Peronista*, Mexico, DF: Editorial Extemporaneos.

Amaral, Samuel and Ben Plotkin (1993) *Perón: del Exilio al Poder*, San Martín, Buenos Aires: Cantaro Editores.

Apiazu, D. (1988) *La Promoción a la inversión industrial en la Argentina. Efectos sobre la Estructura Industrial, 1974–1987*, Working Paper 27, Buenos Aires: CEPAL.

— (1994) 'La industria argentina ante la privatización, la desregulación y la apertura simétricas de la economia', in D. Apiazu and H. Nochteff (eds), *El Desarrollo Ausente. Restricciones al Desarrollo, Neoconservadorismo y Elite Económica en la Argentina*, Buenos Aires: Flacso – Tesis Grupo Editorial Norma.

Apiazu, D, E. Basualdo and M. Khavisse (1986) *El Nuevo Poder Económico en los Años 80*, Buenos Aires: Legasa.

Basualdo, Eduardo (1987) *Deuda Externa y Poder Económico en la Argentina*, Buenos Aires: Editorial Nueva América.

Beccaria, Luis (1993) 'Estancamiento y distribución del ingreso', in A. Minujin (ed.), *Desigualdad y Exclusión. Desafíos Para la Política Social en la Argentina de Fin de Siglo*, Buenos Aires: UNICEF–Lozada.

Ben Plotkin, Mariano (1993) 'La "ideología" de Perón: continuidades y rupturas', in S. Amaral and M. Ben Plotkin (eds), *Perón: del Exilio al Poder*, San Martín, Buenos Aires: Cantaro Editores.

Braun, Oscar (1973) 'Desarrollo del capital monopolista en la Argentina', in O. Braun (ed.), *El Capitalismo Argentino en Crisis*, Buenos Aires: Siglo XXI.

— (1974) *El Plan Económico del Gobierno Popular*, Buenos Aires: Editorial El Coloquio.

Cafiero, Antonio (1961) *5 Años Después*, Buenos Aires: Writers Edition.

Cortés Conde, Roberto (1969) 'El boom argentino: ¿una oportunidad desperdiciada?', in T. di Tella and T. Halperin Donghi, *Los Fragmentos Del Poder*, Buenos Aires: Editorial Jorge Alvarez.

— (1995) *La Economía Argentina en el Largo Plazo. Ensayos de Historia Económica de Siglos XIX y XX*, Buenos Aires: Sudamericana.

Díaz Alejandro, Carlos (1975) *Ensayos Sobre la História Económica Argentina*, Buenos Aires: Amorrortu Editores.

Escudé, Carlos (1983) *Gran Bretaña-Estados Unidos y la Declinación Argentina, 1942–1949*, Buenos Aires: Editorial de Belgrano.

Fernández López, Manuel (1996) 'El ciclo económico argentino: estudios de Raúl Prebisch', *Ciclos en la Historia la Economía y la Sociedad*, 6 (10) (Buenos Aires).

Ferrer, Aldo (1969) 'Devaluación redistribución de ingresos y el proceso de desarticulación industrial en la Argentina', in A. Ferrer et al., *Los Planes de Estabilización en la Argentina*, Buenos Aires: Paidos.

— (1989) *El Devenir de una Ilusión. La Industria Argentina: desde 1930 hasta Nuestros Días*, Buenos Aires: Editorial Sudamericana.

Gerchunoff, Pablo and Juan Carlos Torre (1996) 'La política de liberalización económica en la administración Menem', *Desarrollo Económico – Revista de Ciencias Sociales*, 143 (136), October–December.

Germani, Gino (1955) *Estructura Social de la Argentina*, Buenos Aires: Editorial Raigal.

Girbal Blancha, N. (1998) 'Acera de la vigencia de la Argentina Agropecuaria. Estado y crédito al agro durante la gestión peronista (1946–1955)', paper presented at the 1998 meeting of the Latin American Studies Association (LASA), Chicago, IL, 24–26 September.

Halperin Donghi, Tulio (1972) *Argentina: la Democracia de Masas* (Colección Historia Argentina), Buenos Aires: Editorial Paidos.

Hobsbawm, E. (1995) *The Age of Extremes. A History of the World, 1914–1991*, New York: Vintage.

Kohli, A. (1993) 'Democracy amid economic orthodoxy: trends in developing countries', *Third World Quarterly*, 14 (4): 671–89.

Lang, Tim and Colin Hines (1993) *The New Protectionism: Protecting the Future against Free Trade*, London: Earthscan.

Lemarchand, G. A. (1996) 'Long-wave analysis in the GNP of 56 countries between 1870–1994', paper presented to Expobeca-Expociencia, Universidad de Buenos Aires, September (unpublished).

Maddison, A. (1995) *Monitoring the World Economy 1820–1992*, OECD: Paris.

Marshall, Adriana (1992) *Circumventing Labour Protection: Non-Standard Employment in Argentina and Peru*, Research Series no. 88, ILO, Geneva.

— (1995) 'Mercado de trabajo y distribución del ingreso: efectos de la política económica, 1991–1994', *Realidad Económica*, no. 129, January–February (Buenos Aires).

Mayo, Aníbal (1999) 'El Plan de Convertibilidad (1991–1998): siete años de ofensiva del capital', unpublished document.

McGuire, James W. (1993) 'Perón y los sindicatos: la lucha por el liderazgo peronista', in S. Amaral and M. Ben Plotkin (eds), *Perón: del Exilio al Poder*, Buenos Aires: Cantaro Editores.

Murmis, Miguel and Juan Carlos Portantiero (1971) *Estudios sobre los Orígenes del Peronismo*, Buenos Aires: Siglo XXI.

O'Donnell, Guillermo (1979) 'Tensions in the bureaucratic-authoritarian state and the question of democracy', in David Collier (ed.), *The New Authoritarianism in Latin America*, Princeton, NJ: Princeton University Press.

Sanchez, Miguel A. (1995) 'El empleo en Argentina', *IBAP*, 1, November (Buenos Aires).

Seoane, María (1998) *El Burgues Maldito. La História Secreta de José Ber Gelbard, el Jefe de los Empresarios Nacionales, Ultimo Ministro de Economía de Perón y el Principal Lobbista Político de la Argentina en los Años Setenta*, Buenos Aires: Planeta – Espejo de la Argentina.

Schvarzer, Jorge (1983) *Martínez de Hoz: La Lógica Política de la Política Económica*, Buenos Aires: CISEA.

Soares, María (1998) *El Burgués Maldito*, Buenos Aires: Planeta.

Teubal, Miguel (1961) 'Europa y Latinoamérica ante la integración económica', *Desarrollo Económico*, vol. I, no. 3 (Buenos Aires).

— (1968) 'The failure of Latin America's economic integration', in J. Petras and M. Zeitlin (eds), *Latin America: Reform or Revolution?* Greenwich, CO: Fawcett Publications.

— (1992a) 'Food security and regimes of accumulation', Working Paper Series, no. 123, The Hague: Institute of Social Studies.

— (1992b) 'Hambre, pobreza y regímenes de acumulación: el caso argentino', *Realidad Económica*, 111, October–November.

— (1993) 'Argentina: fragile democracy', in B. Gills, J. Rocamora and R. Wilson, *Low Intensity Democracy: Political Power in the New World Order*, London: Pluto Press.

— (1994a) 'Cambios en el modelo socioeconómico: problemas de incluidos y excluidos', in N. Giarracca (ed.), *Acciones Colectivas y Organización Cooperativa. Reflexiones y Estudios de Caso*, Buenos Aires: Centro Editor de América Latina – Universidad de Buenos Aires, Facultad de Ciencias Sociales.

— (1994b) 'Hambre y crisis agraria en el "granero del mundo"', *Realidad Económica*, 121, January–Febrary: 47–68.

— (1995) *Globalización y Expansión Agroindustrial. Superación de la Pobreza en América Latina?*, Buenos Aires: Ediciones Corregidor.

— (1996) 'Structural adjustments, democracy and the state in Argentina', in A. E. Fernández Jilberto and A. Mommen, *Liberalization in the Developing World. Institutional and Economic Changes in Latin America, Africa and Asia*, London and New York: Routledge.

— (forthcoming) *Structural Adjustment and Social Disarticulation: The Case of Argentina*, New York: Science and Society.

Teubal, M. and R. Pastore (1998) 'Acceso a la alimentación y regímenes de acumulación. El papel de los precios relativos', in M. Teubal (ed.), *Teoría, Estructura y Procesos Económicos. Ensayos en Honor al Doctor Julio H. G. Olivera*, Buenos Aires: Eudeba-CEA.

Torrado, Susana (1992) *Estructura Social de la Argentina, 1945–1983*, Buenos Aires: Ediciones de la Flor.

Tulchin, Joseph (1975) 'Foreign policy', in M. Falcoff and R. Dolkart, *Prologue to Perón. Argentina in Depression and War, 1930–1943*, Berkeley, CA and London: University of California Press.

Villanueva, Javier (1975) 'Economic development', in M. Falcoff and R. Dolkart, *Prologue to Perón. Argentina in Depression and War, 1930–1943*, Berkeley, CA and London: University of California Press.

Whitaker, Arthur (1975) 'An overview of the period', in M. Falcoff and R. Dolkart, *Prologue to Perón. Argentina in Depression and War, 1930–1943*, Berkeley, CA and London: University of California Press.

THREE

The Neoliberal Transformation of Chilean Populism: The Case of the Socialist Party

ALEX E. FERNÁNDEZ JILBERTO

The policies of neoliberal restructuring implemented by the military dictatorship of 1973 put an end to the historical cycle of populism as a political regime. This form of political organization dominated the relations between the state, parties and civil society until 1973. The cycle was initiated at the end of the 1930s with the definitive decline of the oligarchic state based on export of primary products. The stability demonstrated by the political system between 1930 and 1973 was based on three coexisting processes: (1) state-supported industrialization, focused on the internal market (import substitution industrialization, ISI); (2) the progressive incorporation of the social sectors deprived from the benefits of development; and (3) the progressive enlargement of the political system through the co-optation of the communist and socialist parties. The balance between democracy, participation and industrialization was the basis for what has been called the Estado de Compromiso, or Compromise State, which is an underdeveloped form of the Keynesian state. The exhaustion of this system, that clearly suffered a crisis during the political radicalization that gave way to the Popular Unity (UP) government (1970–73), explains the structural origins of the 1973 military coup.

The neoliberal restructuring process is the consequence of the association of the military bureaucracy, transformed into a political class of the authoritarian state, and the neoliberal civil technocracy ('Chicago boys') that developed itself with the help of the ideological influence of the Chicago School of Milton Friedman. Both groups shared the values of the anti-communist doctrine of National Security and critiqued the political incapability of the statist industrial bourgeoisie to protect both the state and the political regime from the dangers of communism. The 'refoundation of capitalism' project that inspired neoliberal restructuring eventually changed the traditional system of relations between state and civil society and led to the breakdown of the democratic political regime that was installed with the transition from oligarchic domination to industrial populism of ISI. In turn, the market not only operated as an essential factor in the allocation of resources in the political system: it also regulated the relations between parties and the state after the re-establishment of democracy in 1990, establishing the limits of economic policy in the framework of 'improvement of competitivness' of the economy in the world market and of the stability of macroeconomic variables. The economism that is so dominant in the relations between parties, state and civil society was one of the most influential factors in the ideological neoliberalization of the Socialist Party of Chile (PSCh). This process, called the 'socialist renovation', started after the division of the party in 1979.

Since its foundation in 1933, the PSCh was, in its original form, part of the structure of the Compromise State. Its political history is characterized by a continuous ideological ambivalence and by the permanent rejection of associations with international social democracy and the USSR during the Cold War. Among its diverse ideological phases we can distinguish its aprist, Titoist, Peronist and nationalist periods and its latest phase in which it constituted itself as a populist party with a neoliberal character (1989–98). The party's relevance for Chile's politics started with the participation of its founding leaders in the 1932 Socialist Republic, its incorporation in the diverse governments of the Popular Front after 1938, and its capacity to constitute itself as one of the decisive political powers that established the Popular Unity government (1970–73). In order to reach this central position the PSCh maintained a conflictive alliance with the Communist Party of Chile (PCCh). This can be seen as an early materialization of the historical compromise within the Chilean way to socialism, which differed substantially from the socialisms of Eastern Europe at that time because of its profound democratic character. The Leninization of the party at the beginning of the 1970s, however, removed it from the initial democratic character of its political programme.

The coup of 1973 put the PSCh not only into a long period of clandestine existence (1973–89), but also into a profound ideological and factional chaos, which it managed to overcome only with the so-called process of 'socialist renovation'. This process, which was inspired by a Latin American version of Gramsci, founded the basis for the abandonment of the political alliance with the Chilean communists that had existed since 1938, in favour of a political alliance with the Christian Democratic party (DC). This new alliance underpinned the first and second governments of democratic transition in the post-1989 period. The abandonment of a Leninist approach and the collapse of the socialisms of Eastern Europe (1989) favoured neoliberal currents within the party. The main aim of this chapter is to discuss the ideological, political, theoretical and historical components that inspired the integration of the PSCh in Chilean politics. To some extent, the history of the PSCh represents the dramatic history of Latin American populism, vilified nowadays by the predominantly neoliberal ideological currents. This fundamentally historical approach will provide the necessary space for the historical context of the political scene of Chilean populism.

From the Socialist Republic to the Popular Front

The explanatory structural framework of the rise of Chile's Socialist Party in 1933 consists of the political and social changes that took place during the crisis of the oligarchic system. These changes occurred as a reaction to the crisis of the state form, the crisis of the political regime and the economic structure aimed at primary exports, which started in the 1920s. Old structures fell apart as a result of the international crisis of 1929. The military victory in the War of the Pacific against Peru and Bolivia in 1879 and in the Civil War of 1891 had facilitated the association of the oligarchy with the English capital that monopolized the mining of Chilean saltpetre (used for the European production of fertilizer). The oligarchy was an agricultural–commercial–financial bourgeoisie that hegemonized the integration of Chile's economy into the world market, through different forms of associations to foreign capital. State control and control of what was left of the so-called saltpetre enclave facilitated a prolonged stability of the oligarchic peace. During the 1920s, when the military intervened in favour of the transformation of the state, the oligarchic state that traditionally received support from the Conservative, Liberal and partly also the Radical parties declined.

Unlike in other parts of Latin America, the definitive collapse of the oligarchic system in Chile and the transition to industrial capitalism (in the form of ISI) did not lead to a prolonged political crisis (Faletto 1972: 18). This partly explains the capacity of the state and the political regime to absorb and co-opt both left-wing parties (communists and socialists) and trade unions, as was demonstrated with the constitution of the Popular Front in 1936, and its victory in the 1938 elections. This process of co-optation was associated with a model of social peace (improvement of salaries and social conditions), implemented in 1927 by the populist dictatorship of General Carlos Ibañez del Campo. This model involved a substantial rise of fiscal expenditure, to a large extent financed by American loans and investments and the help of the First National Bank of New York, which was given the status of official financial adviser of the Republic of Chile (Burbach 1975: 34). In June, 1932, the Socialist Republic was declared and although it did not succeed in alternating the stability of the political regime, partly because it lasted only twelve days, it did lead to the foundation of the Socialist Party in the following year. The Socialist Republic was created with the help of a military sector that, with the slogan 'Food, Housing and Protection', proposed the nationalization of the export sector (copper, cokes and saltpetre industries), receiving support from both the workers of the mining enclaves and the emerging middle class, who were directly affected by the international crisis. A report of the League of Nations (Ellsworth 1945: 23–69) showed that the Chilean economy was severely affected by the world crisis, with world trade showing a decline of 100 to 75 in the 1929–32 period, and the Chilean index dropping from 100 to 24 for exports and from 100 to 25 for imports. This was worsened by the enormous external debt: the value in instalments and interest was about $326 million in 1929 and $394 million in 1930 (Palma 1984: 76–7). Given the impossibility of continuing this pace of debt cancellation, a moratorium and rigid system of exchange rates was implemented on 15 June 1931. This crisis led to the resignation of Ibáñez on 26 July of the same year. The Socialist Republic implemented a political programme of moderate socialism, in which state planning of economic development was far more important than class struggle. Economic intervention of the state was seen as more important than the expropriation of the means of production (Drake 1992: 59). This process was the first experience of a moderate coexistence of the left and the state.

The direct consequences of the world crises such as the ideological heritage, the twelve-day Socialist Republic and the political radicalization of a small military faction were the bases for the foundation of the PSCh in 1933.[1] From the beginning, the party adopted Marxism as the method of analysis of social reality and rejected any kind of international adjustment to the Second and Third Internationals. It also declared its support for working-class dictatorship as the inevitable state form that would guarantee the transition to socialism, the Socialist Republic of Latin America and the anti-imperialist struggle. Anti-imperialism formed the ideological basis of the wish to have a political and economic unification of Latin America, known as the Federation of Socialist Republics of the continent (Pollack and Rosenkranz 1986). Its social representation was based on what the party called the manual and intellectual working class and it declared itself in favour of the natural proletarianization of the small bourgeoisie and the middle class, including craftsmen, small tradesmen, civil servants, peasants, small businessmen and intellectuals. A considerable number of the founding members of the PSCh belonged to the Masonry, which had a substantial intellectual influence, giving the party a humanist and positivist dimension (among them, for instance, was Eugenio Matte, the Grand Master of the Chilean Lodge).

At its Second Ordinary General Congress in December 1934, the party declared itself in favour of nationalism and economic statism as the only way to defend Chile's economic and political independence and to rescue the property of natural resources from the international monopolies of imperialism. Consequently, it defined socialism as collectivism at the economic level, supported by a 'planning state', able to suppress privileges, stressing an anti-clerical, anti-capitalist, anti-fascist and anti-imperialist character (Jobet

1971). A large part of this programme was in concordance with the convictions of the average citizen, who thought that state intervention, economic national-ism and industrialization were the most effective strategies to overcome the effects of the 1929 crisis. The industrial and agronomic business groups, united in the Society for the Promotion of Industry (SOFOFA) and the National Society of Agriculture (SNA) also agreed on the necessary expansion of state intervention in the economy and legitimized this as a necessary support for private industry, without which national economic independence could not be achieved (Drake 1992: 67).

The contradictory relation between socialists and the Communist Party of Chile (PCCh), founded in 1922, was expressed in both an ideological con-frontation and a search for a political alliance. This ambiguity dominated the internal debates in the party from its foundation until the mid-1980s. The Chilean communists had participated in the 3rd Communist International in 1928 as supporters, and were given the status of full members after the party's bolshevization, which in practice meant the elimination of anarcho-syndicalist tendencies and the introduction of democratic centralism and Leninist organization. From the 6th Congress of the Communist International in 1928 onwards, Chilean communists took a political line based on the principle of class against class and, for that matter, agreed upon the thesis of social fascism, to reject the collaboration with the socialist parties. They saw the social democratic leftists as more dangerous than the right and were in favour of the formation of the Frente Unico (FU – United Front) (Gómez 1984), which in the Chilean version included the middle class and was destined to abolish the fascist military dictatorship of Ibañez. The PCCh qualified the Socialist Republic and especially its Junta as reformist and incompatible with the policy of the United Front, implemented by the South American Bureau of the Communist International in 1932. The class against class tactics, the socialization of the latifundio and the armed insurrection of the proletariat prevailed in the agreements of the National Conference of the PCCh in 1933. It was not until after the 7th Congress of the Communist International in 1935 and under the influence of Latin American Comintern officials (the Peruvian official Eudocio Ravines, the Czech Frederic Glaufbauf and the Ecuadorian Manuel Cazón) that the PCCh started a new strategy that helped integrate the party into Chile's political system (Sarget 1994: 133). The creation of an anti-fascist front implied the defence of bourgeois democracy and the acceptance of elections as an acceptable method in the struggle for power. This choice was based on the aspiration to have a democratic, bourgeois, anti-imperialist and anti-feudal revolution. Unlike the communists, the PSCh had first opposed the constitution of the working class United Front. In 1935 it created the Left Wing Bloc (BI) on the parliamentary level, as an instrument in the struggle to increase its political influence in the social movement.

In 1937, despite the incorporation of the Communist Left (IC) (of

Trotskyite origin), the party was much closer to socializing indo-americanist nationalism than to Marxism, and insisted on the rejection of any identification with international social democracy. The socializing nationalism and indo-americanism resemble the ideology of Haya de la Torre's APRA in Peru, at least in its first phases. However, until the 4th Congress in 1937, the Socialist Party showed an ambivalent attitude towards participation in the Popular Front (FP). The arguments for this ambivalence were reinforced by the fact that the Front ended up transforming the working-class parties into political instruments of the radicalization of the small bourgeoisie, at the expense of the abandonment of the political programme of socialism. Besides, the FP insisted upon the necessity to subordinate the strategy of the PCCh to its own programme, even accepting its possible incorporation in the Left Wing Block.

The approach of PSCh and PCCh in the summer of 1936, which would lead to the creation of the FP, was supported by the general strikes of the railway workers, the teachers' strike, the demands for better living conditions and the struggle against the repressive policy of the Alessandri government (1932–38). The cooperation of the PSCh and the Workers' Central of Chile (CTCH) contributed to it as well, as did the international solidarity with the Spanish Republic and the international struggle against fascism. The political alliance between the parties of the Front was further strengthened by a failed coup attempt by the Chilean Nazi party, just before the presidential elections of 1938. In particular the socialists had implemented a policy of direct confrontation with local Nazism. The creation of the FP (1938–47) as a political coalition incorporating the Radical, Socialist, Democratic and Communist Parties was the second most important heritage of the 1929 world crisis besides the foundation of the PSCh. It also marked the climax of the re-adaptation of the Chilean political system to the rise of populist democracy, supported by the ISI process and by the Compromise State.

The strategical change of the PCCh, demonstrated by the substitution of the United Front by the Popular Front, was consolidated in the agreements of the 7th Congress of the Communist International in 1935, at a moment when, like in the rest of the Latin American communist parties, the Stalinization process had been completed. The Stalinization process is defined as the constitution in the party's core of an hierarchical, authoritarian, bureaucratic, leading apparatus, which was organically, politically and ideologically related to the Communist Party of the Soviet Union. It assumed the doctrine of 'revolution in phases' and the block of the four classes (proletariat, peasants, small bourgeoisie and national bourgeoisie) as a model of political alliance, which should bring about the anti-imperialist and anti-feudal national democratic phase (Lowy 1980). The debate that had taken place since 1936 on the reformist character of the Front and the rejection of the proposition of the PCCh to build one national revolutionary party led to its first division during the 4th General Ordinary Congress in 1937 and the second split in the middle of an FP government in 1939. This resulted in the constitution of 1940 of the Socialist Workers' Party (PST), established by the non-conformists. It rejected the class collaboration that was intrinsic in the FP. The members of the PST made the ideological mosaic, which had led to the foundation of the PSCh in 1933, reappear. Anarchists, Trotskyists and members of the IC declared themselves as being the ideological alternative to the party and the FP. They took the proposal of a Workers' Front (FT) as a framework, rejecting all forms of alliance with the bourgeois parties (Drake 1992: 216).

The conflict between socialists and communists took place during the whole period of the Popular Front, until the PCCh was declared illegal by President Gabriel Gonzales Videla in 1948. This was tolerated by a sector of the PSCh. The socialists were not the leading factor in the constitution of the Popular Front, and although they participated in the FP governments with several ministers, Salvador Allende being one of them, they always kept an attitude of reserve and lacked confidence. This was the fruit of the ideological Puritanism that tried to avoid the temptation of class collaboration and its aspiration to build a revolutionary alternative, different from the PCCh (Moulian 1983). However, its rejection of the 'revolution by phases' was halted by the admission that a democratic revolution was necessary as a prelude to the construction of socialism. This revolution was defined as a *sui generis* revolution that could be introduced by a state with a political regime based on a compromise between classes. The disintegration of the FP in 1941 was initiated by the deterioration of the relations between socialists and communists, a result of the 1939 German–Soviet (Molotov–Von Ribbentrop) pact. It culminated in the socialist withdrawal from the FP in 1941, although the socialists continued to take part in the government (Ponce Durán 1994). The withdrawal from the Front was also the result of the failure of the socialist intent to isolate the communists through the acceptance of the American policy towards Latin America in that period. It stressed, in that way, the rejection of the Chilean communists' ideological dependence on the USSR. By leaving the government, the socialists also tried to restore the internal cohesion of the party, which was divided between those in favour and those opposed to the participation in the FP.

The socialists who supported the continuation of the party's presence in the government believed that this was necessary in order to guarantee compliance with its programme. Those who opposed, however, thought that leaving the government was the only alternative to create pressure from outside to install an economic and social democracy. The latter won in the 9th Congress of 1943 and realized the party's withdrawal from government, without its withdrawing as a member of the Democratic Alliance (AD) that had helped the Front government of President Juan Antonio Rio after 1942. After 1944, the socialists stressed their anti-communist policy and were reincorporated into the provisional government of President Duhalde on the basis of the strategy of the Third Front (TF), which tried to create an alternative between the 'reactionary right' and the communists at the political level. Argentinean Peronism and Getulio Vargas' Brazilian Labour Party inspired the TF ideologically. They presented the socialists with a model for a mass party that was able to deal with the dilemma of combining capitalism and Soviet Marxism. The most immediate effect of the socialist policy was the bankruptcy of the Workers' Central of Chile. The interior organization of the CTCh reproduced the conflict between the different currents within left-wing Chile. The socialists' approach was emphasized by Bernardo Ibañez, who guided the Central towards American influence and economic help from the AFL–CIO. The Third Front current was defeated in the 11th Congress of 1946, partly because of the defeat in the 1945 parliamentary elections, in which it got only 12.8 per cent of the vote (having had 20.7 per cent in the 1941 parliamentary elections).

The experience of the Popular Front was one of the most important programmatic and ideological inheritances of the PSCh and to some extent it would use the experience 30 years later in the participation in the Chilean way to socialism, installed by the government of the Popular Unity (UP). From a programmatic point of view, the FP proposed industrialization, accompanied by a process of redistribution of social wealth, as a structural solution to the effects of the 1929 international crisis. It also facilitated the constitution of a scheme for class collaboration between the industrial bourgeoisie, working class and middle class in order to strengthen industrial development. Conflict and instability originated in the question of 'higher wages or more accumulation' or was expressed in the incompatibility of the model of the state-induced accumulation and the demands of the working class for better wages (De Riz 1979: 58). In that model peasants were excluded from the benefits of national development, given the fact that in order to include them, agricultural reforms and a monetary economy should be introduced in the contractual relations of the agricultural sector. Industrialization was state-organized and therefore the socialists were brought closer to the process of reconciliation with the capitalist state, known as the political agent that introduced social rights. The perception of the state as being above society, accompanied by a flexible and open political system that was seen as a negotiation platform for class conflicts, implied that the socialists were reconciled with the 'Compromise State' that they had helped to build in the FP period, even though they showed an ongoing political ambivalence towards the intrinsic value of parliamentary democracy and elections as the means to get access to state control.

The debate on the political consequences of the party's integration into the state during the Popular Front period has been a source of permanent discussion within the PSCh. For some, the incorporation of the party into the state meant the abandonment of its central objective of representing the working class as well as the bureaucratization of the party structure, whose leadership only wanted to serve state interests (Jobet and Chelen 1973). For other sectors, especially those of Trotskyite inspiration, the FP was seen as an enormous political mistake that effected the rehabilitation of the power of the bourgeoisie, partly represented by the Radical Party, and limited the revolutionary potential of the popular masses (Wais 1961). The sharp internal factionalism, consolidated in the FP period, as well as the party's ideological ambivalence and the permanent search for a radical differentiation from the PCCh, marked the history of the PSCh until the 1990s and is expressed in its diverse ideological phases: nationalism, Peronism, Titoism, anti-communism and Castroism, after the Cuban revolution in 1959. However, with the participation of socialists and communists in the FP, the left's rapprochement with the state was initiated. The concept of revolution associated with the destruction of the bourgeois state was replaced by the acknowledgement of its integration into the political arena, regulated by the constitutional frame-work. Although the PSCh always used a revolutionary and insurrectionist vocabulary, especially after the Cuban revolution and the introduction of the Leninist scheme in its political line in the 1970s, its rapprochement with the state was consolidated.

From the Popular Action Front (FRAP) to the Popular Unity (UP)

The collaboration of a certain faction within the PSCh with the Popular Front government of President Gabriel Gonzales Videla caused a major crisis in the party. It managed to overcome this crisis only in 1956, when the Popular Action Front (FRAP) was set up. Between 1946 and 1952, under Radl Ampuero's guidance, the party tried to start a process of reorganization and doctrinal redefinition, which materialized in the 1947 National Programme Conference. At that conference Eugenio Gonzales, author of the so-called Programme of 47, insisted on the party's Marxist character, distancing himself from the totalitarian errors of the Soviet regime and the reactionary character of capitalism. He said it was important to 'socialize the means of production' and to plan Chile's economic development (Jobet 1971). At the same time, through the expulsion of Bernardo Ibañez' pro-American faction in 1948, the party's anti-imperialism (anti-USA) attitude, which opposed Latin American development through major economic state intervention, regained force. The party did not want to raise economic aid to the region to Marshall Plan levels and thus commit the region to the Cold War. Simultaneously, during the Twelfth General Ordinary Congress in June 1948, Chilean socialism condemned the expulsion of Yugoslavia from the Cominform, which was seen as Stalin's offensive to crush the independence of Tito's regime. It also condemned Soviet expansionism by strengthening the anti-Stalinist com-ponents of its programme.

The conceptualization of Tito's regime in Yugoslavia as a third way between capitalism and Stalinism facilitated the creation of a new ideological tendency within the party, known as Titoism, which resembled social democratic ideology and was replaced by 'Third Worldism' at the end of the 1950s. During the 13th General Ordinary Congress in June 1950, the majority of the socialists, under the name PSP, supported the candidature of former dictator Carlos Ibañez del Campo. A section of the party called the Socialist Recovering Movement (MRS) opposed his candidature. In the end, this led to an alliance with the Communist Party in 1951 and the Popular Front (FP), supporting the candidature of Salvador Allende. In the 1952 presidential elections Allende got 5.5 per cent of the votes (Furci 1984: 65). The FP formed the basis for the alliance with the communists that was consolidated with the formation of the FRAP in which, apart from the socialist parties, the PCCh and the smaller Labour Party (PT) and Popular Democratic Party (PDP) took part. The PSP was considered the official socialist party until the congress of unity, and as such it participated in the Ibañez government until 1953.

The FRAP emerged as the result of the popular disillusion after the failure of the government of General Carlos Ibañez del Campo (1952–58). Ibañez had gained an astonishing electoral victory and for the first time received support from marginal urban sectors. Ibañez criticized the inefficiency and the party's and parliamentary system's demagogy in a Peronist way. When it came to the economy, the old dictator stressed the need for monetary stability to control inflation. This notably decreased the income of popular and middle-class sectors. As a mass phenomenon, Ibañism represented a heterogeneous and caudillist populist movement with an Argentinean Peronist style. The strong migration to the urban regions and especially to greater Santiago that took place after 1945 helped create a 'new working class'. This class was much less state independent compared to those of the former periods of the saltpetre enclave, with less interest in group class actions and more interest in the improvement of its material situation, in a type of business in which the paternalist relationships were dominant (Faletto 1973: 6). These new masses formed the electoral support group for the ex-dictator in 1952. Relative employment expansion in the industrial sector in 1954 started a shift towards the construction and service sectors, stressing the labour sector's heterogeneity. This created the popular sector's ambivalence between the social democrat and revolutionary populist alternatives.

The deterioration of the economic situation and the unpopularity of the monetarist programme of applied economic stabilization implemented by the American economic mission of Klein-Sashes provoked the loss of the government's social support and the recovery of the labour movement's autonomy *vis-à-vis* the state. This was expressed in the constitution of the United Workers Central (CUT) in 1953, which survived until the military coup in 1973 and played a decisive role in the economic and political programme of the Popular Unity government. In the beginning the CUT predominantly mobilized public and private sector employees and to a lesser extent industrial workers and peasants (Barria 1971). The unpopularity and the decline of Ibañism was the reason for the resumption of the relations between the popular parties (specially the PSCh and the PCCh) and the trade unions. This was a phenomenon that to some extent triggered the formation of the FRAP in 1956.

The Popular Action Front fought the political decline of Ibañism with a programme that proposed the strengthening of the popular parties' relations with the trade unions. It coordinated actions with its parliamentary representatives and defined the economic and political content of its programme as anti-imperialist, anti-oligarchic and anti-feudal. The programme aimed to improve the conditions for the popular sectors, an important institutionalization of labour rights and the strengthening of national independence through an impulse for industrial development. This was an attempt to put an end to the pre-capitalist forms of exploitation of peasants. Besides, the functioning of the democratic institution would be improved, and the planning of economic development stimulated. At the same time the stress on industrialization would help the development of the national bourgeoisie, which was most related to the financial sector and less dependent on the interests of the agricultural oligarchy. As in the first Popular Front period in 1938, in this FRAP programme the state played a central role in the stimulation of a capital accumulation process through public enterprises. The state had to allocate significant amounts of financial resources to the productive system and to operate as a regulator of the economic differences inherent to development, in particular through investments in health care and education. The programmatic scheme of the FRAP was not much different from others in different Latin American countries, and it was unique only in that it was formulated by the workers' parties that considered themselves the political agents of the working class. They continued to define the principal contradiction of Chilean capitalism as oligarchy versus people, in the same way as in the FP period (De Riz 1979: 70).

For the Chilean socialists, the foundation of the FRAP meant the successful binding of the various working-classes parties, forever abandoning the political alliances with the centre parties. The principal objective was no longer the bourgeois democratic revolution, which would need the support of the progressive bourgeois parties, but the establishment of the Democratic Workers' Republic with a socialist orientation (Jobet 1971: 24). This defined the fulfilment of the bourgeois democratic tasks as a process prior to socialist revolution. At the same time, the socialists ambiguously accepted their integration into the Latin American Consultative Committee of the Socialist International, founded in 1956. They did not affiliate with international social democracy. The integration of the PSP into this Consultative Committee was the result of the party's assumed agreements in the Asian Socialist Conference in January of 1953 in Burma (Rangoon).[2] In this conference the necessity to keep and strengthen world peace through the creation of a third way between capitalism and (Soviet) communism was stressed. It was also declared that the connection of parties to the Socialist International was necessary. This was also manifested in the compromise of those parties when it came to the struggle against colonialism and their solidarity with the national liberation struggle in Africa and in support for Algerian independence. This was the first encounter of the socialists with Third Worldism. It went further than their Latin Americanist nationalism, which had been one of the major focus points in their international policy. It initiated the implementation of an international policy in favour of the non-allied bloc during the Cold War. Nevertheless, the Twentieth Congress of the Communist Party of the Soviet Union, and the announcement of peaceful coexistence and the previous introduction of the non-capitalist way of development, consolidated the approach of the PCCh. It gave an incentive to the political cooperation between both parties (after the congress of socialist unity in 1957). The de-Stalinization of the PCCh led to the implementation of a strategy based on the principle of peaceful transition to socialism and the conviction that the country's liberation of imperialism and the domestic reactionary and oligarchic forces was of immediate importance. At the same time it led to the formulation of the strategy of the National Liberation Front (FNL), which recognized the possibility of political collaboration with the national bourgeoisie. This signified a fundamental contradiction with the socialist strategy of the Workers' Front (FT).

The narrow electoral victory of the right, with Jorge Alessandri (31.6 per cent) against Salvador Allende (28.9 per cent) as the candidate of the FRAP in the 1958 presidential elections, showed that the conservatives and liberals had also gained from the decline of the electoral support to Ibañism. These election results put the left into a new political crisis, accentuated by the influence of the 1959 Cuban revolution, which led to the rise of a new ideological tendency, known as Castroism, within the core of the PSCh. The return to power of the right, for the first time since 1925, was guided by the business technocracy, which subordinated the political right and tried to restructure the state apparatus in favour of the business sector, eliminating the character aimed at assistance and conciliation that it had had since the FP period in 1938. Its economic policy was intended to conciliate the interests of the industrialist and latifundist sector and to support economic development with state resources. At the political level, the idea was to promote a model of development favourable to foreign investment, marginalizing and/or reducing the influence of the popular sectors on economic policy. This gave room to policies that accelerated the internal formation of capital and that supported the monopolistic control of the foreign business sector that predominantly operated in the mining sector, through a general scheme of denationalizing the economy. This rapidly translated into inflation, unemployment, stagnation, higher external debts and the profound weakening of the state's capacity to play an intermediary role in settling disputes and dealing with protests and demands of labour organizations.

After the electoral defeat of the FRAP in 1958, Chilean socialism stressed its ideological differences with the communists, putting the political alliance in danger. Both the ideological influence of the Sino-Soviet conflict and the Cuban revolution played a role in this. The Sino-Soviet debate led to an internal split in the PCCh and, with respect to the Cuban revolution, it took an ambiguous position. The revolution was the result of a non-orthodox strategy, which was not taken into account by any communist party in the region, and which had been adapted and recommended for the Latin American revolutionary struggle by Ernesto 'Che' Guevara in his book *La Guerra de Guerrillas*. Castro represented the Latin American alternative to revolution and allowed the Sino-Soviet debate to be considered as irrelevant to the region's revolutionary movements. The Chilean communists, however, distrusted the non-Marxist character of the organizations that formed the Cuban revolutionary movement and the fact that none of the relevant members of the Cuban communist party, such as Blas Roca and Juan Marinello, had played a role in the revolutionary process (Furci 1984: 84). The Chilean communists' loyalty to the Soviet Communist Party and the international policy of peaceful coexistence, the Leninist concept of the revolutionary process and the party structure, clashed with the Cuban strategy of the guerrillero. According to this strategy the absence of favourable objective conditions for revolution could be compensated for and developed through the effect and the political action of a guerrillero group. The urban character of the revolutionary potential of the industrial proletariat was replaced by the revolutionary condition of the rural regions' poor and the Leninist idea as the leader of the revolutionary process was replaced by that of the guerrillero movement. Only after the end of the 1960s did the PCCh start considering the Cuban revolution as a victory over imperialism, and even then with the reservation that many lessons of the revolution were only valid for and applicable to the Cuban situation.

For the Chilean socialists, the Cuban revolution represented the materialization of what had been one of the basic principles of the party's international policy in that it was a nationalist, anti-imperialist, popular, anti-capitalist and Latin Americanist revolutionary experience. Unlike the experience of Yugoslavia and Titoism, Cuba was a case with which the Chilean socialists could identify themselves at both cultural and political levels. The fact that the revolution was the result of the direct victory of the Cuban revolutionaries over the dilemma between social democracy and Soviet socialism, realized without the help of a foreign military power such as the East European socialisms, reaffirmed the value and specificity of Third World revolutions. The socialists declared complete solidarity with the Cuban revolution, and deplored the aggression of American policy against the country. US policy had led Cuba to look for help from the USSR, thus losing its international independence and having to cope with the Sovietization of its political and economic system. The party reaffirmed the validity of the FRAP strategy during its Eighteenth General Ordinary Congress in October 1959. It re-affirmed its decision to contribute to the ideological and political unity of the world's working class based on the Marxist theories and the independence of the revolutionary movements to choose the most appropriate way to reach socialism (Jobet 1971: 52). This is reflected in the need to recognize the diversity of ways to implement and develop socialism in the Third World countries, depending on the convergence between revolutionary nationalism and socialism that is the result of the experiences of the anti-colonial and anti-imperialist revolutions, particularly represented by the revolutionary struggle of the Algerian National Liberation Front (FLN). Nevertheless, in the second half of the 1960s, a Castroist faction was constructed in the party that afterwards facilitated the Leninization of the Socialist Party. This was inspired by the changes of direction of the Cuban revolution itself. For some authors the new phenomenon of Leninism within the party was a defensive reaction to the rise of a powerful political actor that threatened to occupy the same popular spaces of social representation: Christian Democracy (Sarget 1994: 326). The adoption of Leninism would also have meant an intent to modernize the party's structure, which was excessively controlled by *caudillismo*. At the national level, the PSCh characterized Alessandri's government as an instrument of plutocracy and American imperialism, which had only elevated the country's external debts, unemployment, inflation and misery amongst the popular sectors.

Revolution in Freedom and the PSCh

Apart from the influence of the Cuban revolution, the Leninization of Chilean socialism had to do with the electoral defeat of both the FRAP and Salvador Allende in the 1964 presidential elections, and the victory of the Christian Democratic Party (DC). The DC proposed the Revolution in Liberty, with substantial American support and opposition to the nationalist revolutionism of the FRAP, including the communists. Hitherto, all initiatives for the transformation and restructuring of Chile's society had come from the demands of the popular sectors and/or from the parties that represented them politically. With the electoral victory of the DC, for the first time, it was initiated by modernizing sectors within the economic elites. The DC intended to resolve the economic crisis that was the result of the exhaustion of the ISI and the durable consumer goods production sectors. Its policy was not much different from the strategy applied in Brazil by Juscelino Kubitschek or João Goulart, and in Argentina by Arturo Frondizi or by the military intervention in 1966 that gave way to the so-called Argentinean Revolution. Just as in the cases of Brazil and Argentina, the revolution in liberty tried to resolve the crisis of industrialization by strengthening the internal accumulation of capital through reducing the effects of the changes in the international capitalist system, something that helped the penetration of the national industrial economy by the multinationals. The search for an alliance with international capital was one of the keys of the economic model implemented by President Eduardo Frei (1964–70). His political alliance was based on the support of large social sectors that had so far been excluded from civil society (peasants, marginalized urban population). These social sectors were mobilized in favour of agrarian reform, against the large latifundio and in search of the integration of the marginalized into the benefits of the state policies. Making use of these new political actors that were related to the middle class meant trying to neutralize and eliminate the revolutionary power of the working class and trade union movement, which was traditionally linked to the political actions of the socialist and communist parties. This also implied an attack on the traditional political right, which had supported the election of the DC government, and for that reason it made clear that it was not necessary to restructure political support.

For the implementation of the project the DC needed a drastic redefinition of what until then had been the function of the state, from the perspective of a major efficiency in the articulation of the state with the centres of political and economic decision-making. In order to achieve this, it was necessary to strengthen presidential power, which could give the state more autonomy *vis-à-vis* civil society. Presidentialism had to give way to a business technocracy that would have direct access to state decision-making in order to guarantee the central goal of putting an end to the stagnation of the process of accumulation and of building up the relations of industrial capitalism with the multinationals. The weak state, considered as a political path of the transformations that was supported by a flexible and open political system, had to be replaced by a state that would manage the transformations that needed to be implemented and that would be in favour of an open relation with transnational capital. In this sense the project of the DC was the Chilean model of associated development (Cardoso 1973). This model tried to strengthen the capitalist development that was supported by a reformist political solution. Agrarian reform and the nationalization of the copper industry (51 per cent under state control) were the fundamental supporting elements of the associated development model and, unlike the cases of Brazil and Argentina, its consolidation was hindered by the economic weakness of the monopolistic bourgeoisie, whose hegemonic character depended much more on its ties to the state (subsidies) and on speculation than on its capacity to promote the process of capital accumulation. This was demonstrated by the fall of the investment coefficient, which dropped from 16.4 per cent in the 1964–70 period to 15.6 per cent in the 1965–70 period. In line with the historical tendency of Chile's economic development, the state and foreign investments kept their function of decisive forces in the solution of the economic crisis (De Riz 1979: 82).

The success of the applied economic policy was limited and restricted to economic recovery in 1965 and 1966, based on the improvement of the price for copper on the international markets, and on the old formula of increasing external debt, which ended up accelerating the inflation that, in turn, led to a fall in salaries and a reduction of economic growth. This situation progressively reduced the popular support that had legitimized the DC's project of restructuring in a decisive way, and had facilitated the social pact in favour of associated development. The incorporation of peasants and the marginalized urban population, agrarian reform and the political radicalization of civil society ended up terrifying the middle-class sectors, the political right and the monopolistic bourgeoisie, which had supported the DC for being the only possible alternative to communism. This proves that there was an irremediable contradiction between the objectives of strengthening capitalism and the reformist political solution. It led to the failure of the simultaneous intent to recompose the mechanisms of capital accumulation, together with the political and economic demands of the new social sectors that had been incorporated into political society.

The failure of the DC government radicalized the political conceptualization of the necessary structural reforms of Chilean capitalism, leading to the political recomposition of the left, which had been defeated dramatically in 1964. The PSCh faced the beginning of the DC government with a political and organizational weakness, which arose from the internal fragmentation that generated the defeat in the 1964 presidential elections, and from the strong influence of Castroism amongst an important part of the party's youth. This conflict was made evident during the 20th Congress in 1964, when important sectors within the party did not want to recognize the authority of the central committee, as a result of doctrinary discrepancies. The conflict led to the foundation of the Movement of the Revolutionary Left (MIR) in 1965, ideologically inspired by the Cuban revolution and with the aim of building up the third 'working-class' party in Chile. In the official documentation of the 1964 congress, the internal fragmentation of socialism was being interpreted as the result of the ideological influence of the 'Sino-Soviet crisis' (Maoist), and of the 'romantic bewitching' of the guerrilla actions in other places, in direct reference to the Cuban influence and the rejection of the 'economistic and electoristic reformism' of the traditional left.

Chilean socialism insisted on the rejection of all understanding or collaboration with the national bourgeoisie or its parties, preferring the 'unity of the working class' and class parties. The basic ingredients of its political programme had their origin in the combination of electoral and revolutionary methods, both legal and illegal, that were necessary to confront the possible rejection of the right regarding the electoral victory of the left. The electoral defeat of 1964 caused the party to elaborate a new national political line, in which it categorically rejected the thesis that the bourgeois democratic phase of the revolution is a necessary phase to implement in the future socialism of the backward countries, given the fact that it recognizes the incapacity of the Chilean bourgeoisie to assimilate socialism and of the DC to implement it politically. In the 21st General Ordinary Congress of 1965, the party repeated the need to strengthen the political alliance of the FRAP and stressed that electoral defeat, which derived from the exclusive dependence on the electoral system, did not invalidate the historical necessity for the Chilean revolution. It also declared that the DC government was reactionary and anti-socialist. The DC was defined as the political representative of the bourgeoisie, supported by the American government. The party implemented economic policies to consolidate its economic power and established paternalistic ties with the rural and urban poor. These were, in turn, used to neutralize the revolutionary potential of the organized working class. It was because of this that the party's principal task was to reconquer its political influence in the mass movement (peasants and urban poor). In this respect, the crisis of the bourgeois government of the DC offered a 'revolutionary way out'. In order to strengthen the fundamental socialist/communist axis within the Chilean revolution, however, the FRAP had to transform into a political representative of the socialist line of the Workers' Front and the ideological and programmatical differences within the PCCh had to be resolved.

The debate over the ways that lead to power was accentuated through the presence of the MIR in Chile's political scene. The socialists considered the choice between the electoral and the insurrectional ways to be false. 'The party has one objective, and in order to reach it, it has to use the methods and the means that will be necessary for the revolutionary struggle. The insurrection will have to occur when the leadership of the popular movement understands that the social process, that it promoted by itself, has reached maturity and is disposed to serve as the midwife of the revolution. We can not foresee the concrete form that the insurgency of the masses will take in the future' (Jobet 1971: 111).

The political radicalization of the socialists was also stimulated by their participation in the Tricontinental Conference of the Peoples of Asia, Africa and Latin America, which took place in Havana in 1966. The meeting had the objective to support the revolutionary movements in those continents. In the Conference and in January of the same year, the Latin American Organization for Solidarity (OLAS) was created, initiated by the Chilean socialists, and its first conference was held in July and August 1967. The socialist participation in both conferences had a double effect: on the one hand it made the relations with the PCCh, which had maintained a reserved and distant attitude towards Castroism, more difficult. On the other hand, it radicalized the Leninist tendencies that sharpened the factional conflict in the heart of the party. The socialists criticized the faithfulness of the PCCh towards the international politics of the Soviet Union and its lack of support to the OLAS. At the same time, the socialists rejected the application of the politics of peaceful coexistence in Latin America, given the fact that this concept was interpreted as the domination of Soviet diplomacy over some of the communist parties in the region, leading to the collaboration of classes and the liquidation of the struggle against the oligarchies and American imperialism.

Within the Socialist Party, the factional conflict culminated in a new division of the party in that same year, 1967, giving way to the formation of the Socialist Popular Party (PSP). The consolidation of Leninism in the party and the adoption of armed struggle as a preferable means to power were realized in the 22nd General Ordinary Congress in November 1967. In the resolutions approved by the Congress, it was declared that the PSCh was a Marxist-Leninist organization. Getting to power was a strategical objective, which would lead to the installation of a revolutionary state that initiated the construction of socialism. It declared that 'revolutionary violence' was inevitable and legitimate, and that it was the only way to face the repressive and armed nature of the state class. In the same resolutions, it also stated that the peaceful or legal forms of struggle alone, elections being one of them, do not lead to power. It repeated the validity of the policy of the Workers' Front (FT), formulated in 1957, defined as the unity of action of the proletariat, peasants and poor middle class, under the guidance of the first.

The incorporation of intellectuals and students strengthened the development of the Front and supported the independence of the FT *vis-à-vis* the national bourgeoisie, allied to American politics. The OLAS would continue to be the continental version of the FT and would give the armed struggle an essential value in the Latin American revolutionary process. The FRAP was considered to represent politically the interests of the working class, which was possible because of the mutual understanding of socialists and communists, and it had to unify all anti-imperialist forces that could help the socialist revolution. However, it was the weight of Chile's electoral system (the necessity to save the socialist parliamentary representation) and the chronical ideological ambivalence of the party that made the Leninization of the party purely rhetorical. The socialists thought that the strengthening of the FRAP was necessary because of the success of the new strategy of the Chilean communists, destined to build a popular democratic union, which should achieve a multi-party government with a programmatical and political platform. This was opposed by the socialist agreements of the 22nd General Ordinary Congress.

It is evident that the new communist strategy of democratic popular unity radically opposed the socialist laws of the FRAP, whose strategy was built on a working-class basis, as in the FT thesis. It contradicted, in particular, the communist aspirations of amplifying the political alliance towards the 'bourgeois reformists'' political parties such as the Radical Party (PR). In practice, the revolutionist rhetoric of the socialists faced radical modifications and could not prevent the success of the communist strategy that finally led to the formation of the Popular Unity[3] (UP) and the victory of Salvador Allende, a socialist militant, in the 1970 presidential elections.

The Socialists and the UP

The axis of the formation of Popular Unity was the political alliance between communists and socialists, who had a conflictive co-existence, stemming from the Popular Front period. The unity of the left was progressively consolidated, with communist help, from its clandestine nature to the presidential candidature of Salvador Allende in 1952 and with the formation of the FRAP in 1956. The PCCh had kept its thesis of the peaceful way to power since the 10th Congress in 1957. During the 12th Congress of 1965 it kept repeating this (despite the FRAP's electoral defeat in 1964) to support the strategy of a future constitution of a Popular government (Corvalán 1971). The instrument of the peaceful way was the mobilization of the masses, compatible with the democratic tradition of the political system and of a working-class movement with party representatives (socialists and communists) who had previous government experience and had incorporated themselves into the parliamentary political regime.

The continuity of the communist political line is in contrast with the contradictory and ambivalent policy of the PSCh. This was expressed in the difference between the doctrinary political analysis and the concrete political action during the UP government. During the 23rd General Ordinary Congress in January of 1971, the socialists characterized Salvador Allende's electoral victory as a partial control of the state and defined the UP as a multi-class political alliance. It was a government with working-class, petty bourgeois and bourgeois tendencies. In this context the PSCh claimed it would overcome these contradictions by a strengthening of the popular movement's revolutionary character and the transformation of the party into a revolutionary elite, capable of changing the capitalist character of the system through socialism, during the UP government. This was necessary considering the fact that the conquest of the Presidency of the Republic in the framework of bourgeois institutionality cannot automatically produce the change of a bourgeois government to a working-class government (Jobet 1973: 175).

Unlike the communists, who focused their strategy on the destruction of economic power of the monopolistic bourgeoisie and the multinationals, the socialists tried, through the growth of popular power, to destroy the bourgeois political power reflected in the state. The concept of popular power had been vaguely formulated in the government programme and was defined as the intervention of the popular sectors at different decision-making levels of the state and the economy. During the first days of the government, the existence of contradictory strategical lines between both parties was stressed. For the communists the central problem to resolve was the enlargement of the social base for support for the government, through a policy that was favourable to the middle classes, and petty and middle bourgeoisie. For the socialists the central problem was to strengthen working-class power through the implementation of popular power. The strategical incompatibility of the political lines of both parties persisted during the three years of the UP government, and was expressed in extreme communist economism versus the political voluntarism of the socialists. In the opposition between re-formism and revolution none of these parties succeeded in developing an integral vision of the problem of the state.

The UP government (1970–73) had to cope with a radicalized political scene because of a sum of social and economic demands that were not met by the DC government. These demands were the convergence of three basic conflicts: the opposition between nation and imperialism (nationalization of the American mining companies); the conflict between people and oligarchy (agrarian reforms, nationalization of the banks and the monopoly companies); and the participation in or exclusion from the benefits of development of the popular sectors (employment, salaries and social services). The complexity of this triple dimension of social movements (Touraine 1973) and the complexity that came with the incapacity of the state to offer solutions to these three basic conflicts in the end destroyed the stability of the political system and the social pact that had supported the Chilean state of compromise for almost forty years. The UP's programme of structural transformations was based on the so-called Chilean way to socialism, which tried to change the character of state class without destroying it first, and considered the democratic system as absolutely valid. In his first presidential speech, Salvador Allende himself legitimized the necessity of a peaceful evolution of the old society towards a new one. Particularly in countries where most of the power lies with the popular representation, this should all take place in accordance with the constitutional state (Allende 1972: 7).

The specificity of the programme of the UP was its anti-imperialist, anti-monopolistic and anti-oligarchic character, with the ultimate objective of the construction of socialism in a democratic, pluralist and libertarian society. For this purpose the construction of a new economy, with the formation of an area of social property, was a central priority. This area of social property should consist of state enterprises, together with the expropriated mono-polistic industrial sector, the financial sector, the banking sector and the large mining enterprises that operated in the exports sector (Unidad Popular 1970). To these small and medium-sized private industry were added. These sectors supported the state in the economic and technological development, and the mixed area of association between national and private capital.

The economic strategy that was applied in the beginning period of the government was inspired by the political premise of a necessary enlargement of its social base of support for the modification of the correlation of political powers that were favourable to the UP. For this reason, short-term economic measurements should lead to an effective improvement of the economic situation of the popular sectors and at the same time weaken the economic base of the monopolistic industrial sectors and the latifundist oligarchy. Therefore, a policy of economic reactivation was used, based on the increase of demand as a result of the increase of salaries and public spending. The increase of production was achieved through the reactivation of the unused production capacity of the industrial sector and the assimilation of employment. The results were indeed very good. In 1971, industrial production rose by 14 per cent, GDP growth reached 8.3 per cent and the participation of the employed in total income rose from 53.7 per cent in 1970 to 59 per cent in 1971 (ODEPLAN 1972). The reactivation measurements were accompanied by the nationalization of foreign enterprises operating in the copper, saltpetre and coal-mining sectors. The nationalization of the monopolistic enterprises and the deepening of the agrarian reforms started during the Frei government. The immediate political results of this strategy became clear in the municipal elections of April 1971, in which the UP got 50.7 per cent of the votes. The participation of trade unions in the management of the nationalized enterprises was regulated on the basis of agreements with the United Workers Central (CUT) in July, without ratification of the national Congress.

Nevertheless, in the first year of government problems arose, stemming from the discrepancy between the small increases in political support necessary for the change of production relations and the accelerated rhythm of economic transformations. In addition, American pressure and intervention increased: from the beginning the United States had applied a strategy that aimed to undermine the government and to support the DC opposition and the right (represented by the PN) financially. The slogan to win the production battle and the accelerated nationalization of the economy ended up progressively eroding the initial support of the middle-class sectors for the UP government. As a result of the accelerated income redistribution, the growth of demand had become larger than the growth of supply in a very short time, and the increase of the international prices for import products and the fall of the copper export prices on the world market rapidly increased the budget deficit. This made it clear that at the end of 1971 an economic crisis had begun that would put into doubt the viability of the populist policy of the UP (Castells 1974). The government was convinced that the success and continuity of the economic policy depended to a greater extent on the possibility to transform it into mass-supported policy. The dilemmas that resulted from this were how to make the popular revolutionary mobilization compatible with the presidential obligation to protect the constitutional state, and how to have the executive power (with an adversary parliament and judicial and military powers) transform the state without leading to the destruction of this state. There were no solutions to these dilemmas and for the UP government until the military coup of September 1973.

The government tried to resolve the problems in the UP Conclave in June 1972 through a debate on the continuity of the applied policy but once again there was a confrontation between the communist line, stressing the idea of 'consolidation in order to progress', and the socialist line of 'progress without trade-off'. According to the communists the political radicalization that resulted from rapid nationalization of the economy and the deepening of the strategy of popular power weakened the control and the stability of Allende's government. For them the principal objective of the UP was not the conquest of power, but the radical change of the social structure and the creation of a new economic order and, as a solution to the economic crisis, an increase of production. For this it was necessary substantially to improve economic guidance and central planning. This would lead to a larger partici-pation of the working class, which would bring about a true change in production relations and the recovery of the political support from the middle class. According to the communists the correlation of political and social powers turned out negatively for the working class, due to the errors at the political (popular power) and social (speeded nationalization) levels, which were transgressions to the programme of the UP government itself.

In this context, the principal task was to assume the defence of the continuity of the government. The political mobilization of the popular movement was considered to be a threat to the existence of the government because of the political instability that it might generate. The PSCh claimed that it was crucial to start of with the bourgeois character of the state and stressed that only the mobilization of the masses could generate total control of political power. However, the improvement of the coalition of political powers that were most favourable to the UP could not be based on the introduction of political and economic concessions, to recover the support from the middle class. The enlargement of popular support should increase the deepening of the transformation of class relations. It turned out that the communist economic line was imposed within the UP (in June of 1972), putting an end to the economic policy of the first period. The strategy of popular power, applied by the socialists, was, in mid-1972, more myth than reality, and did not present an efficient political alternative for the con-frontation with the economic crisis.

In order to control the institutional crises that the possibly illegal expropri-ations would generate, the definition of the areas of social property and the nationalization of the economy searched for compromises with the DC. This led to a parliamentary confrontation with the government. In October 1972 the 'paternal strike' took place, which made clear that the popular power was incapable of assuming the defence of power effectively. The government had to accept a cabinet of armistice, assign militaries as members and consolidate the rejection of a policy that was supported by the mass movement. The incorporation of the militaries into the government signified the reaffirmation of the centrist policy that had been formulated by the communists and that looked acceptable both to the DC and the militaries. However, it was not enough to achieve the political isolation of the contra-revolutionary right from the DC, and from that moment onwards the UP government did not achieve the formulation of a coherent economic policy until the collapse of Allende's government in September 1973. The results of the parliamentary elections of September 1973, favourable to the government, made the opposition lose its hope for a 'white coup' that should have been the result of the constitutional collapse through the opposition of the parliament to Allende's government. For that reason the way to a military coup, supported and stimulated by the civil opposition of the right and the DC, was open. For the socialists every search for an agreement with the DC stimulated the sectors that tried to destroy the government, and because of that the gaps with the strategy of the Chilean communists were consolidated.

From Dictatorship to Neoliberalism

After the military coup of 11 September 1973 the party kept its revolutionary vision, stressing the gaps with the Chilean communists, who had initiated two irreconcilable strategic lines in the UP government. In some of their first documents under the dictatorial regime (November 1973), the Chilean socialists stated that the fall of the government was the direct consequence of the lack of confidence in the support of the revolutionary masses (popular power), and the hegemony of the positions of the centre, represented by the PC in the heart of the government, at the expense of the power of the working class. In another document of March 1974, the socialists reaffirmed their Leninist vision on the failure of the UP government, which had been the direct consequence of the insufficiencies of the revolutionary failures (Fernández Jilberto 1985: 310). The necessity and the validity of a Marxist-Leninist inspired socialist revolution, supported by the establishment of the proletarian dictatorship, is also reaffirmed in that document. The socialist revolution had to confront the errors of the right in a successful way, represented by parliamentary cretinism and the childish extremism of the extreme left. The insufficient Leninization of the party and the predominance of the petty bourgeoisie in the government leadership would form the basis for the explanations of the decline of Salvador Allende.

Nevertheless, in spite of the severe critique on communist reformism, the aforementioned document affirms that one of the most significant lessons was the unjustifiable existence of two working-class parties in Chilean politics. This would only weaken the political activities of the working class. The document also proposed the fusion of the PSCh and the PCCh. The influence of this document was underlined by the fact that it was the official version of the party's Internal Department (DI) of Chile. The External Department (DE) in East Berlin, however, was of the opinion that the document would eventually eliminate the Chilean socialists, and would devalue the party's ideological patrimony. The initial conflict between both currents was solved temporarily by the old socialist medicine of permitting the coexistence of the factions. It was regulated by a third faction that represented the party's surviving regional organizations which, for that matter, played a pacifying role between the DI and the DE.

Power relations between the various factions were institutionalized in the Plenary of the Central Committee of the PSCh in Havana in 1975. The conflictive stability that was the result of a pact between the different factions managed to survive until 1979 in the so-called Plenary of Algiers, where the DI questioned the legitimacy of the DE and the General Secretary of the Party. They accused them of sustaining right-wing positions and of stimulating an alternative to the centre-left respect for the dictatorship, through a political alliance with the DC, the Radical Party and the socialists, with the explicit exclusion of the communists. Because of that, the DI thought that the party's right-wing faction intended to eliminate the historical alliance with the Communist Party from the FP period. This Plenary, which ultimately led to a split within the party, faced two tendencies that diverged the policy of future alliances of the party from the perspective of the toppling of the dictatorship and the analysis of the causes of the UP's defeat. The first one was lead by Clodomiro Almeyda and, with the so-called Document of March 1974 as its source of inspiration, declared itself a Marxist-Leninist party and intended to establish a close alliance with the PCCh in the future. The second faction, led by Secretary-General Carlos Altamirano, was known as the Socialist Party of the 24th Congress. For this faction the critical analysis of the experience of the UP, and particularly the absence of a coherent conception of the relations between socialism and democracy, was crucial. This absence was explained by the underestimation of the decisive role that was played by the superstructural factors (ideology of the middle class in the case of Chile) in the process of radical transformations (economic programme of the UP). In the instrumentalist vision of democracy that dominated the political conduct of the PS during the 1970–73 period, democracy was characterized as merely 'formal and representative' and as a means and obstruction to the implementation of the revolutionary transformations. In the opinion of this faction, the PSCh did not succeed in assimilating the principle that the political democracy is not just tactics or an instrument, but a historical conquest of the popular movement of Chile and the structural framework in which the struggle for socialism should take place.

According to the Secretary-General Altamirano, the socialist left had made a historical mistake in not assigning importance to the specific characteristics of the political system of Chile in the twentieth century. In the heart of its socio-political evolution a constitutional state and republican institutions were built. These institutions managed to put military power under the control of the civilian political power of the state. Compared to other countries in the region and in spite of the economic (underdevelopment) and cultural

(Catholic/Hispanic tradition) restraints, the democratic system that emerged from it was much more advanced. The PSCh was particularly attached to an instrumentalist vision of democracy, through the Trotskyite, anarchist and populist influences that managed to dominate its internal political life, which helped its Marxist-Leninization and Cubanization (Politzer 1990).

The faction that was represented by the 24th Congress supported the 'revaluation of democracy' by introducing a Gramscian interpretation of Chilean politics that covered the periods of the UP and the military dictatorship, all of this considering Gramsci as the anti-Leninist. This perspective was reinforced afterwards by what was called the process of 'socialist renovation', meaning the abandonment of the strategy of frontal attack of the state (the moment of domination) and the introduction of a strategy of revaluation of civil society and its institutions (the moment of hegemony) (Walker 1990: 206). During its participation in the first and second democratic governments after 1990, the party progressed to an acceptance of neoliberal politics, abandoning its Keynesian perception of economic policy. The radical ideological change that the PSCh went through in this period can be explained by the growing conviction of the irreversibility of the neoliberal transformations implemented by the dictatorship. Factors that are just as important were the strong external influences that the party assimilated from the crisis, the East European collapse and the influence of the European social democracy, supported by its members in exile (Angell and Carstairs 1987).

It was the socialist section of the 24th Congress that controlled and dominated what was designated as the European connection, which was the totality of relations with social democracy, in a context of significant changes in the situation of the European left, such as Eurocommunism with the predominant role of Enrico Berlinguer; the Italian Communist Party and Italian Marxism, which was strongly influenced by a renewed interest in Antonio Gramsci; access to power by the French Socialist Party under the leadership of François Mitterrand; and the fall of the South European dictatorships and the transformation of social democracy into government parties, as in the case of the PSOE in Spain and the socialist parties of Mario Soares in Portugal and Andreas Papandreou in Greece. The events in Poland in the 1979–80 period, the repression of Solidarity and the Soviet invasion of Afghanistan alienated the socialists from their admiration for the regimes of the 'real socialisms'. All this led to the abandonment of the idea of European social democracy as reformist, and favoured the slow but effective reconciliation with that European social democracy.

The global ideological revision caused by the revaluation of democracy and the rapprochement with European social democracy gave way to a more global vision of ideological restructuring of Chilean socialism, known as 'socialist renovation'. This shows the necessity of a critical analysis of the experience of the UP, which will make the explanation of its failure as the result of the strategic duality of its project evident. This was expressed in the contradiction between the idea of a second model of transition towards the socialism based on democracy, pluralism and liberty (the Chilean way to socialism), and the conception of the parties of the UP that explain the transit from capitalism to socialism according to the 'general laws of the revolution', inspired by the canons of Marxism-Leninism. This last aspect reduced the possibilities of transforming the Chilean way into a hegemonic political project, with ample support for the democratic political regime, and proves that the political alliance of the UP was no longer valid.

The process of socialist renovation, however, was a key condition for the formation of a new political alliance that would form the base for a centre-left understanding, further reinforced by the mutual understanding between renovated socialism and the leadership of Christian Democracy, integrated through the critical sectors during the 1973 military coup. A process of political understanding and agreement began that led to the constitution of the Democratic Alliance (AD) in 1983, and culminated in the formation of the Agreement for Democracy (CD), and its victory in the 1989 presidential elections. The PSCh abandoned its historical alliance with the PCCh, which dated from the late 1930s. Participation in the insurrectional strategy against the dictatorship and integration into the Popular Democratic Movement (MDP) at the end of 1983, together with the Marxist-Leninist faction of the PS, which originated in the 1979 division, characterized this alliance. On 11 March 1990 the PSCh returned to government, from which it had been violently expelled in 1973. It did so in alliance with the principal political adversary of the UP, the Christian Democratic Party (PDC), and remains in power until today, with an electoral capacity of 25 per cent of the votes.

The return of the PSCh to government presupposed the acceptance of the irreversibility of the economic transformations of the dictatorship and the implicit acknowledgement that it did not intend to restore the order of the UP, but that it promoted the establishment of a new economic, social and institutional order. For this reason, it had to accept and promote the deepening of those transformations expressed in the reduction of the role of the state, liberalization of the labour market, flexibilization and internationalization of the production structures, privatization of public enterprises and depoliticization of the social consequences of economic development. The party argued that accepting to govern during the transition to democracy was the only way to make possible the transition of a deregulated neoliberal model to a model of social market economy (Moulian 1997: 73).

Conclusions

The PSCh has played a decisive role in the stabilization and restoration of democracy in Chile since 1990 and has formed part of the government ever since. Its principal virtue has been the facilitation of adjustment of the democratic regime to the model of neoliberal economic restructuring and the assurance of social peace that was necessary for growth while the economy was integrating into the world market. For this reason, far removed from its revolutionary past, it has transformed itself into a political actor of great importance that stimulates and facilitates the transnationalization of the economy, promising that its political role consists of guaranteeing the substitution of 'brutal capitalism' with the 'social market economy'.

The price Chilean socialists have so far paid for their prominent political role is the impossibility of dissolving the model of 'protected democracy' implemented by the dictatorship itself. This model is expressed in a two-party political system that gives the civilian political forces of Pinochetism control over parliament, even when they are permanently destroyed at electoral level. A system of vetoes for the minority is used, based on the constitutional dispositions that limit popular sovereignty in the Senate elections (designated senators). The designated senators operate as guards of the 1980 Constitution, of the model of protected democracy and the constitutional legitimacy of the market economy. The constitutional reforms designed to put an end to the so-called authoritarian enclaves have so far failed, and this allows the existence of a political regime of blocked democracy in which the majority cannot exercise the power emanating from popular will, expressed in the elections.

At the ideological level the PSCh has achieved its electorally successful adaptation to the model of protected democracy, through its ideological transformation from the 1990s onwards. This is reflected in the substitution of Gramscian-style renovated Marxism, through which it managed to abandon Leninism for an ideology of social liberalism. With this transformation it has confronted two big ideological challenges of this era: the abandonment of the state's regulatory functions and the adoration of the market.

Notes

1. The following organizations participated in the foundation of the PSCh: Socialist Revolutionary Action (ARS), Socialist Marxist Party (PSM), New Public Action (NAP), Socialist Order (OS) and Unified Socialist Party (PSU).

2. In this conference the socialist parties of Burma, Ceylon, India, Indonesia, Israel, Lebanon, Japan, Malaysia, Nepal, Pakistan and Vietnam participated.

3. The UP was formed by the PCCh, PSCh, PR, Social Democratic Party (PS), Movement of Unitarian Popular Action (MAPU), and the Independent Popular Action (API).

References

Alba, V. (1953) *Le Mouvement ouvrier en Amérique Latine*, Paris: Editions Ouvrierès.

Angell, Alan and Susan Carstairs (1987) *The Exile Question in Chilean Politics*, London: Latin American Bureau.

Allende, S. (1972) *La Via Chilena al Socialismo*, Santiago: Quimantd.

Bascuzan Edwards, C. (1990) *La Izquierda sin Allende*, Santiago: Ediciones Planeta.

Barria, J. (1971) *História de la CUT*, Santiago: Prensa Latinoamericana.

Burbach, R. J. (1975) 'The Chilean industrial bourgeoisie and foreign capital, 1920–1970', unpublished M.Phil. thesis, University of Michigan.

Caballero, M. (1986) *Latin America and the Comintern 1919–1943*, Cambridge: Cambridge University Press.

Cardoso, F. H. (1973) 'Associated dependent development: theoretical and practical implications', in Alfred Stephan (ed.), *Authoritarian Brazil: Origins, Policies and Future*, New Haven, CT: Yale University Press.

Castells, M. (1974) *La Lucha de Clases en Chile*, Mexico: Siglo XXI.

Corvalán, L. (1971) *Camino de Victoria*, Santiago: Horizonte.

De Riz, L. (1979) *Sociedad y Política en Chile*, Mexico: Universidad Nacional Autónoma.

Drake, Paul (1992) *Socialismo y Populismo. Chile 1936–1973*, Valparaíso: Universidad Católica de Valparaíso.

Ellsworth P. T. (1945) *Chile: An Economy in Transition*, New York: Macmillan.

Faletto, E. (1972) *Génesis Histórica del Proceso Político Chileno*, Santiago: Quimantú.

— (1973) *Clases Sociales, Crisis Política y Problemas del Socialismo en Chile*, Santiago: Flacso.

Fazio, H. (1996) *El Programa Abandonado. Balance Económico Social del Gobierno de Aylwin*, Santiago: Universidad Arcis/Lom.

— (1997) *Mapa Actual de la Extrema Riqueza en Chile*, Santiago: Universidad Arcis/Lom.

Fernández Jilberto, A. E. (1985) *Dictadura Militar y Oposición Política en Chile 1973–1981*, Dordrecht: Foris Publications.

Furci, C. (1984) *The Chilean Communist Party and the Road to Socialism*, London: Zed Books.

Goldenberg, B. (1971) *Kommunismus in Lateinamerika*, Stuttgart: Verlag Kohlhammer.

Gómez, M. S. (1984) *Partido Comunista de Chile. Factores Nacionales e Internacionales de su Política Interna 1922–1952*, Santiago: FLACSO.

Góngora, M. (1981) *Ensayo Histórico Sobre la Noción de Estado en Chile en los Siglos XIX y XX*, Santiago: Ediciones la Ciudad.

Jobet, J. C. (1971) *El Partido Socialista de Chile*, Santiago: Ediciones Prensa Latinoamericana.

Jobet, J. C. and Chelen, A. (1973) *Pensamiento Teórico y Político del Partido Socialista de Chile*, Santiago: Quimantú.

Lowy, M. (1980) *Le Marxisme en Amérique Latine de 1909 à nos jours*, Paris: François Maspero.

Martínez, Javier and Alvaro Díaz (1995) *Chile: La Gran Transformación*, Santiago: SUR.

Moulian, T. (1983) *Los Frentes Populares y el Desarrollo Político de la Década de los Sesenta*, Santiago: FLACSO.

— (1991) *El Marxismo en Chile: Producción y Utilización*, Santiago: FLACSO.

— (1993) *La Forja de Ilusiones: El Sistema de Partidos 1932–1973*, Santiago: Universidad ARCIS/FLACSO.

— (1997) *Chile Actual: Anatomía de un Mito*, Santiago: Universidad Arcis/Lom.

ODEPLAN (1972) *Informe Económico Anual*, Santiago: ODEPLAN.

Palma, G. (1984) 'Chile 1914–1935: de economía exportadora a sustitutiva de importaciones', *Estudios Cieplan* 12: 61–88.

Politzer, Patricia (1990) *Altamirano*, Buenos Aires: Ediciones B.

Pollack, B. and H. Rosenkranz (1986) *Revolutionary Social Democracy: The Chilean Socialist Party*, London: Frances Pinter.

Ponce Durán, P. Oscar Schnake (1994) *Comienzos del Socialismo Chileno 1933–1942*, Santiago: Ediciones Documentas.

Pinto, A. (1959) *Chile, un Caso de Desarrollo Frustrado*, Santiago: Editorial Universitaria.

Tironi, E. (1984) *La Torre de Babel. Ensayos de Crítica y Renovación*, Santiago: Ediciones Sur.

Touraine, A. (1987) *Actores Sociales y Sistema Poliíicos en América Latina*, Santiago: PREALC/OIT.

— (1973) *Vie et Mort du Chili populaire*, Paris: Seuil.

Ramos, J. A. (1969) *História del Stalinismo en la Argentina*, Buenos Aires: Ediciones del Mar Dulce.

Roca, B. (1939) *La Unidad Vencera el Fascismo*, Havana: Ediciones Sociales.

— (1945) *Estados Unidos, Teheran y la América Latina, una Carta a Earl Browder*, Havana: Ediciones Sociales.

Sarget, Marie-Noëlle (1994) *Systeme Politique et Parti Socialiste au Chili*, Paris: L'Harmattan.

Silva, H. (1970) *1935 – A Revolta Vermelha*, Rio de Janeiro: Editora Civilizacao Brasileira.

Thorpe, R. (1984) *The Effect of the 1929 Depression on Latin America*, London: Macmillan.

Unidad Popular (1970) *Programa Básico de Gobierno de la Unidad Popular*, Santiago: Editorial PLA.

Urzda Valenzuela, G. (1992) *História Política de Chile y su Evolución Electoral. Desde 1810 a 1992*, Santiago: Editorial Jurídica de Chile.

Varas, A. (1991) *De la Komintern a la Perestroika. América Latina y la URSS*, Santiago: FLACSO.

— (1996) *El Partido Comunista de Chile, Estudio Interdiciplinario*, Santiago: FLACSO.

Wais, Oscar (1961) *Nacionalismo y Socialismo en América Latina*, Buenos Aires: Editorial Iguazu.

Walker, I. (1990) *Socialismo y Democracia. Chile y Europa en Perspectiva Comparada*, Buenos Aires: Cieplan/Hachette.

FOUR

The Cardoso Administration and Brazil's Transition to the Third Millennium

KARLA LEMANSKI-VALENTE

The year 1985 has been considered the mark for the Brazilian transition to democracy, a process that has unveiled many paradoxes. On the one hand, the changes in the regime has brought renovation, dynamism and hope on political, economical and social levels. It has also changed the country's role in South America with the creation of Mercosur[1] and numerous multilateral agreements inside and outside the region, advancing Brazil's inclusion in the globalization process. On the other hand, democracy has exacerbated many problems and deficiencies that are deeply rooted in Brazilian history and culture.

In the early 1980s, Brazil experienced its worse economic crisis since 1929. The crisis was due to a combination of factors: the exhaustion and delay in abandoning the import substitution industrialization strategy; the debt crisis; the poor management of public finances by the military government; and the oil shocks. Moreover, the irreversible reality of the globalization process, with intense capital and trade flows, and the economic success of Chile and other newly industrialized countries of East Asia, induced Brazil and other Latin American countries to adopt the necessary transformations in order to be included in this process. From the mid-1980s, the shift towards democracy was accompanied by an implementation of neoliberal[2] reforms in Latin America[3] (Haggard and Kaufman 1992), although the degree and emphasis on the adoption of these reforms varied substantially within the region. Since the shift from authoritarianism in the mid-1980s, all governments have struggled to achieve economic stabilization through several attempts that resulted in further economic disarray, a political crisis and high social costs. Brazil went from a 'miracle economy' in the 1970s to a 'lost decade' in the 1980s. Inflation control was achieved only in 1994, with the introduction of the *Real* Plan, which produced many positive outcomes. However, the macroeconomic stability still depends on major structural reforms that have been challenged by the Brazilian institutional framework and decision-making culture.

This chapter analyses the Brazilian situation from various perspectives. First, we discuss the challenges of the democratic transition process. Second, we analyse how the institutional structure and decision-making culture affect the policy-making process in Brazil. Third, we expose the major outcomes of the implementation of neoliberal reforms on economic stability, and discuss the *Real* Plan. We conclude by discussing the latest issues challenges of the current government in shaping Brazil's future in the new millennium.

'Muda Brasil': The Challenges of the Democratic Transition[4]

The democratic transition process produced a dynamic multi-party system, where more than three dozen new political parties were formed, giving voice and empowerment to members of the political community. An interesting example is the creation of the left-wing Workers' Party (PT), up to now the main opposition party in Brazil.[5] During the transition period, the Workers' Party played an important role in the democratic movement and was identified with the desire for change and further inclusion. Its presence has helped to ignite political thinking throughout the country. However, the party suffered some political losses, partially due to its internal fragmentation and its conservative thinking, opposing any major reforms that would lead to the reduction of the size and role of the state in the Brazilian economy.[6]

Another significant change in the political environment is a renovation of leadership. In this case, two interesting political actors deserve attention: Fernando Henrique Cardoso and Luis Ignácio 'Lula' da Silva. Cardoso (PSDB), has been considered the best-prepared president in Brazil in more than a generation, and is the first president to be re-elected in the new democracy.[7] His main accomplishments and political strength came from the successful implementation of the *Real* Plan. Although his administration still has many elements of old political practices such as clientelism, nepotism, patronage, and so on, he is credited with important measures such as: redeeming the national and international trust in the government; his attempts to make the state more consistent, transparent and accountable; and encouraging civil society and other political actors to take in a more active and responsible role in the restructuring process that the country has to go through in order to face the future. The second example of renovation of leadership is Lula, one of the founders of the Workers' Party. He was a charismatic leader of the metalworkers' strike, which became a national event in the late 1970s and won the support of the Roman Catholic Church, as well as that of many students and intellectuals.[8] Both leaders, with very different backgrounds, styles and visions, have greatly influenced society and politics over the last years. This renovation of leadership is very important because it is bringing new dynamics to political practices and thinking. These dynamics, in turn, are helping to move the country through an important, although often painful, learning process.

There is no doubt that since the 1980s political diversity has increased and new relationships have developed, both within the state and between the state and civil society. In addition to political parties and leaders, perhaps one of the most significant characteristics of Brazil's transition to democracy has been the involvement and participation of civil society through an increased number of social movements, political, business and grassroots organizations. In terms of social movements, the example of the 'Diretas Já' and the demonstrations for Collor's impeachment are remarkable moments in Brazilian history.[9] During these events, the whole country, in spite of its social fragmentation, presented an unusually unified front. In fact, during the 1980s, social movements initially started at local level promoted the emergence of independent labour initiatives that were disconnected from the control of the state, which allowed the popular sector to experience active political participation, and increased political mobilization in urban areas (Graham 1994).

One of the most controversial and active grassroots movements in Brazil is the Landless Movement (MST – Movimento dos Trabalhadores Rurais Sem-Terra).[10] The organization represents the displaced rural workers in Brazil and has about 600,000 members. MST has drawn international attention over recent years by pressuring the government for agrarian reform, politically a very delicate issue in Brazil.

There has been a rise of non-governmental organizations and mobilizations dedicated to numerous issues such as urban violence; hunger; indigenous rights, women's rights; environmental awareness and conservation (specially protection of the Amazon), and so on. Some other important actors, either new or renewed, include labour organizations such as the Central Workers' Organisation (CUT – Central Única dos Trabalhadores[11]), the Sindical Force (FS – Força Sindical) and the National Confederation of Workers in Agriculture (CONTAG – Confederação Nacional dos Trabalhadores na Agricultura). It also includes employers' organizations such as the National Confederation of Industry (CNI – Confederação Nacional da Indústria), the National Confederation of Commerce (CNC – Confederação Nacional do Comércio) and the Federation of Industries of São Paulo (FIESP – Federação das Indústrias do Estado de São Paulo).

The Brazilian government has increasingly been forced to negotiate and interact with different interest groups. This democratic aspect is healthy because it guarantees that the government maintains a balance of interests as well as decision-making transparency and accountability. In addition, civil society can exercise more control, inducing the state actors to build a more unified front (Hintze 1981) and to become, therefore, a more effective channel of representation. Nevertheless, democracy can also intensify the existing expressed ideological divergences and fuel partisan conflict, which was limited under the authoritarian regime (O'Donnell and Schmitter 1986). In general, the experience of democratic transition in Brazil did not increase cohesion within the state, among interest groups, social movements or political parties (Weyland 1996). Further, it has not renewed party organization and did not improve it in terms of a well-defined ideology and programme. There has also been little change in the political culture characterized by corporativist and clientelistic[12] practices within the state and society. In fact, democracy, combined with the institutional framework, political culture and social fragmentation found in Brazil, made policy-making very complicated, usually delaying critical reforms and spreading scepticism about the country's future. In the next section we will discuss some of the major aspects of the Brazilian institutional framework and decision-making culture that are still critical obstacles to reaching a compromise on the restructuring needs and processes.

Institutional Structure and Decision-making Culture

For the last 20 years, democratic consolidation, economic stabilization, state restructuring and many social policies have been limited by the institutional features and decision-making culture prevailing in Brazil. These characteristics pose enormous obstacles to the implementation of major reforms that are essential to guarantee future growth, international competitiveness and the further inclusion of society. According to Mainwaring (Mainwaring and Shugart 1997), these institutional features are: a robust federalism[13]; strong presidential powers; a large number of weak and fragmented parties with no clear ideology; and undisciplined and disloyal politicians. Moreover, there is the problem of the constitutional structure increasing inefficiency through power-dispersion. The 1988 Constitution, written during the early years of the democratic transition, is often criticized for being a product of populism. Sarney's administration, trying to please different interest groups in the midst of a very delicate political environment, ended up with an extremely complex document, often endorsing bureaucratic and inefficient decision-making. Finally, in addition to the internal segmentation of the state apparatus, with open rivalries among governmental agencies and leaders as well as states, there is a high fragmentation of the social forces.

The institutional characteristics mentioned above make consensus among diverse sociopolitical forces very difficult to achieve (Huber et al. 1993; Weyland 1996). Below we discuss how structural configuration and political practices have limited the democratic government's ability to gain political support for further restructuring.

Federalism

Federalism was proposed as an ideal option to guarantee the national unity and balanced economic development in a country with the continental dimensions and huge socioeconomic disparities of Brazil. In a democratic system, federalism could help to increase the regional and local governments' powers, giving the federal government more freedom to delegate routine tasks, such as basic health care and basic education (Domingues and Giraldo 1996).

However, Brazil's combination of federalism and presidentialism enhances the dispersion of power and the strength of interest groups to oppose change. For many years the strongly centralized power of the federal government has made the state and municipal governments financially and politically dependent. Although the new Constitution has transferred some resources from the federal level to the state and municipal levels, it did not clearly transfer the responsibilities that were financed by those resources. In order to increase efficiency, it is necessary to restructure and balance the level of tasks and responsibilities across all levels of government.

Federalism has also shaped the logic of politicians in a very unproductive way, limiting party programme orientation. Usually, the loyalty of the politicians and their agendas are focused on electoral strategies as well as local and regional interests, weakening the building of a broad national level policy and making a reliable government coalition difficult. In sum, federalism did not advance regional and local interests effectively and the differences between states enhance clientelistic and populist practices, which continue to be widespread. Politicians continue to use a populist rhetoric and rely on large-scale clientelistic networks in order to control resources and use them in their political bases (Geddes 1994).

The Political Party System and Decision-making

The fragmentation of the party system is another major obstacle. Since parties are weak, do not present a clear ideology and are formed by politicians who lack accountability and loyalty, they can be used as an efficient channel of representation and compromise neither by society nor by the government. In fact, the parties' weakness and lack of discipline makes it difficult efficiently to aggregate and organize social interests (Desposato 1997), and gives way to narrow interests and widespread clientelistic practices. Consequently, many interest groups and leaders choose not to use political parties as a channel of representation. They prefer to use their personal influence to pressure and close deals directly with state agents.

For the last 20 years, major structural reforms have been postponed because clientelistic politicians refused to give up patronage resources. As stated by Schneider (1991: 381): 'A major obstacle resides in the peculiar electoral system – one that not only minimizes both the degree of responsibility of representatives to constituencies or meaningful party discipline, but also encourages alliances of transitory electoral convenience at the state and local levels. These are often contrary to the parties' positions on the national level.' In order to change the electoral system, Brazil needs further political reforms that require constitutional transformation, which has been a political struggle for the last five years.

Low loyalty and lack of discipline has also made the relation between the executive and the legislative powers very unpredictable (Mainwaring and Shugart 1997: 81) and therefore vulnerable. This increases the uncertainty of support for the president, making the relationship between him and the coalitions too fluid (Novaes 1994). One of the ways in which Brazilian politicians have demonstrated their lack of commitment is frequently switching party affiliation[14]. These career-oriented politicians refuse to accept any kind of party discipline and have shown little interest in supporting a well-defined programme. This individualistic action is perpetuated not only by the institutions, but also by the fact that the voter typically 'has no knowledge of the candidate he votes for. Usually, he doesn't know anything about the candidate's proposals, ideas, or behaviour' (Rabinovich 1990). In the congressional elections of 1998, for instance, the success or failure of the candidates depended on their fame or obscurity, and the 'issue-content was almost zero.'[15] It is true that democratization has in general improved the level of interest and awareness of voters, but such improvement varies between regions and social classes and has not made a significant overall impact. Since political parties do not present a clear programme and society in general does not understand specific issues (for example, the tax system), voters tend to follow charismatic leaders who use populist rhetoric that focuses on short-term projects addressing the immediate needs of the voters. Collor's campaign, with its anti-corruption and modernization speech, was a good example of a populist rhetoric responding to an immediate need of the society at the time. His strategy was based on the perception that society during the democratic transition strongly rejected corruption and the 'old guard' politicians. In addition, voters were also afraid of the radical and socialistic views of Collor's opponent (Lula, of the Worker's Party), preferring Collor's promises of modernization and corruption eradication. Ironically, after winning the election, Collor choose to implement most of his programme in a very authoritarian fashion and was impeached on corruption accusations.

Some voters, especially in large cities, are more informed about politicians running for high-level positions, but still know little about politicians who may represent them more directly. Usually, after the election, the representatives have little or no accountability to the voters. One reason for this is that there is a lot of confusion about the responsibilities at municipal, state and federal levels, as well as the tasks and actual decision-making power of the different kinds of representatives. In addition, the level of education of the voters has complicated the process even more, since they have limited access to information, which is usually manipulated.[16] Education and awareness are essential if society is to be able to choose and evaluate its representatives more efficiently. Moreover, decentralization of power and simplification of the system in general would help to focus on the right means to address local needs.

Presidentialism

Traditionally, the president can accomplish many things through, for instance, building coalitions, governing by decree, and winning the support of individual legislators through patronage (Mainwaring and Shugart 1997). In Brazil, since presidents almost always have a minority of seats in Congress and consequently are unable to gain reliable and broad support, they have extensively applied their decree power in order to implement unpopular reforms. Indeed, most of the economic plans adopted in Brazil during the 1990s were implemented that way.[17]

On the one hand, these powers have helped the presidents to implement measures that were considered urgent due to the economic crisis. With the present institutional structure, it would take too long to reach a compromise, and the delay might deepen the problems. On the other hand, the extensive use of such power has increased the level of national and international insecurity and distrust in the government, especially after the repeated failure of those plans. Collor, for instance, resorted to the drastic act of a temporary retention of private financial assets. The trust lost by these radical measures, implemented overnight, is taking years to regain. Cardoso, aware of the importance of the trust of the investor and the fragility of the economy once the government is not trusted, has pledged since the beginning of his first term that his administration's main characteristic will be a 'lack of surprises' and disclosure.[18] Presidents also frequently appoint and fire ministers according to their level of popularity, personal relationship and outcomes of the policies implemented.[19]

Leadership

The results of the presidentialism in Brazil during the 1990s have not been promising, although the country chose to keep the same system of government when given a chance to change in the 1993 referendum.[20] Many authors stress that the outcomes of past administrations and the behaviour of the presidents have been greatly shaped by the Brazilian institutional framework. Since it is difficult to reach a compromise and since the behaviour of legislators, governors and parties is usually unpredictable, they maintained and extensively used their decree power, appointment power and patronage relationships. Nevertheless, the leadership style seems also to influence the results of each administration, since most of the reforms depend on the leader's ability to overcome popular and interest group pressure. Below, we briefly discuss the leadership style of the four presidents after the end of authoritarianism.

Sarney's government failed to control inflation and to implement the necessary structural reforms. There were many conflicts in response to the agrarian reform project[21] and criticisms of his populist handling of the new

Constitution Assembly of 1988. As a leader, he did not present strong determination. He also lacked legitimacy due to the fact that he assumed office after the death of the indirectly elected Tancredo Neves.[22] In addition, he was not trusted because he and his party (PDS) were strongly connected with the authoritarian government.

Collor made important advances in terms of implementing neoliberal reforms in the midst of nationalistic and protectionist reactions, sometimes even violent demonstrations. There is no doubt that these advances favoured later reforms, but his drastic style and accusations of corruption in his government increased uncertainty and distrust. He implemented the stabilization plans in an authoritarian style and refused to discuss them with Congress, parties and interest groups. During his populist speeches, businesses were often accused of not making sacrifices to improve the country's economy.

Franco made some progress towards constitutional changes that were necessary to pursue structural reforms, and backed Cardoso in the creation of a short-term fiscal stabilization plan and the implementation of the *Real* Plan. As a leader, however, he lacked a clear vision and broad thinking, was unable to build political support and explicitly maintained strong ties and special interests in his home state, Minas Gerais, which raised suspicion among politicians and society.

Cardoso's leadership was legitimized by the success of the *Real* Plan and the economic predictability it generated. In large part his two presidential election victories are due to his success as well as his increased bargain power (which weakened the opposition), and his credibility with national and foreign investors. Equally important is his consensus-building leadership style, as well as his consistency and openness. In 1995, for instance, he gained support for a number of constitutional amendments eliminating state monopolies in telecommunications, gas and petroleum industries and ending discrimination against foreign investments. Since he faced the same institutional framework and resistance found by previous presidents, his ability to win congressional majority in this matter was notable. Many of his achievements resulted from his ability to seek and win the support of key individual legislators and build coalitions. He won the elections supported by a heterodox alliance between a variety of parties ranging from the centre-left to the right of the spectrum. Despite its lack of political consistency, this coalition has been fairly successful in holding members to their commitment to support economic and state reforms.

Cardoso's speeches are in general less popular than those of his predecessors. He promises consistency and transparency but, at the same time, stresses the limitations of the central government to solve all the social problems. He constantly reinforces the point that in order to address the social problems the involvement of civil society is fundamental,[23] as is the participation of different levels of government. Cardoso's emphasis on the limitation of the power of the central government and the concept of shared responsibility through partnerships has often been misunderstood and criticized, since it challenges traditional ways of thinking. Society is asked to participate and cooperate in a more organized way. His position also forces society to change the perception that the government is responsible for all development, financing and implementation of social projects. The following section will look at Brazil's civil society in order to understand its resistance to the changes proposed.

Civil Society

There is no doubt that democratization has brought important advances in terms of civil society interest and organization. Nevertheless, in spite of its new dynamics, civil society is still highly fragmented because of the socio-economic heterogeneity that characterizes Brazil. This heterogeneity supports division between social sectors as well as between members of the same class, hindering an efficient pressure from below. Although democracy has brought greater autonomy to many social groups, they still have not developed strong mechanisms of political coordination and remain highly fragmented, especially in the case of business and labour. Business associations and syndicates do not present an effective united front representing a collective interest as a class (Weyland 1996). Labour, the most targeted and controlled class under the authoritarian years, still does not have the organizational strength needed for effective policy pressure to improve its position. In fact, some leaders from labour and business organizations prefer to negotiate directly with the governmental officials. The middle class, which has suffered a great decline in living standards following years of inflation and occasional recessions, continues to have a very low degree of solidarity and is divided along political lines.

All these patterns of fragmentation combined to the institutional framework have made it difficult for Brazilian civil society to obtain a considerable degree of self-sustaining cohesion and to promote effective group actions to influence government decision-making. With rare exceptions, most of the time different groups look at each other with suspicion, avoiding networking and cross-sector coalition. Some non-governmental organizations, for instance, are targeted by critics for being funded by government or international resources.

Unfortunately, but not surprisingly, the organization and action of civil society over the last years reflect the same problems of clientelism, bureaucratization, and the influence of special isolated interest groups as practised in the political sphere. In order to influence government decision-making and eventually help to improve the institutional framework, civil society has to learn how to organize and express itself in a more efficient and cohesive way. In this context, it is critical that a social restructuring process accompanies the economic and political reforms. Civil society needs to understand that its role and participation are vital to correct many problems resulting from the economic crisis. It needs to change the belief and acceptance 'of a natural hierarchy of social groups, each with its ordained place and its own set of prerequisite and responsibilities' (Schmitter 1971). Furthermore, it needs to overcome its unwillingness to participate and cooperate and its attitude of 'leave it to the government' when it comes to social policies. This behaviour pattern results from a history of paternalism and patrimonialism that 'has made association leaders and followers ready to leave initiation to higher authorities and to regard the government as the supreme patrão (boss) of the society' (Schmitter 1971: 380–1). If these patterns persist, the improvements the society needs in order to enhance equality and justice and prepare itself to face global competition will continue to be postponed. Economic and political restructuring pose a great challenge in view of the exisiting institutional framework and decision-making practices. An equally important challenge is to reform a culture that exercises inefficient, self-interest-driven behaviour on individual, social and institutional levels.

Neoliberalism and Economic Stabilization

According to the neoliberal approach (Williamson 1990), the economic crisis in Brazil and other Latin American countries was a result of years of economic populism during the authoritarian regime, as well as the excessive intervention of the state, marked by over-protectionism, over-regulation and the over-large public sector. It should therefore be addressed by fighting economic populism and reducing the size of the state apparatus. Once those measures had been taken and the state reached macroeconomic stabilization, promoted trade liberalization and privatization, then growth would automatically resume (Bresser Pereira et al. 1993). In addition, those market-oriented reforms should improve resource allocation across sectors and processes (Williamson 1990) and increase overall economic efficiency. However, the implementation of neoliberal policies in Latin America has shown that the regulatory framework and macroeconomic incentives may not be enough for the domestic businesses to acquire competitiveness. Furthermore, the neoliberal approach works as a stabilization model, but does not offer a development strategy, which is a very important step once stabilization is achieved.

As proposed by Ramos (1997: 16), there are two typical attitudes to the neoliberal reforms: 'one attitude considers the structural reforms inspired by neoliberalism to be quintessence of good economic policy, while the other considers that this model involves excessively high costs, especially as regards its impact on distribution'. Many authors have argued that success on the adoption of many non-neoliberal policies depends on how the central role of the state and market orientation is maintained (Kingstone 1997). Neo-structuralists, for instance, question the neoliberal claims that the set of measures would automatically result in growth and equity because it has critical flaws that should be corrected by state intervention (Sunkel 1991).

In the case of Brazil, for instance, Bresser Pereira (Bresser Pereira et al. 1993: 64) has argued that the neoliberal approach assesses the problem wrongly because it 'does not sufficiently acknowledge the gravity of fiscal crisis, compromises excessively with internal and foreign creditors, does not provide for reasonable burden sharing, is based on a misguided assessment of the nature of inflation, proposes stabilisation programs that are too costly, and, most important, because even if it succeeds in stabilising, it does not offer effective strategies to recover public savings and promote the resumption of growth'. Further, he suggests that the Brazilian crisis should be addressed by an alternative 'pragmatic approach', which does not over-emphasise the economic crisis resulting from state intervention and economic populism. In addition to stabilization and reduction of the role of the state, the pragmatic approach includes the need to address the fiscal crisis and to define a new growth strategy through 'a new pattern of state intervention' where the state's economic role, although reduced, is still active.

The neoliberal policies adopted in Brazil were often unconventional, using a combination of liberal and social democratic elements, and retained a central role for the state. The state is still considered important in coordinating the whole economic and political restructuring process and, more importantly, remedying the consequences of the economic crisis, such as increased poverty, social and regional disparities, deterioration or stagnation of income distribution and infrastructure, unemployment, rising urban violence, and so on. However, in order to further the restructuring process and address social needs, the state, civil society and the institutional framework will need to find a new *modus operandi*.

The *Real* Plan

Since the beginning of the 1990s, there has been a growing consensus on the benefits of a reduced state apparatus and a more open economy. Especially after the *Real* Plan[24] (1994), significant advances in economic reforms were carried out, which included trade liberalization, privatization[25], deregulation of state monopolies, and opening up to foreign investment.

One of the most important factors influencing those macroeconomic advances has been the control of inflation through the *Real* Plan, considered the most successful stabilization plan since 1985 (Figure 4.1). Only one year after its implementation, inflation reduced from 2,489 per cent in 1993 to 22 per cent in 1995. With inflation under control, GDP increased by 17 per cent between 1994 and 1997, an average of 4 per cent a year as opposed to 0.2 per cent during the four previous years. In terms of foreign direct investment, the country received R$24 billion in 1998, compared to R$ 1 billion in 1993[27]. Internationally, Brazil has expanded its participation at regional and global levels, which sometimes required the adoption of new laws in areas such as anti-dumping and intellectual property. The *Real* Plan

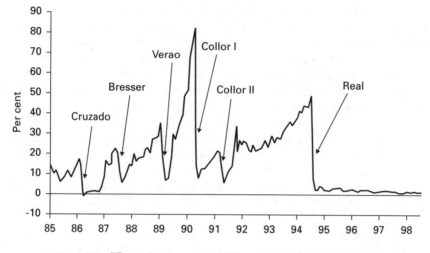

FIGURE 4.1 The main economic stabilization plans[26] and their impact
on inflation, 1985–98 (*Source*: IBGE)

also helped to bring benefits to new segments of the population, particularly
the poor. The government estimates that a very important outcome was to
help about 13 million Brazilians to cross the poverty line and be integrated
in the consumers' market.

There are several reasons for the success of the *Real* Plan. First, the
government had learned from previous failures and aggregated three basic
elements that were not used by the previous plans: a monetary and fiscal
policy; structural reform; and a coordinated policy with regard to contracts
and revenues. Second, the *Real* Plan had the benefits of being launched after
significant structural reforms were initiated by Collor's government, resuming
capital flows. Third, the *Real* Plan was based on an initial fiscal adjustment
through the implementation of the Immediate Action Programme[28] in June
1993 and the Social Emergency Fund. Fourth, an agreement rescheduling the
foreign debt (1994) re-established normal relations between Brazil and its
international creditors. Fifth, there was a growing consensus on neoliberal
policies and the need to restructure the state. Finally, the political will and
Cardoso's leadership played an important role.

Although the *Real* Plan has lasted longer than any previous plan, the
future of the economy depends on the government's ability to stabilize its
fiscal accounts. Recent international events – the Asian crisis and Russian
default – have revealed that the economy is still vulnerable and that fiscal
stabilization and key reforms are urgent. By the end of 1998, Brazil had
negotiated a rescue package with the International Monetary Fund, which
included more than US$41 billion in financial assistance.[29]

The government also needs to remedy the consequences these political and economic events have had on society. One of the most critical problems is the rising unemployment due to changes in production and industrial relocation. Many industries, especially multinationals, are receiving incentives to operate in different regions of the country and therefore help to promote a more even development in the different regions. However, this will take a long time and the 'temporary' consequences of the relocations need to be addressed. Other problems, such as escalating urban violence and the deterioration of basic services, need urgent attention. With inflation under control, Cardoso's government has been able to accomplish more in terms of social policies than those of his predecessors. An interesting innovation is the 'Comunidade Solidária'[30] (Community with Solidarity) programme, through which the community cooperates with the government to address problems on local levels more efficiently. Other programmes in the areas of education, housing, agriculture, health,[31] and so on, have made some progress, but for most groups in society that have suffered a considerable decline of living standards the government still has not done enough. In addition, the problem with the fiscal balance and the vulnerability of the economy to international events is pushing the government to focus on structural reforms. The nature of the reforms and their urgency are likely to influence political behaviour, increase opposition and delay social programmes. Cardoso's second term promises to be more difficult than the first, and his ability to compromise and move forward his political and economic agenda will be in check.

The Path Ahead

Over the last decade Brazil has undergone intensive changes characterized by the transition to democracy and economic reforms. Significant advances were made in terms of macroeconomic stabilization, regional and global integration, opening the country to many opportunities and at the same time forcing further reforms. The consolidation of these achievements in recent years, the strong and sustainable development of the economy, and the policies addressing social problems depend on the ability of Cardoso's government to pursue critical state restructuring as well as institutional reforms. Although macroeconomic stabilization is a precondition for many of the reforms, it is not sufficient to guarantee the future strength of Brazil. Many of these reforms had already been postponed by previous governments, and it is not possible for the present government to overcome all the obstacles. The structural reforms are concentrated in several areas, such as administration, social security, tax and labour. There has been a growing consensus on the need for restructuring, and many projects are likely to be approved by Congress. The delays in the process so far have been caused not only by disagreements on strategy and goals and an unwillingness to give up patronage resources, but also by the fact that career-oriented politicians have little interest in backing up projects that will generate results only in the long run and may not continue after the next election. Commitment and continuity, however, depend on concurrent institutional reforms, starting with the electoral and party systems.

Cardoso's second term started by focusing on the fiscal equilibrium, without which the present and future stability are at risk. In order to achieve that balance, the government announced on October 1998 (immediately after Cardoso's re-election) a Fiscal Stabilization Plan, including a package of measures designed to collect $28 billion in public funds in 1999 and continue structural reforms. The package is a two-part programme including a work agenda aimed at structural measures and institutional changes, and a 1999–2001 action plan designed to ensure a successful transition process. The work agenda encompasses the implementation of the administrative reform already approved by Congress and the approval of additional social security, fiscal and labour reforms.

The tax reform, a very unpopular measure with strong opposition, focuses on the reduction of the number of taxes and simplification of the current tax system. It is an important measure to help with the balance of public finances. At present, the tax system is difficult to understand, unfair, allows tax evasion, conflicts with other tax systems, and complicates the distribution of resources and the relationships between the different levels of government. The social security reform is equally important and will establish a new regime for public and private sector employees, reshaping the organization and functioning of the social security in all levels of government. By the end of 1998, Congress had approved key aspects of the new legislation for the private sector, including minimum age limits for retirement. The system has maintained along the years many distortions, especially in the public sector, where retirement salaries are based on the last salary and not the employees' level of contribution. According to the government, in 1996 the average pension of public sector retired workers was almost eight times higher than the pension of their private sector counterparts. Those of public sector workers from the Legislative and Judiciary branches were roughly sixteen times higher.

The globalization process, the state, and economic restructuring are changing the labour market and a reform in the area is vital. The main objectives are to preserve and create job opportunities, to reduce manpower turnaround as well as informal sector activities, to produce growth and to support the unemployed. Basically, labour legislation will be redesigned in its approach to employment contracts, dismissals and collective bargaining. In order to achieve some of the goals and improve the country's competitiveness, the government will have to develop measures and invest heavily in education, training and technological modernization. Education has been continuously neglected and the few improvements made by Cardoso's government, such as teacher training and investment in equipment and materials, are still not enough to overcome the deficiencies in the system.

The success of the reforms and the implementation of new programmes will not be enough if they concentrate only on structural changes. It is important that the public sector adopts a new management structure that can increase efficiency, transparency and accountability. The current government is suggesting the application of management models used by the private sector, oriented towards results and using appropriate evaluation instruments such as indicators, goals, costs, and so on to verify their achievement. The results of the evaluation of the programmes would serve as guidelines for allocating resources and directing the attention to society's priorities. In theory, the proposition is positive and logical, but the actual implementation of this kind of management model will take a long time and face enormous cultural resistance. It will be a challenge to change a culture that has shaped the decision-making practices, organization, productivity, working relations, and so on, not only in the public but also in the private sectors. The political and economic crisis of the past years and the complexity of the reforms ahead have made clear that the government will be unable to solve the social problem in the short run. Continuity by future administrations and further participation of the civil society are critical.

Notes

1. Mercosur is a common market between Brazil, Argentina, Paraguay and Uruguay established by the Treaty of Asunción, 26 March 1991. The trade pact took effect as a customs union and partial free-trade zone in January 1995. Many other Latin American countries, such as Chile and Bolivia, are joining the market. The aim of the agreement is to allow the free movement of capital, labour and services between the members.

2. Basically, the neoliberal approach included the following: explicit measures to liberalize trade, characterized by the elimination of quantitative restrictions and the establishment of moderate tariffs; fiscal discipline (reduction of fiscal deficit); redirecting and prioritization of public expenditures; tax reform; monetary discipline; financial liberalization; privatization of most state enterprises; deregulation of financial and labour markets; elimination of trade barriers to the entry of direct foreign investment; legal and institutional framework strengthening property rights (Williamson 1990).

3. Neoliberalism, a perspective that has its roots in the collapse of the Keynesian consensus (Bleaney 1985) and in the crisis of development economics (Hirshman 1979), is difficult to analyse not only because the term has many ideological connotations, but also because the commitments and extent of the neoliberal reform in Latin American countries vary substantially (Gwynne 1997).

4. 'Muda Brasil' (Change Brazil) was the campaign slogan used in 1985 by the civilian presidential candidate, Tancredo Neves from the PMDB (Brazilian Democratic Movement Party – centre). The campaign was a democratic alliance (Aliança Democrática) between the PMDB, PDS (Social Democratic Party – right centre) and the PFL (Liberal Front Party – right).

5. The party was founded in 1980 as a consequence of the efforts to establish an independent position and raise the level of political consciousness of the urban industrial working class.

6. The most relevant losses were during the elections for president, when Luis Ignácio

Lula da Silva was the main candidate for the PT. The first loss (1989) was in a run-off against Fernando Collor de Mello, a right-wing candidate for the PRN (Party of National Reconstruction). This typical right–left division was represented by Lula with a socialist agenda on the one side, and Collor with a neoliberal programme on the other. Collor, who had only 16 per cent in the first round, got 46.9 per cent in the second as a result of the voters' fear of the PT's radicalism. The second (1989) and third (1998) time Lula lost to Cardoso, a representative of the centre-left PSDB (Brazilian Social Democracy Party). In both presidential elections Cardoso got about 53.06 per cent of the votes, while Lula had 31.71 per cent. There was no run-off in either case. (Source: TSE [Superior Election Tribunal].)

7. The PSDB is a centre-left party formed in 1988 by dissidents of the PMDB, PFL, PDS, PDT (Democratic Labour Party), PSB (Brazilian Socialist Party) and PTB (Brazilian Labour Party). (Source: TSE.)

8. At the end of the 1970s, the strikes in the state of São Paulo (ABCD region) were the first attempts of collective bargaining since 1964.

9. The 'Diretas Já' was a national campaign with a large street demonstration asking for the withdrawal of the military government and for direct elections for president in 1985. However, the first direct presidential election in 29 years took place only in 1989, with the victory of Fernando Collor de Mello, who was also the first president in Brazilian history to be impeached.

10. Over the years the group has staged many invasions and other violent manifestations, making negotiations with the government difficult. Seligman, the current president of the National Institute of Agrarian Reform and Colonization (INCRA), has said that the problem in negotiating is the fact that the MST is split into two movements: one social, and one political, which disrespects the law and represents political candidates and motives (*Washington Post*, August 1998, 'To Brazil's poor, land is up for grabs'). The MST has the sympathy of the Catholic Church, some labour unions, the PT, and several members of society who share the criticism against the government's economic and social policies.

11. Founded in 1983, CUT was the first central union body to be organized since 1964.

12. The clientelistic interpersonal relationship in Brazil is based on inequalities and power differences. Democracy has maintained the clientelistic practices in the government, which increased the waste of resources and expenditures of many administrations. Personnel spending of the federal government between 1986 and 1989, for instance, went from 2.5 to 4.5 per cent of the GDP. Between 1985 and 1990 at state and municipal level, personnel spending increased by 44 per cent (MARE 1996; Varsano 1996).

13. By robust federalism Mainwaring means that during democratic periods 'mayors and governors have been powerful actors with significant autonomy *vis-à-vis* the federal government and with significant resources' (Mainwaring and Shugart 1997: 83).

14. Between 1987 and 1990 there were 197 cases of party affiliation change among congressmen. Between 1991 and 1995 this number increased to 262 (Mainwaring and Shugart 1997: 81).

15. *The Economist*, August 1998.

16. A recent survey conducted by the TSE indicated that 66 per cent of Brazilian voters are either illiterate or received very basic education (TSE 1998).

17. According to the 1988 Constitution, Brazilian presidents can issue decrees (called provisional measures) that have the same power as ordinary laws, but need to be ratified or defeated by Congress within 30 days. Until May 1995, for instance, the civilian presidents issued 1,004 provisional measures – Sarney (147), Collor (160), Franco (505), Cardoso (192) (*Veja*, 'A explosão das MP', 31 May 1995). One of the reasons for these large numbers is that decrees can be (and almost invariably are) reissued whenever Congress has not yet decided whether to reject the decree or pass it into law.

18. In an interview given to *Veja* (17 January 1996) Cardoso reaffirmed that his decision was to show that there was a direction, that we did not have to go back and forth and there would be no frights nor surprises. 'Eu tomei uma decisão: mostrar que há rumo, que não se faz ziguezague, que não há sustos nem surpresas.'

19. Governments before that of Cardoso (who has surprisingly kept several initial key governmental members, including Finance Minister Pedro Malan) changed an outrageous number of cabinet officials in relatively short periods of time. Sarney, for instance, had four finance ministers, one for each stabilization plan. Collor, in two years, changed most of his administration. Franco, in only six months, had four finance ministers – Cardoso was the fourth, leaving the position before the end of its term to run for president in 1994.

20. The 1993 referendum generated numerous debates. Various segments of the society, intellectuals and politicians did actually support parlamentarianism. However, the average voter did not follow or understand most of the debates and was already traumatized by the recent political and economic events. Consequently, the voters preferred to stick with presidentialism, an already known system that was presented by the media in a more accessible way.

21. This agrarian reform project did not include the lands of the Church and the state. In addition, the government granted land to the military (about 6.2 million Brazilian acres). The action resulted in many violent protests by peasants and landless people as well as the organization of the UDR (Democratic Rural Union), a strong lobby influence during the elaboration of the new Constitution.

22. Tancredo was elected by the 'Colégio Eleitoral', an institution controlled by the military. In fact, the military relinquished control after several informal negotiations and Tancredo's promise that the military would not be punished for human rights violations (Stepan 1988; Barros 1985).

23. Previous presidents have appealed to social involvement, for example, to control the freeze on prices and force businesses to issue receipts, increasing tension between consumers and businesses.

24. Very basically, the *Real* Plan consisted of three phases: 'fiscal reform; the introduction of the Real Unity of Value (URV), design to bring a complex system of indexetion in line with a single price adjustment mechanism; and the conversion of the URV into a new currency called *real*' (*Latin Finance*, August 1998).

25. In April 1990, during Collor's administration, the PND (National Privatization Program) was created. The first 17 company privatizations under his administration faced strong, sometimes violent, opposition. Part of the opposition came from an important segment of the society that had representation in Congress. Up to 1997, 56 companies were sold, including steel mills, petrochemical plants and electric power utilities, totalling about US$26,075 billion. In 1998, the Telebras (Brazilian Public Telecommunication System, serving about 90 per cent of the country's telephones) was sold for about US$19.01 billion – the second largest privatization in the world in this sector.

26. The Sarney administration launched the Cruzado Plan (February 1986), the Cruzado Plan II (November 1986), the Bresser Plan (June 1987) and the Summer Plan (January 1989). Collor launched the Collor I Plan (March 1990) and the Collor II Plan (February 1991). The *Real* Plan was implemented in 1994 during Franco's government.

27. Sources: IBGE (Brazilian Institute of Geography and Research), Procom (Programme for the Defence of the Consumer) and Dieese (Inter-union Department of Statistics and Social Economic Studies).

28. The programme included the following: (1) a draft law proposing a reduction of US$6 billion in current and capital expenditure by the Federal Government for 1993; (2)

some tax management measures; (3) rescheduling debt payments from the States and Municipalities to Federal institutions; (4) closer supervision of state banks; (5) restructuring of federal financial institutions; (6) measures to expand the privatization programme.

29. The package was funded by the IMF, the World Bank, the Inter-American Development Bank and countries in North America, Europe and Asia through the Bank of International Settlements (BIS).

30. 'Comunidade Solidária' is a programme launched in 1995 that aims to promote partnerships between the different levels of government and between governments and civil society. It addresses many issues, such as education, infant mortality, agriculture, employment and housing. According to the government, illiteracy, for instance, was reduced from 16.5 per cent in 1992 to 13.8 per cent in 1996. School evasion went from 13.4 per cent in 1992 to 8.8 per cent in 1996.

31 In terms of health care, Brazil's spends about $230 to $250 per person, a low per capita expenditure relative to other countries. Reforms opening to foreign competition in insurance and health care management anticipate a shift from public to private sector, but the benefits for the majority are still unclear.

References

Barros, A. (1985) 'An option for the Brazilian military?', *Third World Quarterly*, 7 (2): 63–77.

Bleaney, M. (1985) *The Rise and Fall of Keynesian Economics*, London: Macmillan.

Bresser Pereira, L. C., J. M. Maraval and A. Przeworski (1993) *Economic Reforms in New Democracies: a Social Democratic Approach*, Cambridge: Cambridge University Press.

Desposato. S. (1997) paper presented at the 20th International Congress of the Latin American Studies Association, 17–20 April, Guadalajara, Mexico.

Dominguez, J. and J. Giraldo (1996) 'Parties, institutions, and market reforms in constructing the democracies', in J. Dominguez and A. Lowenthal (eds), *Constructing Democratic Governance: Themes and Issues*, Baltimore, MD: Johns Hopkins University Press.

Geddes, B. (1994) 'Economic development as a collective action problem', in B. Geddes, *Politician's Dilemma: Building State Capaacity in Latin America*, Berkeley and Los Angeles: University of California Press.

Graham, L. (1994) 'Rethinking the relationship between the strength of local institutions and the consolidation of democracy', unpublished document.

Gwynne, R. N. (1997) 'Neoliberalism and regional development in Latin America', paper presented at the 20th International Congress of the Latin American Studies Association, 17–20 April, Guadalajara, Mexico.

Haggard, S. and R. R. Kaufman (eds) (1992) *The Politics of Economic Adjustment*, Princeton, NJ: Princeton University Press.

Hintze, O. (1981) *Beamtentum und Bürokratie*, Göttingen: Vandenhoeck & Ruprecht.

Hirschman, A. (1979) *The Rise and Decline of Development Economics*, Cambridge: Cambridge University Press.

Huber, E., C. Ragin and J. Stephens (1993) 'Social democracy, Christian democracy, constitutional structure, and welfare state', *American Journal of Sociology*, 99 (3) November: 711–49.

Kingstone, P. R. (1997) 'Neoliberalism: business, the state, and democratic consolidation in Brazil', paper prepared for the 20th International Congress of the Latin American Studies Association, 17–20 April, Guadalajara, Mexico.

Matos Filho, J. C. and C. Oliveira (1996) 'O processo de privatização da empresas estatais Brasileiras', Brasília, IPEA, texto para discussão 422.

Mainwaring, S. and M. S. Shugart (1997) *Presidentialism and Democracy in Latin America*, Cambridge: Cambridge University Press.

MARE (Ministério da Administração Federal e Reforma do Estado) (1996) *Boletim Estatístico Mensal*, May.

Novaes, C. A. M. (1994) 'Dinámica institucional da representação: individualismo e partidos na câmara dos deputados', *Novos Estudos*, 38, March: 99–147.

O'Donnell, G. A., P. Schmitter (1986) *Transition from Authoritarian Rule. Tentative Conclusions about Uncertain Democracies*, Baltimore, MD: Johns Hopkins University Press.

Rabinovich, S. (1990) *Comportamento Eleitoral do Brasileiro*, São Paulo: Gráfica e Editora.

Ramos, J. (1997) 'Neoliberal structural reforms in Latin America: the current situation', *Cepal Review*, 62, August: 16–39.

Schneider, R. (1991) *Order and Progress: A Political History of Brazil*, Boulder, CO: Westview Press.

Schmitter, P. C. (1971) *Interest, Conflict and Political Change in Brazil*, Stanford, CA: Stanford University Press.

Stepan, A. (1988) *Rethinking Military Politics: Brazil and the Southern Cone*, Princeton, NJ: Princeton University Press.

Sunkel, O. (1991) *El Desarrollo Desde Dentro: Un Enfoque Neostrucuralista para América Latina*, Mexico City: Fondo de Cultura Economica.

Varsano, R. (1996) 'De ônus a bônus: política governamental e reformas fiscais na transformação do estado Brasileiro', Brasilia, IPEA, Texto para Discussão #417.

Weyland, K. (1996) *Democracy Without Equity – Failures of Reform in Brazil*, Pittsburgh: University of Pittsburgh Press.

Weyland, K. (1996) 'How much political power do economic forces have? Conflicts over social insurance reform in Brazil', *Journal of Public Policy*, 16 (I): 59–84.

Williamson, J. (1990) 'What Washington means by policy reform', in J. Williamson (ed.), *Latin American Adjustment: How Much Has Happened?*, Washington, DC: Institute of International Economics.

FIVE

Populism and Authoritarianism in Peru: An Old Vice in the Neoliberal Era

GIUSEPPE SOLFRINI

After the presidential elections of 1990, Peru went through a policy process of drastic economic adjustment that completely changed the previous state-centred economic model. The shift of the economic paradigm was carried out by the newly elected president, Alberto Fujimori, who implemented a radical neoliberal policy and far-reaching state reform. On 5 April 1992 he suspended democratic warranties and closed the parliament. Only when international pressure became overwhelming did Fujimori agree to hold elections. Despite his authoritarian shift Fujimori remained very popular and in 1995 he won the election, gaining 64.4 per cent of the votes in the first round, with none of the traditional parties gaining more than 5 per cent. Fujimori's adjustment programme stabilized the economy and brought inflation under control, but at the same time it lowered the standard of living of a large part of the population. Nevertheless, none of the Peruvian political parties or organizations of civil society was able to articulate any efficient opposition.

What makes the Peruvian case interesting is the rapidity of change of the political scenario and the economic paradigm. In fact, during the 1980s, the centre-left party Revolutionary American Popular Alliance[1] (Alianza Popular Revolucionaria Americana – APRA), and the leftist coalition United Left (Izquierda Unida – IU) represented more than 75 per cent of the electorate, and the popular sector was animated by myriad grassroots organizations tied to the left. At the beginning of the 1990s this situation changed: the left did not manage to present itself as a united electoral force; its state-centred approach lost its legitimacy due to the disastrous heterodox policy of APRA; and the mobilization capacities of leftist grassroots organizations lost much of theirs. The crisis of the left is a key factor in understanding the political changes in Peru and the implementation of neoliberal policy. The inability of the left to build an effective opposition enabled an economic restructuring process without comparison in the Latin American region.

Many observers saw the division of the left as one of the main causes of its defeat. However, it is important to understand why the left became split at such a crucial time, and why it was not able to represent a viable alternative to Fujimori's neoliberal agenda and his authoritarian populist rule. While the Peruvian left passed through an important phase of ideological renewal, the economic crisis, social fragmentation and political errors caused the collapse of this popular force. The internal divisions and the attempts at unification were part of a long process that started at the beginning of the 1980s with Peru's transition to democracy. The economic problems, dramatic social injustice and the fragility of democratic institutions reinforced radical currents and weakened the capacity of the left to present itself as an electoral alternative.

To analyse this process I will start from the political scenario that emerged after the military regime, which withdrew in the last years of the 1970s; in particular I will focus on the policy of the two main political forces that claimed to represent popular interests, the IU and APRA, and their incorporation into a democratic regime. I will then analyse the different projects that matured inside the left, and the long series of divisions that opened the door to a new political scenario. These events are crucial to understanding the political peculiarities of the regime under which neoliberalism was implemented in Peru.

The Military Revolution and the Rise of the Left

After a long period of authoritarianism and controlled elections, interrupted by several coups, in 1963 Belaúnde Terry, leader and founder of Popular Action (Acción Popular – AP) was democratically elected with a reformist programme. His government raised high expectations among the Peruvian population, but the strong opposition of the conservative bloc allied with APRA, and discrepancies within the AP itself, inhibited the reforms (Cotler 1978). The democratic institutions failed in their attempts to respond to people's needs and the entire political system suffered a strong de-legitimization. Military forces led by General Velasco resolved the political stalemate by overthrowing Belaúnde, and they established the Revolutionary Government of Military Force.

The new military regime of Velasco embarked on an ambitious programme of political and economic reforms, which has become known as the Peruvian Revolution. The military experiment redefined state–society relations and put an end to the oligarchic system (Stepan 1978). The state went through a transformation, becoming the major economic actor: it enforced a radical land reform and allowed industrial workers to participate in enterprise management (so-called Communities). In particular this last reform was considered an important step in promoting the building of a society without class, but it met strong opposition from the corporate sector. The reforms were designed to create a 'real democracy' in which social property would predominate over other forms of property. Velasco's regime wanted to differentiate this project from the 'real socialism', in which state property predominated, and from the Leninist approach, in which the power of the capitalist class would be replaced by the dictatorship of the proletariat. The regime thus defined itself as 'neither communist nor capitalist'. It tried to incorporate the excluded masses into the political process by opening channels of popular participation. Traditional forms of representation were contested: the liberal democracy in which parties represented people's interests would be replaced by a 'fully participatory social democracy'. This *democracia social de participación plena* became the title of the military political project. Elections and parties were considered an obstacle to the creation of a society free of conflicts of interest. The political parties were accused of manipulating people and restraining them from taking direct part in the process of political decision-making. The critics of the party system and representative democracy found support for their view in the historic inability of these institutions to solve Peru's dramatic social injustice and poverty. The alternative would be a society organized around their corporative organizations (Dietz and Palmer 1978).

Despite all its limitations and its authoritarian methods, the Peruvian Revolution opened an intensive debate on social justice and popular participation. This animated political climate promoted a flourishing of leftist organizations, which were mostly critical of the political project of the military, accusing it of implementing a bourgeois revolution (Letts 1981). Only the Peruvian Communist Party (Partido Comunista Peruano – PCP) 'critically' supported the military junta. However, none of the traditional political parties was able to represent a real opposition to the military project. APRA, the oldest and strongest Peruvian party, which for decades had represented the principal opposition to the oligarchy, embarked on alliances with conservative parties that had blocked social and economic reforms at the end of the 1950s and in the 1960s. These alliances allowed APRA to return to legality, but created a serious ideological crisis that was not resolved until the mid-1980s (Graham 1992: 37). Although APRA had abandoned its revolutionary programme of the 1930s, it accused Velasco's regime of having stolen APRA. On the other side of the political arena, the reformist parties AP and Popular Christian Party (Partido Popular Cristiano – PPC) were unable to overcome the lack of prestige they suffered, having ruled from 1963 to 1968 without implementing the reforms they had promised.

The economic crisis and internal political dissension enlarged the conflicts within the military. These tensions gave way to the coup of August 1975, during which General Velasco was replaced by General Morales Bermúdez. With the deterioration of the economic situation the regime implemented an economic adjustment programme that met with strong popular opposition. This opposition contributed to the unification of the workers' movement and other grassroots organizations in the Unitarian Command for Struggle

(Comando Unitario de Lucha), which organized an impressive national strike in July 1977. It was one of the first attempts at coordination of the left, but it did not live long. Popular opposition to the stabilization policy, the worsening struggle within military institutions (Mauceri 1989: 12) and the lack of support from conservative and liberal sectors persuaded the military to return power to civilians. Democratic transition was not the result of political demands of the left, nor of the popular movement, which mainly wanted to continue the reforms started by the Revolution. In fact electoral democracy was only a priority of liberal forces such as the AP, which considered democracy a guarantee of correct economic decisions.

APRA had the biggest chance of winning the elections, but it did not want to put the transition to democracy in danger by accelerating the process. It therefore supported a gradual transfer of power in two stages: first, the election of the Constitutional Assembly and then, after two years, general elections. The attitude of the left towards democratic elections was more complex. The PCP remained a supporter of the revolutionary process started by Velasco. For this party the economic crisis would be resolved not through elections but by accelerating the reforms. Its main preoccupation was the deterioration of the economic situation of the workers, not the type of government. The various organizations of the so-called new-left were very critical of the military government. Their criticism concerned not its authoritarian connotation but its reformist political nature and its populist approach in dealing with the economic problems through class cooperation. The majority of the left was convinced that Peru was in a pre-revolutionary situation, and that the organization of the popular movement, not participation in the electoral process, should be the political priority (Nieto 1983). From the very first moment the discussion on this issue revealed the ideological dogmatism of the Peruvian left: most of the discussions focused on the Russian elections held in 1906 and 1912, with little understanding of the situation in Peru. Those who opposed elections believed that they were a reactionary instrument that would divert the party from the organization of revolution. Later on a more pragmatic position prevailed, in which participation in the elections was considered as a stage from which to amplify the revolutionary message of the left, or the elections were supported simply because non-participation would be difficult to explain to young people and illiterates. Furthermore, for the first time in Peruvian history, the elections were open to all political parties.[2]

In 1978 APRA won the elections with 35 per cent of the votes, and its leader Haya de la Torre became the president of the Constitutional Assembly. The Christian PPC, with its strong critics against the military regime, gained the second position. In the following years the new-left (the new formations that were critical of the pro-Soviet PCP, with Maoist, Trotskyist or Castrist orientations) gained great influence among grassroots organizations and unions, but the left-wing movement remained highly fragmented. Together, the four major leftist parties combined achieved good electoral results, obtaining one-third of the total vote (Tuesta 1994). The more radical and sceptical about the electoral process, the Trotskyist FOCEP, gained 12.3 per cent and ex-guerrilla leader Hugo Blanco received the highest preference. This result convinced the leaders of the fragmented left to reopen the debate started in the 1960s to unify in a common alliance and to organize a Unitarian Revolutionary Front (Frente Unitario Revolucionario – FUR). However, the process of unification of the fragmented archipelago of the left appeared to be more complex than expected. The first agreement was reached at the end of 1979, when the Left Revolutionary Alliance (Alianza Revolucionaria de Izquierda – ARI) was constituted, but just before the elections of 1980 ARI split into five different groups. The process of unification continued despite reciprocal accusations and the electoral defeat of a loss of 15 per cent of the votes compared to the previous elections. From then on unification became one of the main issues for the left-wing political organizations.

Also APRA lost its dream of governing in the house of Pizarro (the presidential palace). A few months after the promulgation of the Constitution, Haya de la Torre, the leader of APRA, died. This loss had dramatic effects on the party, overburdening the ideological crisis and inflaming internal political conflicts. The political factions, which had never come to the surface due to the iron discipline imposed by Haya, began a struggle to achieve leadership after the death of their charismatic leader. In particular, a progressivist, revolutionary faction with a strong state-centred ideology opposed a more liberal faction that was willing to forge an alliance with the national bourgeoisie.

The elections of 1980 were won by the liberal AP leader Belaúnde Terry, the same president who had been overthrown by the military twelve years before. For many observers his victory was due more to the weakness of APRA and of the left, and less to the strength of the right (Tanaka 1998: 105). In fact, when the left presented itself as being united and APRA's internal struggle for leadership was resolved, these two forces expanded again. A new alliance between left-wing parties was presented for the municipal elections that were held a few months later. Even though the Unified Left (Izquierda Unida – IU) was no more then an electoral cartel without a definite programme, it managed to gain 23.3 per cent at the national level. This convinced even the more sceptical among the left that a united front could obtain more electoral support. At the margin remained the ultra-radical Maoist Shining Path (Sendero Luminoso – SL) that opted for armed struggle. Its actions started with the bombing of a polling station in the Ayacucho.

The Democratic Challenge

The slogans 'Health', 'Education' and 'Work' of Belaúnde Terry were very effective, despite his vague liberal programme and electoral campaign. From the very beginning the government wanted to accelerate the liberal policy started during the last phase of the military regime. The promotion of industrial production for export was one of the main priorities of the government's economic policy (Schydlowsky 1986). The government was aware that the national manufacturing sector had to improve its quality and reduce the costs of production in order to be competitive in the international market. According to this idea protectionism would create distortions that would limit the natural capacity of market expansion. Tariffs were reduced from 60 per cent to 32 per cent, and there was a drastic reduction of state subsidies. Despite all efforts Belaúnde's policy did not achieve good results: in 1983 industrial production declined to 17.2 per cent; in 1984 unemployment reached 68 per cent of the active labour force; and between 1979 and 1984 wages lost 30 per cent of their purchasing power.[3]

Unlike other countries of the continent, such as Chile, in Peru liberalism was not yet the hegemonic economic paradigm. As was noted, 'Belaúnde's commitment to neoliberalism was not ideological but highly instrumental ... determined largely by his desire to cultivate good relations with international lending institutions like the World Bank and the International Monetary Fund' (Conaghan et al. 1990). In fact, Belaúnde gave high priority to structural projects, as he had done in his previous government in 1963 (Kuczynski 1980), and for this he needed security to obtain credits.

The government's liberal policy was attacked from different sides. The heavily subsidized national bourgeoisie, represented in the National Industrial Society (Sociedad Nacional Industrial – SNE) and in the Exporters Association, strongly opposed the liberalization of the market. The left was very critical of orienting the national economy to the external market, which was considered to be intrinsically fluctuating. At this time, however, the left did not represent a real obstacle to the government's policy since it had lost much of its mobilization capacity. The unions were particularly debilitated after the confrontation with the military government (Parodi 1986).

Weakened by internal struggle, APRA was also unable to organize any efficient opposition. At its 14th Congress the discussion was not on the organization of a reliable alternative to liberalism but rather on electoral strategy: all matters concerning a political programme were left aside (Gonzáles 1983). Despite the opposition of the establishment, with a slight majority the young moderate Alan García was elected secretary of the party.[4] García wanted to change the party's violent and radical image, and oriented the political discourse to those sectors traditionally excluded from the attention of APRA. The results of these changes arrived quickly: during the 1983 municipal elections, having conducted a moderate but clearly reformist campaign, APRA became the first party at the national level.

The United Left was going through an internal leadership struggle. Each party tried to impose its hegemony over the coalition. In the end, Alfonso Barrantes was chosen as the secretary of the IU. He was an independent and moderate candidate and able to stand above the different factions. This choice showed a new concern for electoral support, which was approved by the electorate: the IU emerged as the second national political force with 29 per cent of the votes, and Barrantes was elected mayor of Lima.

The participation of the left in local governments was very important for the development of a different perspective on democracy and political struggle. It eroded the Utopian tone and gave way to concrete forms of action (Calderón and Valdeavellano 1991). Also, the international situation encouraged the ideological debate. From the other side of the ocean, the congressional thesis of the Italian Communist Party – the major communist party in Europe – pointed at the necessity of rethinking the socialist perspective as underlined by the famous sentence 'this phase of socialism, started with the October Revolution, has exhausted its propulsive force'. The Peruvian left was acquainted with this debate. However, the internal situation did not help the development of a fruitful ideological review to present the IU as a new democratic electoral force. Several factors inhibited the development of this debate. First of all, the left remained a minor force with little chance of allying itself with APRA, the other reformist force. Second, a large section of the left considered the democratic institutions as too weak to resist the opposition of the conservative national bourgeoisie when structural reforms – needed to overcome social injustice and inequality – were implemented in a democratic context: sooner or later the bourgeoisie would show its true violent face. Furthermore, the expansion of the armed struggle of Shining Path and the violent reply of the state, which blindly persecuted many militants of the democratic left as well, radicalized the political scenario. A more moderate attitude would have left space for the revolutionary discourse of the armed movement. The electoral defeats in 1985 and 1986 reinforced this general radicalism and the position of those who believed that socialism could not be achieved by democratic processes. The insurgency of the armed groups was not clearly condemned, but was considered as a response against the structural violence of the state. This ambiguous position on political violence strengthened the critique that the IU would not commit itself to democracy (Pásara 1990).

In 1985, the right-wing parties had little opportunity of regaining the presidency, even though they presented themselves under the new Convergencia Democrática (CODE). The right was still paying for the consequences of Belaúnde's government and could not attract support outside its traditional electorate. APRA was the force with the highest chances of winning the electoral competition and the left represented the most dangerous competitor. The strength of the leftist bloc could put democracy in danger: the military, which always had conditioned the Peruvian political arena, might oppose an elected left-wing government. While APRA had improved its relations with the military from the time of democratic transition, the left was still viewed with suspicion. In an interview in *Que hacer* (1985, 11), a left-wing fortnightly magazine, Minister of War General Julián Juliá declared that in the case of a victory of the left, the military would not overthrow an elected government. The critique on Marxism raised by the general was not in terms of moral values against communism and did not oppose any specific economic project, but it was rather related to its attitude towards the military institutions, which usually suffered deep restructuring and a lack of autonomy under Marxist government. The most interesting aspect of this debate was the lack of criticism of the political programme of the left, underlining the lack of an autonomous political project of the Peruvian military forces after Velasco.[5] Immediately the IU stated in its programme that it would respect the independence and internal military ascendancy rules. Despite these mutual declarations, the situation remained strained due to the left's vague condemnation of armed struggle.

Another major issue in the political debate involved foreign capital and the nationalization of natural resources. The IU clearly stood for the expropriation of some foreign companies to reduce their monopoly and their capacity to control prices. Such expropriations would reduce the monopoly of foreign capital and increase the national capacity for negotiation. The left was aware of the importance of foreign investment but believed that nationalization did not automatically prevent the inflow of capital. If the state offered political stability and guaranteed market protection in order to reduce external competition, investors might find this a good opportunity for investment, better than the economic incentives in a highly competitive market offered by the right wing (Sánchez 1985). As to the speculative nature of capital, the left rather realistically assumed that Peru would not obtain investments on the basis of a nationalist pact as proposed by APRA.

The electoral campaign of García was cautious. He aimed to win over the left-wing moderate electorate that was deceived by the radicalization of the left. With the slogan 'my commitment is to all Peruvians', García directed his speeches to the entire nation in the messianic style of the classical populist leaders. But instead of building his political alliance with the working class, as in the classical forms of populism, he shifted his attention to the informal sector (Cameron 1991). The leader of APRA accused the working class of being a 'privileged minority', and he called the informal sectors 'the future of the nation', offering them political representation (Ballón 1986). García carefully avoided talking about property structures and centred the debate on innovative reforms designed to enlarge the national market. This successful campaign brought García into power with 53.1 per cent of the votes and after more than sixty years APRA became the ruling party.

The candidate of the left obtained 24.7 per cent of the votes, which was a good achievement for a political force that had entered the electoral competition only seven years before and maintained a suspicious – if not ambiguous – attitude to the formal democratic institutions. However, the left did not expand outside its traditional electorate. Under attack from the previous liberal government, the IU attempted to protect its traditional task of demanding more job security and an increase in wages. There was little understanding of the specific problems of the informal sector, which felt itself to be excluded from the programme of the left. Alan García took advantage of this lack of attention, addressing the specific requests of the informals, and thereby obtaining extensive support from this side.

APRA's Heterodox Experiment

In his inaugural speech García proclaimed himself the president of the 'other 70 per cent' of the population. He was critical of the Unified Left, accusing it of being corporatist and of protecting only the interests of an organized minority. García's political project was based on the organization of a large solidarity pact among the popular masses, national entrepreneurs and the state. He asked the national capitalists to guarantee investments, with the state assuming the role of arbitrator of the concertation process. The state would subsidize the local industries, while the redistributive policy would enlarge the national market by revitalizing consumers and production. Redistribution would then become not only a matter of social justice, but also a condition for economic development.

Despite this apparently well-organized political view, there was no clear policy on basic concepts like private property, underlining the persistent ambiguity of APRA's political programme (Graham 1990: 100). APRA appeared to be a highly ideologized party lacking ideological clarity. This apparent contradiction is explained by the fact that APRA remained more like a religious sectarian movement than a political party. Nevertheless, García raised great expectations among the population and even the MRTA (Movimento Revolucionario Túpac Amaru) guerrilla movement by declaring a temporary truce to allow for the implementation of his government's reforms. The IU, however, was sceptical from the beginning and criticized García's project for not tackling the base of property structures. In its view, without radical reforms it would be impossible to reduce the deep social inequality that not even the structural reforms implemented by Velasco had been able substantially to diminish.

Lacking stable support both from his own party and from popular sectors of society, García vacillated between revolutionary rhetoric and tactical reformist attitudes. These changes in the political discourse were also the result of contradictory relations with the national bourgeoisie (Durand 1988). From the beginning the government had the support of national capital: in two years private investments doubled, and the economy grew by 8 per cent in the first and around 6 per cent in the second year (Thorp 1987). But Peru was a difficult country to govern. At the beginning of García's mandate the GNP of Peru was about $1,010 per capita, the lowest on the continent after Bolivia. García strongly attacked the economic imperialism of the IMF and

World Bank. In order to reinforce state intervention, he unilaterally reduced the external debt repayment to 10 per cent of the value of the exports. In this way he saved the currency, but closed the door to further credit.

García's 'social populist' project was implemented when deregulation was triumphing in other parts of the world. Liberalization and transnationalization of the economy increased the government's difficulty to implement social reforms in favour of the lower classes. International capital rejected any state control and began to threaten to withdraw investment. Capital flight became a real weapon in the hands of the capitalists. It was clear that the policy of concertation would not last long. The relations between the president and the national investors remained uncertain. In fact after the first signs of crisis, the capitalists reduced their investment drastically. García felt betrayed by the national bourgeoisie and changed his policy. Then, following the example of the Mexican President López Portillo in 1982, García announced the nationalization of the banks in July 1987. This decision put an end to any further agreement with the national bourgeoisie. This 'courageous' manoeuvre was also prompted by García's ambition for re-election. Since in Peru it was not possible to be elected for two consecutive terms, García had to reinforce his position inside his own party against the ambitions of other leaders, obtaining support in Parliament from sectors of the moderate left by promulgating this new law and reinforcing the support of public opinion (cf. Tanaka 1998: 150–5). In this climate of polarization, right-wing forces organized an opinion movement, the Movimiento Libertad (ML) led by Mario Vargas Llosa, which in a short time became the electoral cartel of the right. García's nationalization law basically fell due to the opposition from within his own party.

One of the brightest representatives of the emerging new right was Hernando de Soto, a social scientist who had conducted a study on the new features of Peruvian society. De Soto ascribed an important political value to the economic activities of the informals: they were considered vigorous and fanciful entrepreneurs limited by several constraints. State bureaucratization and labour politics were responsible for producing further obstacles to the emergent market. The aim of the liberal project was to remove institutional rigidity and excessive administrative obstacles that prevented the formal private sector or the public sector in the cities from creating jobs, which were rapidly needed to absorb the peasants arriving from rural areas (De Soto 1989: 211).

De Soto's analysis received strong criticism from the left, which perceived the rapid growth of the informal sector as resulting from the economic crisis and a lack of social justice, and not as a desire for entrepreneurial freedom. The informals were simply workers without stable employment and assured income, but with the same interests and needs – and also political identity – as formal workers. This idea was supported by the whole of workers' movements, and neighbourhood, informal and other grassroots organizations, which were considered part of the same popular movement, and whose leaders attempted to bring their efforts together (Grompone 1991).

The left managed to maintain some influence and links with the organized groups of informal workers such as the Federación de Vendedores Ambulantes de Lima (FEDEVAL), but this was largely based on the political past of their leaders.

Due to the lack of legislation and the unofficial nature of their work, traditional unions had little to offer to the informal sector. As a result, informals formed pressure groups that were active outside the formal unions. This situation clearly played against the reinforcement of relations with left-wing parties. Without any political force that could fully represent their interests, the political identity of informal workers became more vague and ambiguous. Nevertheless they remained politically oriented to the left: a public opinion poll conducted in 1988 revealed that the leader of the IU, Alfonso Barrantes, was the most favourite candidate for the presidential elections, with 36 per cent, followed by Vargas Llosa with 25 per cent, and APRA's candidate Luís Alva Castro with 22 per cent.[6] The left appeared to be an ascendant political force capable of being the principal challenger against the right in the 1990 presidential elections.

Despite all the efforts at unification, the IU remained a loose electoral coalition that lacked both a solid common identity and the ability to reach full agreement on a basic programme. One major point of contention was the viability of institutional democracy versus a revolutionary tactic and the empowerment of the popular movement. The radical faction never considered the consolidation of democratic institutions a political priority. Rather, it believed that democracy would serve to consolidate the organization of the popular sectors. On the contrary, the moderate faction led by Barrantes wanted to keep the party within the institutional democratic framework and to implement a more reformist programme. Between these two tendencies the communist PCP and the leftist Christians tried to mediate and avoid division. To overcome this political stalemate, a few months before the elections Barrantes decided to run with an independent faction called the Socialist Left (Izquierda Socialista – IS). He hoped that such a drastic decision would marginalize the extreme Left and force hesitant groups to join the IS. This political gamble did not have the expected results: Barrantes remained without any organizational support, which effectively decreed his political demise. The difficult relations between the different parties of the IU were well known, but it remained difficult for the electorate to understand why the IU had split at such a crucial moment.

On the contrary, the right wing concluded a process of unification after the opinion movement Libertad was transformed into a new political force called the Democratic Front (Frente Democrático – FREDEMO). The neoliberal programme of FREDEMO was simple and clear: reduce state intervention in the economy, privatize state companies, cut public service costs and create labour flexibility. A shock therapy was proposed to save Peru from the disastrous crisis provoked by the mismanagement of APRA.

One of the most distinquished economists of the left, Iguíñez, argued that the neoliberal project to reduce state intervention would worsen social inequalities and create yet more economic injustice. The state inefficiency was a result not of its intrinsic inability, but of too many private interests being involved. On the contrary, state capacities should be reinforced. In a country like Peru, with low fiscal revenue, it was necessary to maintain the state as a central economic actor to enlarge the infrastructure required for economic development. The social situation in Peru needed a strong state to protect the country's national interests, provide social justice and give political stability. This would encourage international investment, but its speculative interventions had to be limited (Iguíñez 1991: 18–24). The attitude of the left towards national and international investors was pragmatic. The IU saw the monopolistic concentration as the main source of social injustice, preventing the rise of other economic forces such as small enterprises, cooperatives and the development of the working class. The aim of its political project was to create the conditions for a more democratic society, in which different forms of property could coexist. Leaving aside the appeals for the construction of socialism – which were never repudiated – the left proposed itself as a responsible ruling force. The experience of local governments strengthened the pragmatism of one of the most powerful left-wing movements of the Latin American subcontinent (Pease 1989).

The new IS group of Barrantes proposed instead to mitigate social conflict in order to overcome the crisis. Economic stabilization would be achieved only through the reaffirmation of cooperation between capital, the workers' movement and the state in a clear democratic context (cf. Gamero 1990). To make any agreement possible, all these components would have to be strong, and the workers' movement in particular had to be reinforced and unified. For this reason Barrantes tried to build an alliance with the left-wing sectors of APRA. The most radical sectors of the left strongly criticized Barrantes for his intention to reinforce democratic institutions to build an alliance with APRA, since APRA's clientelistic programme of reforms was considered incompatible with the grassroots empowerment project of the left. Barrantes, however, never explained on which basis this cooperation would be founded, and the previous attempt by the García government had failed. The political project of IS in the end convinced neither the other political forces of the left nor the Peruvian electorate.

Crisis of the Left-wing Alternative

In the mid-1980s the left-wing leaders were quite confident that they would win the upcoming elections, as the electorate was clearly shifting to the left. Even though APRA (with its well-organized electoral machine) gained the presidency in 1985, the entire left was experiencing a positive response in the municipalities and had the opportunity to reinforce its relations with social movements (Cardenas et al. 1991). However, the clientelistic policy of APRA in the barriadas,[7] and the disastrous economic performance of the heterodox policy of García's government rapidly reduced the appeal of the statist programme of the left and added to the political legitimacy of the neoliberal project. At the end of 1989 the right-wing front FREDEMO appeared to be the most favoured party, with a viable economic alternative and a respected candidate. However, none of the political forces was hegemonic over the others following the presidential elections of 1990. This balance of forces could have been favourable for cross-party coalitions. Also, the ballot system introduced in the Constitution of 1978 facilitated the formation of political alliances, such as the one between APRA and the PPC during the Constituent Assembly. The left and the centre-left could theoretically unify their strength to present an anti-liberal front with a candidate who could easily get through in the first round. Due to the radicalization of politics, however, this was not possible. The left itself, as described above, presented two different presidential candidates: Henry Pease for the IU and Barrantes for the IS, leaving a large part of the left-wing electorate astonished and confused. Together, the two candidates gained only 13 per cent of the votes, while APRA, with 22.6 per cent, proved it had maintained the support of its traditional electorate. All these anti-liberal forces could have easily confronted Vargas Llosa's liberal front, which obtained 32.7 per cent. This polarization of the political arena left a great void, which was easily occupied by the independent candidate Alberto Fujimori (of Cambio 90), who reached the second position with 29.1 per cent of the votes (Grompone 1990).

Fujimori's programme was vague, but it was characterized by simple slogans that captured the public imagination: 'Work', 'Honesty' and 'Technology'. While the leader of Cambio 90 proposed a stabilization programme, unlike Mario Vargas Llosa he supported gradual economic reforms, which were to be implemented together with measures to compensate for the social costs of stabilization. Vargas Llosa criticized job security laws and attacked the inefficiency of the public sector, and this created fears that structural adjustment would create widespread unemployment. Fujimori opposed an anti-shock plan, as proposed by the right, that would drastically increase the price of goods and services (Iguíñez 1991). The centre-left advisers of Fujimori opposed any austerity programme because it could intensify the concentration of income, lower private investments and retard economic growth. APRA and the left, having been defeated in the first round, believed that Fujimori could represent a viable alternative to the neoliberal project of the right, and offered their votes for the second round. A series of tactical mistakes during the electoral campaign of Vargas Llosa (Cameron 1994), mistrust of the traditional political class, and, not least, the votes received from the left and APRA, allowed Fujimori to win the second round with 62.5 per cent.[8] However, his Cambio 90 remained a minority in the Congress.

In 1990 the left lost almost two-thirds of its votes. How can this defeat be explained? The split in 1990 was clearly one of the elements that discredited the IU. But is this a sufficient explanation, or do we need to analyse the reasons behind the split? As stated above, a series of structural causes prevented a left-wing ideological review, and this conserved a large part of the left's radical, highly ideologized and sectarian nature.[9] We should ask whether there were conditions for political change in Peru or, conversely, whether the so-called radicalism could have had another possible political strategy. The acute economic crisis, the political polarization and the closed and conservative national bourgeoisie prevented the left from widening its discourse on social justice and including other forces. The experience in governments of municipalities did not encourage an open debate with other forces – in fact left-wing municipalities were often boycotted or marginalized.

Societal cleavages, the weakening of democratic institutions and a capitalist sector closed to any dialogue prevented the development of a reformist programme. In this context, the revolutionary option remained all the more appealing and effective when compared to a more moderate one. This was demonstrated by the behaviour of the unions: radicalism remained the only tactic possible against a bourgeoisie deaf to any compromise, and confrontational tactics proved in many cases more fruitful than other means. The unions, for example, could not have a meeting with the management of a company without organizing a strike first. In the end, class struggle and confrontation became political values in themselves (Balbi and Parodi 1984). The economic crisis and unemployment, however, made this form of struggle not only useless but devastating.

At the end of the 1980s, Peruvian society reached a high level of informalization. Whereas in 1981 this sector represented 39 per cent of the economically active population, in 1990 the majority of economically active Peruvians was working in the informal sectors. This social decomposition was not favourable to stable political representation. Furthermore, the crisis created a climate of emergency in which any long-term project seemed to lose validity. In a situation of drastic crisis generally only contingent answers are sought, rendering political identity vague and fluctuating. The legal left had little to offer in these extreme conditions.

The social and economic situation reinforced the already existing radical political tendency of the left. The controversy over armed struggle versus democratic institutionalization was never resolved, and in general the left remained ambiguous regarding political violence. A moderate programme could leave space for the ascendant attraction of Sendero Luminoso and its call for popular revolution. Part of the left criticized SL only because it embarked on an armed struggle without the existence of the right social and political conditions, and for its lack of ties with the masses (Pásara 1990). From this perspective, democratic elections were just a contingent strategy, nothing more. The dramatic situation of social injustice, the insurmountable structural problems, and the long history of failures of democratic reformist governments (the only government able to carry out structural reforms was the Revolutionary Government of the Armed Forces in 1968) made it difficult for left-wing militants to accept a different form of struggle. Even those who supported elections as the main vehicle to conquer power believed that the capitalists would not peacefully accept a democratic government that would damage their interests, as Peruvian history has shown (Pease 1988).

In reality, Sendero's armed struggle had disastrous effects on the left and popular organizations: on one side they underwent the political erosion of the armed groups and on the other they suffered from the restriction of democratic participative space. Left-wing militants were the target of violence of both SL and the military. In this radicalized scenario the moderates, who could easily prevail under normal conditions, did not succeed in constituting a new hegemonic front. On the contrary, they were marginalized, losing all ties with popular organizations. However, political violence did attract attention to human rights issues and consequently democratic principles and institutions.

Finally, the decline of the Peruvian left cannot be fully understood without taking into account the disastrous economic performance of García's heterodox experiment, which put the state-centred model in crisis. As a result, for the majority of people the state meant only corruption and inefficiency. At the beginning of the 1990s, then, the left had a fragmented social base and a weak organization, with inefficient tactics and an unattractive political project.

The Implementation of Neoliberal Policy and the Authoritarian Shift

Contrary to what was expected by left-wing leaders, in 1990 the Peruvian electorate, instead of adopting a radical attitude, preferred the moderate project of one single man who appeared to bring something new to Peruvian politics.[10] The left did not win, but at least the neoliberal project presented by Mario Vargas Llosa was beaten by the more moderate programme of Fujimori. Part of the left supported the newly elected president and opted to join the government. Gloria Helfer of the IU took over the Ministry of Education and two members of the IS became ministers of agriculture and of energy and mines. At the same time, liberals joined Fujimori's cabinet – for example, Hurtado Miller of the AP assumed the position of minister of the economy. The Partido Mariáteguista Unificado (United Mariateguist Party – PUM), led by Diez Canseco, firmly opposed the admission of a member of the IU into the cabinet. The PUM believed that Fujimori would not keep his 'no-shock' promise and did not want the left to become involved in a drastic economic restructuring with high social costs. The presence of left-wing personalities in the cabinet would create confusion in public opinion on the very nature of the government and would give the impression of the absence of any alternative to liberalism. This different perception of the new government created a further rupture in the IU when the PUM decided to leave the directive committee.

The new government inherited a disastrous economic situation. The external debt exceeded US$19 billion and Peru's GNP contracted by 10.4 per cent in 1989, without any sign of recovery. As the Bolivian president Paz Estenssoro had done in 1985, a few months after Fujimori had established his cabinet, a drastic stabilization programme was implemented, which contradicted all the economic analyses presented during the electoral campaign (Stokes 1997).[11] Just before this shock, in which almost all of Vargas Llosa's long-term economic proposals were implemented by his rival, the left-wing ministers abandoned the government. In a short time, making ample use of government decrees, job security laws were eliminated and labour relations were liberalized. The prices of basic goods and services were increased: for example, the price of potatoes increased ten-fold and petrol thirty-one-fold. After the shock, real wages halved and out of a population of 22 million, 12 million fell below the line of extreme poverty. Tanks were sent into the streets to prevent riots but they did not meet with any protest. In the eyes of the majority, the gravity of the economic crisis made the shock inevitable.

To explain this shift, Fujimori claimed that he became informed of the dramatic fiscal conditions of the state after he came into office, only then discovering the current account shortfalls, mismanagement and widespread corruption in state institutions. Of course this explanation is rather questionable (Stokes 1997: 218).

Fujimori was not the leader of a historical political force with specific support and interests to defend, and he transformed this weakness into his strength. He sought alliances with forces known in Latin America as de facto powers: national capitalists, international economic organizations and the military (López 1995). The latter became the most powerful supporter and partner of the new government after Fujimori fully accepted the military's anti-terrorist strategy (Rospigliosi 1994). This marked a radical change in the military political perspective. In past decades, national security had been linked to the idea of social justice and the reinforcement of state control over the economy, and the military's nationalist project was to reinforce the role of the state and to limit the intervention of foreign capital. In the 1990s, however, following the Chilean example, Peru's military institutions were strongly advocating neoliberal policy.

The only opposition came from Parliament, where the president did not have an overall majority. The entire left accused the government of de-industrializing the nation and transforming Peru into an exporter of raw materials, leaving the country vulnerable to international crises and damaging small and medium national enterprises. The PUM presented an alternative economic plan called Plan Amaru, designed by the economist Oscar Dancourt, in which the weakest sections of society would be protected from the costs of a necessary adjustment. Among other things, wages would be linked to the dollar to reduce the impact of devaluation. The plan had many similarities to the policy implemented in Brazil by Cardoso, which maintained a selected protectionism and tried to coordinate the influence of international and national capital without cancelling out the economic role of the state.

At the institutional level Fujimori had only the support of his weak movement and on several occasions his project was put at serious risk. FREDEMO supported the liberal policy but remained sceptical of Fujimori, mainly due to his attitude of attacking democratic institutions and his support for the military strategy against the insurgency. After Congress had blocked several decrees, on 5 April 1992 Fujimori closed down parliament and other state institutions. Before this coup, he attacked the parties and their behaviour in parliament for hampering his economic policies. A series of events played in favour of Fujimori. Just when Sendero Luminoso increased its actions of terror, especially in the capital, and declared the so-called strategic equilibrium with the military forces, its sanguinary leader Abimael Guzmán was captured by the Security Forces. Fujimori's authoritarian shift could not find a better legitimacy. Several Peruvian experts on insurgency argue that the strength of the SL was overestimated in order to justify such special measures and political restrictions (cf. Rospigliosi 1994 and Tapia 1997). In fact the Intelligence Service, which prepared the coup together with the president, was sure to be close to inflicting a hard blow to the SL. As Machiavelli taught, luck does not come by itself.

Meanwhile the economy started to show signs of recovery. It grew by 6.3 per cent in 1993 and by 12.9 per cent the following year, while inflation remained under control. The two most important national problems, hyper-inflation and political violence, appeared to have been defeated. The popularity of the president rose to 71 per cent. Only because of international pressures did Fujimori start the process of restoring democratic warranty, implementing first a new constitution, then general elections.

Again, the left-wing opposition appeared to be divided. Patria Roja, FOCEP and PUM, former members of the IU and other moderate forces of the opposition did not participate in the election of the Constituent Assembly as they did not want to provide any legitimacy to the government. A group of independent left-wing personalities dissented from this position and formed the Democratic Movement of the Left (Movimiento Democrático de Izquierda – MDI). This force stood for the elections, believing in the necessity of reconquering democratic institutional spaces. The MDI did not achieve the expected results, obtaining only a few seats in the Assembly. As a result of the weakness of all the forces of opposition, the power of the executive was reinforced in the new Constitution, providing the possibility for the president to be re-elected for two mandates. After some months the new constitution was passed with a reduced majority, which made it appear that there had been a rebirth of opposition to the regime.

In 1994 a new force appeared in the political arena: the Union for Peru (Unión por el Perú – UPP), led by Pérez de Cuéllar, former UN secretary-general. The UPP assembled people with different ideological backgrounds, representing a wide spectrum of civil society (economists, jurists, retired military, etc.). The left-wing MDI converged with this new formation. The UPP campaign was based mainly on restoring the rule of law and reinforcing democratic institutions, but it did not represent a real alternative to Fujimori's neoliberal economy. Pérez de Cuéllar showed timid opposition to the nationalization of certain companies such as Petroperú, but generally he maintained a liberal view on the economy. In the 1995 elections none of the traditional parties obtained more than 5 per cent of the votes. The strong support for Fujimori meant the end of the party system. The Peruvian electorate clearly approved of the authoritarian government of Fujimori, demonstrating how representative democracy had lost against the so-called *política del éxito* (politics of success).

Fujimori's personalist leadership, a 'top-down' political mobilization in which the relationship between the leader and the people does not pass through autonomous political institutions, as well as his anti-elitist political discourse and redistributive policy beg for a comparison with classical populism (Roberts 1995). As a typical populist leader, Fujimori found legitimacy in his claim that he represented the interests of the whole nation and stood above particularistic interests. The populist leader presents himself as the mediator of a social-political pact between strong actors such as the national bourgeoisie and the working class. Fujimori's case, however, shows two novelties. As has already been underlined in the literature (cf. Weyland 1996), Fujimori readjusted the populist political style to a new model of development. What have been less considered are the very nature and political implications of the alliances between the actors. In Peru the political actors involved were weak and difficult to define, and the ties between the president and the masses precarious and loose (Grompone 1998). This was important for Fujimori's policy. Apart from the military, he received support from an indeterminate mass with no clear economic interests. Fujimori had to readjust his alliance continuously. Also, the relations with national capital were contingent and controversial. As has been noted by Graham and Kane (1998), in such circumstances clear corporatist or clientelistic policies are difficult to implement. Politically oriented public expenses do not translate into a blind support for the president, creating the necessity for Fujimori to carry out a continuous political campaign. This may in turn create difficulties for the coherency of the adjustment programme.

Fujimori's success has been based on a precarious alliance. However, the absence of any strong alternative ensures its continuation. A questionable interpretation of the Constitution might allow Fujimori to present himself as a candidate in the elections of 2000. After the Constitutional Court gave an opposite response in 1997, half of their members were dismissed. The protests against the authoritarianism of the regime was organized around the civic association Foro Democrático, which collected 1,200,000 signatures for a referendum against the re-election (this was rejected by the Parliament). This and other manifestations, such as marches in different parts of the country, show the emergence of a dynamic opposition against the government. After a decade, Fujimori's popularity is at an all-time low, despite the fact that his regime reinforced its power outside the conventional channels of democratic institutions. Finally, all the other political forces seem to have become convinced that there is no alternative to democracy. With the exception of debilitated fringes of the left, they have generally come to support neoliberal policy with no substantial differences from the economic course of the regime.

Conclusion

The elections of 1990 were a watershed in Peruvian political history. The left and all traditional parties suffered a historic defeat. After decades of economic swings from one economic policy to another (González and Samamé 1994), drastic liberal adjustments were implemented, opening the door to an independent candidate, who after his election shifted from a moderate programme to a radical liberalism and institutional breakdown. In 1990, however, the majority of Peruvians rejected neoliberal policies. As stated above, the left was defeated not by a more powerful political project, but by its own inability to construct the political foundation for a viable alternative. In the 1980s much emphasis was put on social movements that instead turned out to be short-lived political phenomena, unfit to be translated into strong political identities.

The division of the United Left came at an inopportune moment and was certainly one of the important factors leading to this electoral defeat. The Peruvian left has often been criticized for the personal ambitions and sectarianism of its leaders, and its extreme ideologization. The left's division has been perceived as a result of this sectarianism or simply as an erroneous political choice. However, little attention has been paid to the ideological development of the left. In my opinion, the division of the left was one of the consequences of this process of political development: the split that occurred in 1990 followed from the final confrontation of two incompatible political options, which took place at a crucial (and inopportune) political moment. It occurred during the electoral campaign because it involved a fundamental difference between two political positions: one tending to reinforce institutional channels, and the other remaining oriented to strengthening social movements, following a less institutionalized form of conducting politics. Why is it that in Peru the radical option remains dominant among the left, while in other parts of the continent the left has developed more moderate options that prevail in the electoral arena? The dramatic social cleavages, the ongoing economic crisis and political polarization can provide an explanation for this persistent radicalism.

When describing the political experiences of left-wing parties in Latin America, Roberts characterizes as innovative what he calls the radical democratic project of the Workers' Party of Brazil. This project directed the struggle to transform capitalism into different forms of struggle and political action, emphasizing the role of grassroots organizations (Roberts 1999). The Peruvian left could also fit into this category, even though orthodox Marxist orientations coexist with more innovative currents. Unfortunately, the theoretical contribution of the Peruvian left, its rich experience of popular organization and its political project of social empowerment have not been sufficiently recognized. The highly ideological tone of the political debate demonstrated an important innovation in the political evolution of the archipelago of the Peruvian left.

Nevertheless, a long tradition of mass exclusion from political participation reinforced forms of conducting politics outside the conventional channels. This explains the emphasis given to the so-called popular movement by the left throughout the 1980s as the only possible alternative to a reformist social democratic project. The empowerment of grassroots organizations had great political and cultural value. The left considered popular organizations to be the agents of social transformation and organs of popular power, but it failed to translate the struggle of the grassroots movements into a national political alternative (Pásara 1990). Several factors, such as political violence, were responsible for the demobilization of the 1990s, which not only eclipsed the importance of these political experiences, but also created a deep crisis in the left.

At the same time the social democratic model failed to impose itself as a fruitful alternative. It proved difficult to implement a policy of cooperation in a country with dramatic social contradictions that can not be resolved without structural reforms that inevitably harm capital interests. The reformist policy of Barrantes failed because it was formulated during a period of strong political radicalization when there was no chance of conquering the terrain of the centre-left, and when a more radical alternative seemed to be a more fruitful strategy. The popular movement was still dynamic, even though it started showing signs of weakening, and the ultra-radical choice of armed struggle was gaining ground.

It has often been said that the collapse of the party system created the conditions for the emergence of political outsiders in Peruvian politics (Crabtree 1994), and the imposition of plebiscitarian authoritarism (Cotler 1994). In my view, the organizational crisis of the left and the failure of its alternative political model of grassroots self-organization created a political vacuum. Fujimori presented himself as a viable alternative to the discredited traditional political system. In this sense, Fujimori's victory may be seen as the final result of the institutional breakdown and political crisis rather than as its primary cause.

The dramatic economic situation, the social fragmentation that made it difficult for political forces to represent popular interests, and the resurgence of political violence that ultimately closed the political space for popular participation together created the conditions for the emergence of a charismatic leader with a messianic stance. Fujimori's success is not the result of an irrational choice by the Peruvian people. Rather, he represents the alternative to a generally discredited political class that did not present any viable political project. Fujimori's famous sentence 'I first act, then I inform' not only shows a contempt for democratic procedures, it also manifests the popular wish for efficiency and order. The authoritarianism of such a modern *caudillo* can gain ground only when the normal channels of political representation are ineffective, when democracy has completely lost its appeal, when the social fragmentation prevents political organizations from functioning as a vehicle of social interests, and when conventional means seem unable to solve social problems.

The devaluation of Peru's democratic institutions was essential to the neoliberal project of Fujimori's regime. From the start, Fujimori relied on the military and large enterprises linked with international capital. He ensured the loyalty of the armed forces first by following their propositions on national security, especially in the struggle against terrorism, and on the conflict with Ecuador. Then, with a cautious insertion of the president's straw men, and the help of the Intelligence Service, Fujimori reinforced his control over the military and increased his political strength.

Recently all Peruvian political actors critical of the present government have had as their political priorities the reinforcement of democratic institutions and the restoration of the rule of law. Public opinion polls show the re-emergence among the population of democratic sentiments. The debate among new political forces and self-critics of the left shows the emergence of a new political conscience and projection. However, unless the political struggle moves from simple criticism of political forms to criticism of the present economic model of development, the opposition will have little chance of winning.

Notes

1. It is difficult to define the exact political collocation of APRA. Sometimes it is considered to be a social democratic party, but this definition is not entirely correct as one can hardly transpose this Western political notion to Latin America (cf. Sanborn 1991). APRA shifted from a revolutionary discourse during the 1930s to an alliance with right-wing parties in the 1950s and 1960s (cf. Graham 1992).

2. For a long time APRA and the PCP were excluded from elections, and the left was excluded until 1978.

3. *Coyuntura Laboral*, October–December 1984, DESCO.

4. García won with 55 per cent of the votes over Carlos Melgar, who represented the progressive current willing to reinforce the relation with the left. The lack of support of

the party establishment partially explains García's later distant attitude towards the high-ranking party members.

5. The national security project was limited to the struggle against insurgency. Despite the armed forces putting pressure on the government to combine military repression with social-political measures to combat insurgency, the military of the 1980s lacked any real project for national development. When they spoke of sociopolitical strategy they simply meant confronting terrorism, also in the political arena (Rospigliosi 1989; Mauceri 1989).

6. See *Debate*, March–April 1988, p. 10.

7. Militants of several local social movements, whom I interviewed, accused APRA of boycotting their activities by giving gifts and money to people who joined APRA's organizations.

8. Tanaka (1998) believes that the real collapse of the Peruvian party system became evident after the election of Fujimori. In fact until that moment traditional parties still received the highest amount of consent and took part quite efficiently in the political process. I believe that Fujimori was a clear symptom of the demise of the party system (cf. Crabtree 1994; Cotler 1994).

9. Przeworsky (1986) argues that it is difficult to have democracy when there is no room for class compromises, as in a highly conflicting society. The same argument can also be applied to the process of de-radicalization of parties. Can a party stand for political mediation when there are no conditions for such a policy?

10. I assume that in this election the style of the campaign played a greater role in orienting people's consent, than did the content of the political programmes.

11. It is important to underline a main difference between the Peruvian and Bolivian cases in which both presidents (after their election) drastically changed their economic strategy. When Paz Estenssoro was elected for the fourth time in 1985, he represented the political establishment. On the contrary, Fujimori was an independent candidate who played the card of discrediting state institutions, parties and unions to gain legitimacy for himself (Cotler 1994). Whereas in Bolivia the neoliberal policy did not undermine democratic consolidation, in Peru liberalism proceeded together with an authoritarian shift and with the collapse of the political system.

References

Balbi, R. and J. Parodi (1984) 'Radicalísmo y clasísmo en el movimiento sindical Peruano', *Socialismo y Participación*, 26: 85–98.

Ballón, E. (1986) 'Alan, la pirámide y el movimiento social', *Que hacer*, 41.

Calderón, J. and R. Valdeavellano (1991) *Izquierda y Democracia: Entre la Utopía y Realidad*, Lima: CENCA.

Cameron, M. A. (1991) 'The politics of the urban informal sector in Peru: populism, class and "redistributive combines"', *Canadian Journal of Latin American Studies*, 16 (31): 79–104.

— (1994) *Democracy and Authoritarianism in Peru: Political Coalitions and Social Change*, New York: St. Martin's Press.

Cardenas, L. O., M. Piazza and R. Vergara (1991) *Municipios: Desarrollo Local y Participación*, Lima: DESCO.

Conaghan, C., J. Malloy and L. Abugattas (1990) 'Business and the "boys": the politics of neoliberalism in the Central Andes', *Latin American Research Review*, 25 (2).

Cotler, J. (1978) *Clases, Estado y Nación en el Perú*, Lima: IEP.

Cotler, J. (1994) 'Crísis política, outsiders y autoritarismo plebiscitado: el fujimorismo', in J. Cotler, *Política y Sociedad en el Perú: Cambios y Continuidades*, Lima: IEP.

Crabtree, J. (1994) 'La crísis del sistema partidario peruano (1985–1995)', *Apuntes*, 35: 19–34.

De Soto H. (1989) *The Other Path: The Invisible Revolution in the Third World*, New York: Harper & Row.

Dietz, H., and D. S. Palmer (1978) 'Citizen Participation under Innovative Military Corporativism', in J. Booth and M. Seligson (eds), *Political Participation in America Latina*, New York and London: Holmes & Meier.

Durand, F. (1988) 'Alan García y los empresarios: alianza y conflicto', special issue 'La burguesía peruana', *Cuaderno DESCO*, 11: 43–75, Lima: DESCO.

Gamero, J. (1990) 'Estabilización: gradualismo o shock?', *Que hacer*, 63.

Gonzáles, R. (1983) 'Los secretos del Señor García', *Que hacer*, 21: 40–7.

González de Olarte, E. and L. Samamé (1994) *El Péndulo peruano: Políticas económicas, gobernabilidad y subdesarrollo, 1963–1990*, Lima: IEP.

Graham, C. (1990) 'Peru's APRA party in power: impossible revolution relinquished reform', *Journal of Interamerican Studies and World Affairs*, 32 (3): 75–115.

— (1992) *Peru's APRA: Parties, Politics and the Elusive Quest for Democracy*, Boulder, CO and London: Lynne Rienner.

Graham, C. and C. Kane (1998) 'Opportunistic government or sustaining reform? Electoral trends and public-expenditure patterns in Peru, 1990–1995', *Latin American Research Review*, 33 (1): 67–104.

Grompone, R. (1990) 'Perú: la vertiginosa irrupción de Fujimori. Buscando las razones de un sorprendente resultado electoral, *Revista Mexicana de Sociología*, 52 (4): 177–205.

— (1991) *El Velero en el Viento: Política y Sociedad en Lima*, Lima: IEP.

— (1998) *Fujimori, Neopopulismo, y Comunicación Política*, Lima: IEP.

Iguíñez, J. (1991) 'Perú: ajuste e inflación en el plan Fujimori', in J. Iguíñez (ed.), *Elecciones y política econónica en América Latina*, Buenos Aires, CEDES and Thesis.

Kuczynski, P. (1980) *Democracia Bajo Presión Económica: el Primer Gobierno de Belaúnde (1963–1968)*, Lima: Ediciones Treintitrés & Mosca Azul.

Letts, R. (1981) *La Izquierda Peruana*, Lima: Mosca Azul.

López, S. (1995) 'Perú: una pista de doble vía: la transición entre el autoritarismo y la democratización (1992–1995)', *Cuestión de Estado*, special issue, Lima: IDS.

Mauceri, P. (1989) *Militares: Insurgencia y Democratización en el Perú, 1980–1988*, Lima: IEP.

Nieto, J. (1983) *Izquierda y Democracia en el Perú, 1975–1980*, Lima: DESCO.

Parodi, J. (1986) 'La desmovilización del sindicalismo industrial peruano durante el segundo belaundismo', Documento de Trabajo 3, Lima: IEP.

Pásara, L. (1990) 'El doble sendero de la izquierda legal peruana', *Nueva Sociedad*, 106: 58–72.

Pease, H. (1988) *Democracia y Precariedad Bajo el Populismo Aprísta*, Lima: DESCO.

— (1989) *Democracia Local: Reflexiones y Experiencias*, Lima: DESCO.

Przeworski, A. (1986) 'La democracia como resultado contingente de los conflictos', *Zona Abierta*, 39–40.

Roberts, K. (1995) 'Neoliberalism and the transformation of populism in Latin America: the Peruvian Case', *World Politics*, 48: 82–116.

— (1999) *Deepening Democracy: The Modern Left and Social Movements in Chile and Peru*, Stanford, CA, Stanford University Press.

Rospigliosi, F. (1989) 'Izquierdas y clases populares: democracia y subversión en el Perú', in J. Cotler (ed.), *Clases Populares, Crisis y Democracia in América Latina*, Lima: IEP, pp. 103–41.

— (1994) *Las Fuerzas Armadas y el 5 de Abril: la Percepción de la Amenaza Subversiva como una Motivación Golpista*, Lima: IEP.

Sánchez, F. (1985) 'El tratamiento al capital extranjero', *Que hacer*, 34: 55–7.

Sanborn, C. (1991) ' The democratic left and the persistence of populism in Peru: 1975–1990', PhD thesis, Harvard University.

Schydlowsky, D. (1986) 'The tragedy of lost opportunity in Peru', in J. Hartlyn and S. Morley (eds), *Latin American Political Economy: Financial Crisis and Political Change*, Boulder, CO: Westview Press.

Stepan, A. (1978) *The State and Society: Peru in Comparative Perspective*, Princeton, NJ: Princeton University Press.

Stokes, S. (1997) 'Democratic accountability and political change: economic policy in Fujimori's Peru', *Comparative Politics*, 29 (2).

Tanaka, M. (1998) Los Espejísmos de la Democracia: El Colápso de Partidos en el Perú, Lima: IEP.

Tapia, C. (1997) *Las Fuerzas Armadas y Sendero Luminoso: dos Estratégias y un Final*, Lima: IEP.

Thorp, R. (1987) 'The APRA alternative in Peru: a preliminary evaluation of García's economic policies', *Bulletin of Latin American Research*, 6 (2).

Tuesta, F. (1994) Perú Político en Cifras. Elite Política y Elecciones, Lima: Fundación Friedrich Ebert.

Weyland, K. (1996) 'Neopopulism and neoliberalism in Latin America: unexpected affinities', *Studies in Comparative International Development*, 31 (3): 3–31.

SIX

Neoliberalism, Economic Crisis and Popular Mobilization in Ecuador

JEAN CARRIÈRE

Popular protest of an increasingly violent character is on the rise in Ecuador. Since the beginning of 1997, the country has witnessed wave after wave of marches and demonstrations spreading throughout the country. At the beginning of the period, the demands of the demonstrators focused on constitutional renewal and an end to the corrupt politics of the party hierarchies. By early 1999, militant marchers in Quito, Guayaquil, Cuenca and other urban centres were demanding an end to the economic austerity measures being imposed by President Jamil Mahuad. Students, trade unions, peasant organizations, indigenous groups and other social movements joined together on 4 February 1999 in a bitter confrontation with the authorities. After years of falling wages, increasing unemployment and steep rises in the price of basic necessities, the people were telling the political leaders that they had had enough.

The spark was a package of austerity measures adopted at the beginning of January, which included a 35 per cent increase in electricity tariffs, an end to price control on fuel including bottled gas used by low-income families, and a government announcement that wage increases for teachers and other groups of workers that had already been agreed would not be paid after all. This national protest, and others that had taken place in previous weeks, were more alarming than the traditional protest marches of the past. Some of the marchers covered their faces and were armed; there was a massive army presence in all the major cities. Violent confrontations, especially around the campus of the University of Cuenca, which was occupied by troops, led to an unknown number of casualties and dozens of arrests. On 20 January, anticipating the protests announced for the coming weeks, President Mahuad compared the course the country was on to a ship about to hit an iceberg and said Ecuador was facing its worst crisis in 70 years. He did not refer to a recent survey showing that over half of the Ecuadorians blamed the captain: it was the president, they said, who was steering the ship on the wrong course.

However, like many of his predecessors, President Mahuad can also be considered a victim of Ecuador's permanent state of economic crisis. In January 2000, he announced a programme of dollarization that set off a massive rise in inflation, with some prices going up by 200 to 300 per cent. The popular response was swift. On 21 January he was faced with a massive occupation of Quito and all the major provincial capitals by members of the Confederation of Indigenous Nationalities of Ecuador (Confederación de Nacionalidades Indígenas del Ecuador – CNI). In one of the most bizarre developments in the country's history, a group of army colonels joined the indigenous leaders and occupied the Presidential Palace, forcing President Mahuad to take refuge in a neutral airforce base. The *de facto* regime that emerged from what had in effect been a coup was forced to resign shortly thereafter, after heavy American pressure for a 'constitutional solution'. Congress was convened and swore in Vice-President Noboa, thus giving a veneer of constitutional continuity to this dramatic political crisis. The indigenous leaders strongly opposed the US-imposed solution; they will in all probability rise again when the opportunity presents itself.

This is Ecuador at the dawn of a new century, a country much favoured and visited by travellers attracted by its rich colonial architecture, picturesque Indian markets, ancient Amazonian tribes and its wealth of plant and animal species. However, in recent years, the country has also attracted the attention of social scientists seeking to understand the roots of its growing societal crisis. This chapter is a modest contribution to that endeavour.

A central theme running through this volume is the response of populist regimes to the structural adjustment packages and other austerity measures pressed upon the nations of the South over the past 15 years. The view that emerges from political developments in Ecuador in recent decades is that the Andean variant of populism to be found there exhibits contradictions that, since the early 1980s, have made it impossible for any kind of coherent response to the neoliberal agenda to emerge. To flesh out this argument, I must first provide some historical context to the question of Ecuadorian populism.

Ecuadorian Populism in Historical Perspective

The whole of the Latin American subcontinent was shaken by the Great Depression of the late 1920s and 1930s, and Ecuador was no exception. As a commodity- and resource-exporting economy in a world disrupted by a major collapse of international trade, Ecuador was hit particularly hard. During the early years of the Depression, all of the country's major exports experienced a dramatic decline in terms of both demand and international market prices. By 1931, export revenues were less than half what they had been four years earlier.

The combination of soaring unemployment and bankruptcies associated with the collapse of trade opened the way for a prolonged period of popular protest and political instability. Urban labour and the peasantry, whose livelihoods before the crisis could be described as modest and austere, sank to the level of destitution and widespread life-threatening malnutrition. This was a threshold moment in twentieth-century Ecuadorian political history. The economic crisis and the widespread popular mobilization it sparked off during the early and mid-1930s provided the opportunity for a charismatic populist leader to emerge. This was José Maria Velasco Ibarra, a liberal deputy and powerful personality in the mould of the old civilian *caudillos*. Velasco won the presidency for the first time in 1934 supported, among other groups, by the rapidly growing impoverished urban masses, a scenario that was to be replayed in Argentina a few years later by Perón.

There is no space here for a full account of political developments in Ecuador since the 1930s; however, the arrival of Velasco Ibarra on the political scene was an event of profound political significance that continues to influence the course of Ecuadorian politics. His emergence was the outcome of a crisis that took place at a time when the popular sectors were both socially unstructured and politically unorganized. He used a variety of devices to win, retain and, where necessary, regain power after losing it, usually at the hands of the armed forces. These included a fierce nationalism that, at times, took on a xenophobic character, as a means of uniting the nation behind his leadership; a willingness to use mob rule and street violence to intimidate opponents; a thorough contempt for political parties, which he regarded as wasting their time on petty squabbles rather than being dedicated to the interests of the nation; and a total incapacity to put forward – let alone implement – social and economic policies that could even begin to address the serious economic and social issues facing the country (Corkhill and Cubitt 1998; Acosta 1997).

Through the skilful practice of this kind of ruthless populist style, Velasco Ibarra dominated Ecuadorian politics from 1934 to 1972, a total of 38 years during which he was in and out of office several times. His significance for twentieth-century politics derives from his political longevity and – more importantly – from the type of populist rule that was his legacy. Although his towering presence over the best part of four decades is by no means the only factor to be considered, he did much to perpetuate a political style that could provide only weak, unstable and usually ineffective governance for Ecuador, one that during the 1980s and beyond was essentially unable to generate a coherent response to the clash between popular mobilization on the one hand, and the imperatives of the neoliberal agenda on the other. I shall return to this point towards the end of the chapter.

The 1970s: Proximate Causes of the Economic Crisis

There is thus a clear historical-political dimension to the crisis of the 1980s and 1990s in Ecuador. The Andean brand of populism introduced by Velasco into Ecuadorian politics in the 1930s pre-empted the development of a more potentially effective system of governance that could have generated better policies and solutions when faced with the economic crisis that came later (CORDES/PNUD 1996). However, it is possible to trace causal factors associated with the crisis that are more direct and specific. To understand these, we must look at economic and political developments during the 1970s: the transformation of Ecuador into an oil-exporting economy, complete with full OPEC membership; a military coup that brought to power a left-nationalist regime with populist characteristics; and the slide into economic crisis including a gaping balance of payments deficit, an increase in the external debt and a chronic fiscal crisis of the state.

PETROLEUM COMES ON STREAM Exploration for oil deposits had been going on in the Oriente province of Ecuador throughout the 1960s and by 1972–73, crude oil from concessions controlled by Texaco had begun to come on stream. Within a few years, oil had overtaken bananas and other commodities to become Ecuador's largest (by far) export and source of foreign exchange. This rare good fortune – as everyone then believed – was to have an enormous impact on economic policy, development strategy and indeed on all aspects of Ecuadorian society.

Among the first political consequences of the oil boom was a coup that overthrew the ailing government of Velasco Ibarra in February 1972. Such illegal transfers of power rarely spring from a single motive, but two reasons behind the coup stand out. First, there was the matter of Assad Bucaram, the populist leader and head of a major political clan in Guayaquil. His volatile political style and ideological confusion, coupled with his spreading popularity, which made him a favourite to win the 1972 elections, persuaded the military of the need for a pre-emptive coup. Velasco had been bad enough, but the prospect of this totally unpredictable populist leading the nation was simply too much for the military.

But the other main reason for the coup was the prospect of huge oil revenues coming in during the 1970s and beyond. The generals knew very well which oil concessions were due to come on stream from the mid-1970s onwards, and they were aware that most of the soaring revenue from future petroleum exports would be controlled largely by the state. The corrupt, populist regimes such as the one they wished to overthrow and the one they feared would succeed it would mismanage this new source of wealth; were it to be left in the hands of the populist party politicians, the fruits of the oil boom would disappear in a whirlwind of corruption, incompetence and clientelism. Moreover, the military had its own ideas about how the revenue generated by oil exports should be used. The coup, as already mentioned, took place in February 1972; at just about the same time, soaring revenues began to flow into government coffers, driven upwards not only by the rapidly rising volume of oil exports but also by rapidly rising prices on international markets (a result of the 'oil crisis' of 1973 linked to events in the Middle East).

Confident that the boom would last for many years, the military governments of the early and mid-1970s increased public expenditure to dizzying heights, each day finding new destinations for what appeared to be a limitless source of funds available to the public sector. They bought new and costly military hardware, raised military salaries and financed lavish pension schemes for officers. They invested in commercial real estate on an unprecedented scale, partly for their own benefit, and to this day the commercial districts of Quito are burdened with empty office buildings. They invested heavily in infrastructure in the hope – partly justified in this case – of attracting foreign investment in manufacturing and services rather than in plantation agriculture or extractive industries. And most costly of all, they surrendered to their populist instinct and launched a series of subsidy schemes affecting basic foods and energy for the masses, and soft credits for industrial investors (Acosta 1997; de la Torre 1997).

However desirable some of these initiatives may have seemed, they proved, in the end, to be largely ineffective. While the middle and upper classes were using their new-found wealth to indulge in conspicuous consumption and imported luxury consumer goods, both rural and urban poverty remained stubbornly high and rising. In the mid-1970s, a full three-quarters of the rural population were living under the poverty line while the urban informal sector – the group closest to continuous destitution – rose from 45 per cent to 55 per cent in the seven years that the generals were in power. And as well as being ineffective, some of the more populist initiatives, such as subsidies on basic food and energy, were proving to be extremely costly. A year before the generals were forced to abandon power and make way for a new phase of formal democratic politics, the proportion of the government's budget spent on such schemes reached almost 50 per cent, a dramatic figure that pre-empted the financing of potentially more effective poverty alleviation measures.

In one area only, the objectives of the military regime seem to have been achieved to some degree. A variety of incentives-based investment promotion measures led to a rise in non-agricultural foreign investment from $60 million to $250 million between 1970 and 1976. However, the effects of that rise were limited for a variety of reasons, including poor management, a limited internal market and the capital-intensive nature of much of the new manufacturing activity. The operation was a brilliant technical success, but the patient remained critically ill.

THE GENERALS AND THE RISE IN THE EXTERNAL DEBT The period just described witnessed major changes in the Ecuadorian economy. Two essential elements of that change were a rapid rise in public sector investment and an even more dramatic increase in public sector investment and state-owned enterprises on the one hand, and the creation of costly subsidy schemes created to meet the basic needs of the poorest sectors of the population on the other. These, in addition to the vast amount of public expenditure designed to meet the demands of a whole series of lobbies and particularistic interests (including the armed forces themselves), raised budgetary commitments to levels that could not be financed from oil-based export revenues.

It would not be the first time that an oil boom has had the paradoxical effect of aggravating the economic plight of a country that finds itself unexpectedly sitting on top of billions of dollars in black gold: both Venezuela and Mexico suffered that fate. For the effect of the black gold is not only to increase the state's ability to finance public sector projects and particularistic demands of all kinds, it is also to raise expectations that government will carry out its social and economic agenda, and meet the demands of the strongest particularistic interests, by dipping into its bottomless purse. At the same time, if we are to believe the accounts of lending practices during the 1970s, when international banks were actively looking for borrowers that would take the billions of dollars of recycled petro-dollars from the Middle East off their hands, it was not at all difficult for a country – especially one with present and anticipated oil revenues – to run up a substantial foreign debt. And that is exactly what the generals had to do during the 1970s in order to finance the huge public sector commitments they had made in the early years of their rule (Acosta 1997).

In 1971, the year before the generals took power, the total external debt stood at $260.8 million, most of it in the form of loans granted to the

TABLE 6.1 Ecuador: external debt, 1970–82 (millions of dollars)

Year	Public sector	Private sector	Total
1970	229.3	12.2	241.5
1971	248.0	12.8	260.8
1972	324.6	19.3	343.9
1973	366.2	14.2	380.4
1974	377.2	32.8	410.0
1975	456.5	56.2	512.7
1976	635.8	57.3	693.1
1977	1,173.7	89.9	1,263.6
1978	2,478.4	456.2	2,974.6
1979	2,847.8	706.3	3,554.1
1980	3,530.0	1,121.5	4,651.5
1981	4,415.9	1,452.3	5,868.2
1982	4,557.3	1,629.5	6,185.8

Source: Baldivia et al. 1993: 75.

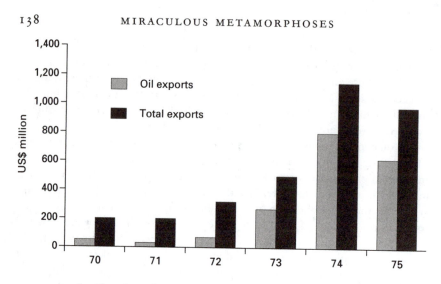

FIGURE 6.1 Ecuador: oil exports and total exports, 1970–75 (millions of US$)
(*Source*: Baldivia et al. 1993: 68)

public sector, and debt service accounted for about 10 per cent of export
revenues. In subsequent years, new credits from external sources, again most
of them going to the public sector and happily agreed by the international
financial organizations, caused the total debt to rise to $380.4 million in
1973, $512.7 million in 1975, then a large jump to $1263.7 million in 1977
and a whopping $3554.1 million in 1979. During the same period, debt service
as a per centage of export revenues rose from approximately 10 per cent in
the years up to 1975, about 22 per cent in 1977 and over 60 per cent in 1979,
the year the generals departed. There was worse to come and, as we will see
further on, in 1982, the year the crisis exploded in everyone's face, debt
service as a per centage of export revenues reached a crippling and unprecedented 90 per cent (Acosta 1997).

I shall be arguing further on that since the end of the military regime in
1979 and the dramatic rise in Ecuador's foreign debt through the 1970s, the
prospect of any government being able to carry out a development strategy
able to combine sustained growth and social equity while carrying the burden
of debt servicing has all but disappeared. In this sense, the 1970s were a
threshold period for Ecuador, and indeed for a large number of highly
indebted Third World states, which face a bleak future. It is therefore worth
taking a moment to reflect on the distribution of responsibilities for this
situation. It is clear that the high-spending military regimes of the 1970s in
Ecuador must bear a share of the responsibility for the rapid debt build-up.
But let us remember the context in which all Third World governments were
operating at that time. Domestically, they were subject to intense pressures
from various constituencies and lobbies – some of them popular, some

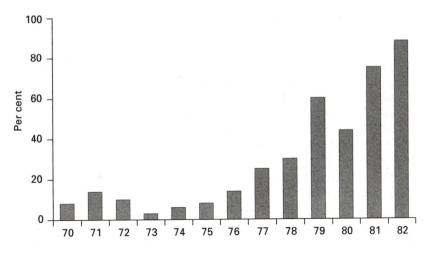

FIGURE 6.2 Ecuador: debt service ratio (debt service as a percentage of export revenues), 1970–82 (*Source*: Baldivia et al. 1993: 78)

capitalist and some bureaucratic – who believed that this was the moment – *now or never*, as many union leaders argued forcefully at the time – for their urgent needs to be met.

Internationally the banking community was sitting on a surplus of capital that it actively tried to foist upon bewildered Third World finance ministers eager to cooperate. It has been said that much of the Third World debt was built up as a result of irresponsible loans contracted by spendthrift governments to finance non-viable projects and programmes. But for every irresponsible borrower there was, inevitably, an irresponsible lender, eager to relax lending criteria (you could borrow money to pay civil service salaries) in order to unload funds for which there were no alternative destinations. This was, in a sense, the origin of the globalization of financial markets, and it suited both the banks and the major capitalist states that capital should be disposed of in this manner. Given this climate of forced optimism and general approval by institutions that had a reputation for financial prudence (the commercial banks, the IMF, the World Bank, the IDB, etc.), it is no surprise that the Ecuadorian military governments of the 1970s should have accepted the poisoned apple and set the country on a pathway to economic decline and political polarization. In the circumstances, it is difficult to imagine any government doing anything else.

The Last Chance for Social Reform: 1979–84

The bulk of the discussion that follows will examine the years 1984 to 1996, during which a runaway economic crisis hit Ecuador with full force and compelled the governments in power to give priority to the neoliberal agenda. Before that, however, we must briefly consider the fate of the last Ecuadorian government to be elected under the banner of social reform. This was the administration of Jaime Roldos, sometimes referred to as a 'sensible' reformist politician, whose name was put forward by the populist party Concentracion de Fuerzas Populares (Concentration of Popular Forces), and Osvaldo Hurtado, leader of the moderately reformist Christian Democratic Party. Campaigning on a platform of democratic restoration and social reform to meet basic needs, they won a convincing victory in the 1979 elections, gathering more than two-thirds of the votes cast. Roldos and his running mate thus seemed to have the electoral legitimacy necessary to institute much-needed policy changes.

Yet, in spite of favourable economic circumstances during the first year of their administration (oil prices rose by 300 per cent and export revenues reached almost one billion dollars), the new government failed to prosper. The brief period of high oil prices helped Roldos buy time and political support among the popular sectors by helping to finance wage increases and subsidize domestic industrialists – the last gasp of the old import-substitution strategy. However, these temporary achievements contributed little to the government's support and credibility in the face of its inability to create a reliable alliance of parties on which it could count to support its legislation programme in Congress. Here again, the confused and erratic face of populism contributed significantly to the failure of this final attempt at social reform, since many of the attacks and betrayals that prevented Roldos from achieving much-needed support in Congress came from rivals from within his own party, including a prominent member of the Bucaram clan.

Roldos died in an air crash in 1981 and the rest of his term of office was served by Vice-President Hurtado, as provided for in the Constitution. The years leading up to the 1984 elections were marked by a visible turn to the right by Hurtado. The mini oil boom of 1979–80 was over, labour militancy was on the rise and, to make matters worse, a major economic crisis, unprecedented in its depth and disruptive effects, hit the country in 1982. Both oil revenues and the value of exports fell by approximately 10 per cent and a serious balance of payments crisis was visible on the horizon. In what looked like a forerunner of the austerity packages forced on Ecuador after 1984, the government devalued the sucre by almost one-third, removed subsidies originally aimed at meeting basic needs such as food and household fuels, and tried to save foreign exchange by raising tariffs in order to curtail imports. But it was too little too late. Inflation soared to almost 50 per cent in 1983 and a series of controversial cuts in public expenditures – some of them hitting labour and other parts of the popular sectors – were implemented (Chislett 1991; Acosta 1997; Corkhill and Cubitt 1998).

Neoliberalism Systematically Applied

The following twelve years (1984–96) were dominated by a seemingly permanent crisis coupled with vigorous attempts – ultimately doomed to failure – to solve the problem by restructuring the economy. The pioneer of this neoliberal revolution in Ecuador was a prominent businessman from Guayaquil and chairman of its Chamber of Industry, Leon Febres Cordero. Febres was a visceral neoliberal, dedicated to markets as the only effective engine of economic development and equally dedicated to the principle that the social costs associated with the unbridled operation of markets were a price worth paying. His economic vision is sometimes referred to by Ecuadorians as Andean Thatcherism.

True to the Ecuadorian tradition of elections run along personalistic lines and based on slogans rather than ideas or programmes, Febres won the 1984 elections with the slogan 'Techo, Comida y Trabajo' (Shelter, Food and Work). The facts that not a word was uttered during the campaign about how these noble objectives were meant to be achieved, or that Febres' political career showed scant attention to such basic values, did not prove an obstacle to his victory. Once in power, he began to implement the most far-reaching series of measures designed to restructure the economy that had ever been attempted.

In contrast to his predecessors, who had focused their economic 'reforms' on currency devaluation and mild cuts in public expenditure, Febres attacked the two principles that had been cast in stone over the previous decades. The first was the protection of domestic industry – the last expression of the old import-substitution model – which he placed under threat by limiting the amount of tariff protection it could enjoy. The number of banned imports of products that competed with domestic manufacture was also reduced by almost half. These measures, designed – as they had been in Pinochet's Chile – to transform domestic industry into an efficient, internationally competitive sector threatened to bring about an industrial collapse – again, as they managed to do in Chile under the Chicago Boys – along with a massive rise in urban unemployment. The second sacred principle violated by Febres went not much further than a legislative change: he introduced amendments to existing legislation to make the privatization of public sector enterprises possible. This key chapter in the neoliberal bible was to take on more importance in later years, and we return to this point further on.

Fearing the onset of a long period of declining oil prices, the Febres regime implemented a new round of adjustment measures in 1986. They included further cuts in public expenditures applied in a way that paid little regard to the collapsing living standards of the popular sectors. This was followed by new tariff reductions on imported goods and higher interest rates designed to attract foreign capital. The cost to what was left of the domestic industrial sector in terms of bankruptcies and unemployment continued to rise as a consequence.

Although I will be touching on the social question further on, it is worth pointing out at this stage that popular protest also reached new heights as one of Ecuador's major union federations, the Frente Unico de Trabajadores (the Workers' United Front) launched a series of general strikes, the last of which brought out over three-quarters of the workforce for several days, during which the economy was at a standstill (CORDES/PNUD 1996).

Even the gods seem to have turned against Febres, as one of the worst earthquakes in Ecuadorian history ravaged the country in March 1987. Hundreds were killed, thousands went missing and almost a hundred thousand people were made homeless. Particularly worrying was the loss of the Trans-amazonian oil pipeline. Barely a month before, the Febres regime had been obliged to suspend payments on the external debt because of a foreign exchange shortfall caused by low oil prices. The earthquake added almost one billion dollars to that shortfall: this was the total cost of getting the pipeline back on stream and of making up for lost export revenues during the months in which the pipeline was out of action.

Studies of the last years of the Febres regime outdo each other in their search for a terminology sufficiently pejorative to describe its economic failures. However, low oil prices, the effects of the earthquake, rising inflation and unemployment were not the most far-reaching aspects of Febres' legacy. Of greater long-term significance was his fundamentalist neoliberal vision, encouraged by US President Reagan, pressed upon the country by the international economic organizations and proudly defended by Febres himself. The policies issued from that vision caused a further opening of the economy, greater vulnerability of the export sector to international price volatility, and what amounts to a 'reprimarization' of the external sector (as Ecuadorian economists sometimes refer to it) – that is, a return to a high degree of dependence on primary exports after a period of increasing diversification. These problems, generated at a time when neoliberalism was achieving a quasi-religious status among the most powerful sections of global business and political elites, continue to plague the Ecuadorian economy.

The two regimes that were in power between 1988 and 1996 had superficial differences in political rhetoric, but they were subject to similar external economic constraints and comparable domestic political dissent. Rodrigo Borja Cevallos was a cautious social democrat who used the rhetoric of reform to consolidate his position *vis-à-vis* the popular sectors, but completely failed to deliver policies aimed at achieving effective social reform – some clumsy attempts at economic re-structuring merely served to generate opposition from the left without advancing the neoliberal cause. He left office with an aura of hypocrisy hanging around him as the gap between the ideology that he articulated and the reality of empty, unfulfilled promises became increasingly obvious.

Sixto Duran-Ballen, on the other hand, headed a more consistent government, convinced that Ecuador had to fall in with the general movement towards economic restructuring, whatever the social costs. His administration was, at times, highly praised by the international economic organizations for several initiatives that they regarded as highly desirable and long overdue. This included advancing the privatization programme, reducing the public sector deficit to less than 0.5 per cent at mid-term, reducing public sector jobs by 35,000 (about 10 per cent of the total) and maintaining an open economy by ensuring that tariffs remained at a historical low: 5 to 10 per cent (except for automobiles) with an average of 11 per cent. Despite the successful negotiation of a debt and debt service reduction agreement with commercial creditors, the country still ended up during Duran-Ballen's administration with one of the largest per capita external debts in Latin America, one that swallowed 16 per cent of export revenues (Economist Intelligence Unit 1996).

After Duran-Ballen left office, Ecuadorian politics plumbed the depths of ridicule with the unexpected election in 1996 of Abdala Bucaram, a populist leader from Guayaquil and a leading member of the clan of the same name. Bucaram's campaign concentrated on attacking Ecuador's rich and powerful elites, whose interests had been served and privileges confirmed by Duran-Ballen's revival of neoliberal policies. In typical populist style, he promised the urban and rural poor increases in subsidies on basic foods and fuels and improved social services such as health and education. Not a word was said about how this programme would be paid for. His campaign rallies included singing, dancing and stand-up comedy featuring the candidate himself. To the astonishment of Quito's respectable burghers, this judicious combination of empty promises and popular entertainment not only attracted the support of large numbers of the rural and urban poor, but also won him the election.

Only a few months into his term, Bucaram announced a sudden and unexpected change of course in the form of a draconian austerity package, parts of which, such as the substantial increases in electricity and public transport fares, hit the poorest sectors of the population harder than the rest. One could fill a book of anecdotes illustrating his outrageous behaviour and his ability to alienate every social sector and every political organization – left, right or centre – in the country. In an unprecedented move, Congress voted to impeach him on the grounds of 'mental incapacity'. With the withdrawal of army support and a general strike supported by both business and labour, it was clear that Bucaram's presidency had come to an end. He was hustled out of the country and went into exile in Panama.

Mahuad and the Economic Legacy of the Past

An interim administration took over after Bucaram's departure, headed by Fabio Alarcon. Alarcon's failure to deal with the now permanent economic crisis was as spectacular as it had been predictable as his administration ran into the kinds of contradictions that had wrecked the reform plans of his predecessors in office. Attempts to reduce the fiscal deficit by cutting subsidies on food, fuels and electricity were opposed by Congress and led to massive protest demonstrations, forcing the administration to withdraw the measures. There is an air of déjà vu about Alarcon's short, sharp defeat by both legislative obstruction and popular resistance, a point to which we will return.

From the beginning of 1998, attention turned to the preparations for the May elections. These were won by a narrow margin by Jamil Mahuad, the establishment candidate with a support base among the middle classes of the Sierra region, determined to tackle the problems of the economy in a pragmatic and less politicized manner, with the help of a technocratically inclined cabinet. The *Andean Group Report* announced the results of the elections in an article headlined 'Mahuad's victory should usher in a period of much needed stability', a prediction the editors will have lived to regret as events unfolded over the following months.

Mahuad took office in August 1998 with 51.2 per cent of the vote against his populist opponent's 48.8 per cent, thus starting his period of office with a weak mandate and a low level of legitimacy. The fact that he did not have control of Congress seriously limited his ability to get his legislation through. In addition to these political handicaps, Mahuad inherited an economy that was still deteriorating after many years of failed reform efforts by his predecessors. At the time he came to office, the fiscal deficit stood at 7 per cent of GDP, inflation was among the highest in Latin America at 45 per cent and unemployment was 14 per cent. The unemployment figures do not fully reflect the deteriorating livelihoods of the popular sectors, since half of the labour force did not have a full-time job and 60 per cent of families were beneath the poverty line. In addition, oil prices were at an all-time low at around $7 a barrel of crude and, not surprisingly, the current account deficit was projected to more than double from $746 million in 1997 to $1.75 billion in 1998. To make matters worse, the damage caused by El Niño would require additional infrastructural investments of nearly $300 million to put right, and the cost of debt servicing – the largest single item of public expenditure – was absorbing 41 per cent of the budget.

During his electoral campaign, Mahuad had been compelled to match the optimistic outlook and promises his populist opponent had made his own. He spoke of thousands of new jobs, new homes for the homeless and new hospitals for the health service. He was even more specific on the question of inflation, which he said he would not contemplate, and on subsidies, which he said he would target on the poorest sectors. Within weeks of taking office, the cold reality of the economic legacy he inherited – especially the deepening fiscal shortfall and the deepening balance of payments deficit – left Mahuad little choice but to ignore the promises he had made to the electorate and adopt a series of highly unpopular measures. These included devaluing the sucre by 15 per cent, which had the effect of raising the domestic price of gas and diesel, and removing subsidies on cooking gas and electricity, a daring gesture since his predecessors had tried to do this without success, being forced to withdraw the measures by massive popular protest (*Latin American Newsletter*, various issues, 1998).

If Mahuad thought that, unlike his predecessors, he could get away with such impoverishing measures this time, he was badly mistaken. This attack on the livelihoods of the middle and lower sectors of society had an enormous mobilizing effect and led to the unprecedented popular protest, at times of an increasingly violent nature, described at the beginning of this chapter. Once again, political stability and governance seemed to clash with what the government felt were essential measures to get the country out of the crisis.

Austerity in Historical Perspective

There is an air of familiarity about the economic legacy inherited by Mahuad and his early failure to deal effectively with this legacy. Similar points have been made about the economic record of just about every administration since the 1981 crisis, when everyone understood that the oil boom and the good times that went with it were truly over.

Since then, during the years up to the impeachment of Bucaram and the subsequent elections in 1998, successive Ecuadorian governments have had to increase public sector borrowing to meet the cost of essential imports, but most of all to meet the payments on old debts. IMF conditionalities appeared in every structural adjustment loan (SAL) negotiated during that period. Their essential components tend to reappear from one SAL to the next: cuts in public expenditures, usually hitting basic services such as health and education; the reduction or elimination of subsidies on food, transport and household fuels, again hitting the poorest sectors of society; cuts in public sector jobs amounting to tens of thousands; trade liberalization measures such as tariff reductions leading to industrial bankruptcies and increasing urban unemployment; and the privatization of some state industries.

Whatever the political colour of the government in power at the time, at no point during these years did the measures achieve their stated purpose, which was to stem inflation, correct balance of payments deficits, stimulate growth and attract investment. Nor, I would argue, were they meant to do so. Their true purpose was to ensure that Ecuador would not default on its foreign debt. Creditors had to be repaid, the rules of the international financial system had to be obeyed so that the system would retain credibility, and Ecuador, like the rest of the nations of the South, had to open its economy and accommodate itself to the thrust of globalization and increasing foreign control.

Moreover, the stated purposes of the structural adjustment packages could not be achieved for two reasons. Again, we find that governments of a left/populist character such as those of Jaime Roldos (1979–81) and Rodrigo Borja (1988–92), who tried to implement a degree of redistributionist social reform, ultimately failed to prosper as inflation, balance of payments deficits and pressures from creditors became unmanageable .

Other administrations, such as those of Febres Cordero (1984–1988) or Duran-Ballen (1992–96), gave priority to implementing the structural adjustment programme to the point, in the case of the former, of being labelled the Thatcher of the Andes. In these cases, however, implementation of the economic 'reforms' came up against popular resistance and congressional divisions, so that by the end of the terms of office of these neoliberal regimes, the 'reforms' had either gone into reverse or else were implemented in a partial, distorted and ineffective manner as a result of backroom deals with Congress and the leaders of the popular protests.

Conclusion

In the end, the lessons to be learned from attempts at neoliberal 'reform' in Ecuador must start from the fact that they ended in a combination of failure and paradox. The responsibilities for their failure in the macroeconomic sphere and the catastrophic effects they had in the social sphere must be attributed to two interacting factors: the external constraints coming from the thrust of globalization, and domestic limitations associated with a long history of poor systems of governance.

Weak governance is an element of national specificity, and it is expressed to a substantial degree by the fragmented, corrupt and thoroughly ineffective variant of populism that developed from Velasco Ibarra in the 1930s to 'El loco' Bucaram in the 1990s. This was a populism that never found an ideology as the Apristas had done in Peru or the Peronistas in Argentina. Moreover, it was a populism that never got beyond the ephemeral lure of charisma, the squabbles among rival politicians based in Quito and Guayaquil, and the ever-deepening corruption, especially from the 1970s onwards, generated by substantial oil revenues flowing through the political and administrative institutions of the state. At no time was this left/populist constellation able to put forward a potentially effective counter-project to that of the Thatcherite right supported by the international financial institutions. They would rather destroy the government they had helped to elect, as in the case of the elder Bucaram's attacks on the Roldos government in the early 1980s, than see a faction other than their own achieve a degree of success. The combination of ineffective, sectarian populism with increasing mobilization of the popular sectors (as discussed further on) generated a permanent crisis of governance that Ecuador has not yet managed to overcome.

As far as external constraints are concerned, the thrust of globalization expressed by the neoliberal agenda promoted by international economic institutions failed in achieving its macroeconomic objectives but had un-intended and unanticipated social and political consequences that have perverted development in both the economic and the political spheres. In the economic sphere, the neoliberal measures[1] that were intended to produce prosperity when they were first introduced almost twenty years ago were never in a position to achieve their assigned objective because they could never be 'properly' implemented. Congress (usually for reasons of partisanship) and the popular movement (to defend existing modest livelihoods from further deterioration), formed a kind of double veto-group that forced successive governments either to water down or to abandon their neoliberal agenda. The result, in the economic sphere, is that little was done to tackle a whole host of economic ills including low growth, high inflation and unemployment, a chronic and rising fiscal deficit and a degradation in the public provision of basic services.

Meanwhile, in the political sphere, the incorporation of the popular sectors into democratic politics, their political empowerment through their own recognized organizations, are being distorted by the collapse in their living standards and their growing alienation from the institutions and practices of formal democratic politics. The sense of alienation suffered by the popular sectors comes from a growing awareness that, although they enjoy a measure of influence by their ability to block the neoliberal agenda, or at least slow down its momentum (a negative, veto-group function), they are unable to drive through an alternative agenda that could arrest the decline of their living standards. As a consequence, some of the casualties of the economic crisis, perhaps a growing number, are driven by desperation to acts of collective and individual violence, and democratic politics itself may be under threat. In one fell swoop, neoliberalism in Ecuador has managed to take the country to the brink of economic collapse while simultaneously putting at risk the uncertain democratic transition initiated some twenty years ago.

What we find in Ecuador since the 1970s is a paradox or vicious circle. The neoliberal agenda cannot be effectively implemented because of popular resistance, and no alternative (popular) agenda can be accommodated by the international system as it is presently constituted and ideologically controlled. The result is a permanent deadlock from which there seems no escape within the system. This author is convinced that there are only two pathways out of the type of permanent, structural crisis suffered by Ecuador and many other countries of the South. The first would be for the neoliberals to admit that their model requires such high social costs, for such a large proportion of the population, for such a very long period of time, that it is impossible to implement it by consent. Only a highly authoritarian form of government could impose such costs on the population in the hope of achieving its restructuring objectives. We could call this the Pinochet/Chicago Boys option. Its (limited) economic 'success' has been widely praised in Thatcherite and other conservative economic circles, but few are willing to admit that the implementation of the neoliberal agenda actually requires a good dose of authoritarian government. To try to drive it through within a formally democratic political environment leads inevitably to the paradoxes and contradictions shown by the recent history of Ecuador. In this sense – and I know some will quarrel with the terminology – there is a fascist core or logic to neoliberal restructuring: it destroys lives and livelihoods by the millions and must be imposed from above by highly authoritarian means.

The other pathway may be regarded by some as either a dated, old-fashioned idea or else Utopian nonsense. It implies, first of all, a paradigm shift that would have us target the source of the problem, not primarily in the domestic economic policies of individual countries of the South but in the way in which the international economic system is managed for the benefit of the richest and most powerful nations. And it implies different rules of the game in the areas of trade, market access, investment and particularly financial relations (including debt management) between North and South, changes that, in many senses, would reverse the trends of the last ten or twenty years. Not long ago, such major reforms were simply not on the agenda. Now, however, since the Asian crisis of 1997 and 1998, and Brazil's currency crisis of 1999, the need to 'do something' is being voiced by cautious, conservative institutions represented at such eminent gatherings as the Davos Forum and others. The forces advocating such a paradigm shift are gathering strength, but that is the subject beyond the scope of this chapter.

Note

1. To call them neoliberal 'reforms', a term that denotes something that is progressive and desirable, would be to use language as a means of legitimizing a questionable ideology.

References

Acosta, Alberto (1997) Breve História Económica del Ecuador, Quito: Corporación Editora Nacional.

Baldivia, J., F. Racines and I. Mendoza (1993) Ajuste Estructural en los Andes: Impactos Sociales y Desarrollo, Quito: Abaya-Yala.

Chislett, Michael (1991) Ecuador: The Economic Transformation, London: Euromoney.

CORDES/PNUD (1996) Ecuador: Un problema de Gobernabilidad, proceedings of an international seminar organized by the Corporación de Estudios para el Desarrollo y el Programa de las Naciones Unidas para el Desarrollo, Quito, 22–24 July.

Corkhill, David and David Cubitt (1998) Ecuador: Fragile Democracy, London: Latin American Bureau.

De Janvry, Alain et al. (1991) Adjustment and Equity in Ecuador, Washington, DC: OECD Publication and Information Centre.

Economist Intelligence Unit (1996) Country Profile: Ecuador, New York: EIU.

Torre, Carlos de la (1997) 'Populism and democracy: political discourses and cultures in contemporary Ecuador', Latin American Perspectives, 14 (3): 12–24.

World Bank (1995) *Ecuador Poverty Report Part I: Components of a Poverty Alleviation Strategy*, Washington, DC: World Bank, 30 June.

Zirker, Daniel (1998) 'José Nun's middle class military coup in contemporary perspective: implications of Latin America's neoliberal democratic coalitions', *Latin American Perspectives*, 25 (5): 67–86.

Other sources

Various web sites including the World Bank, the International Monetary Fund, the government of Ecuador, the Institute of Latin American Studies of the University of Texas at Austin, and Ecuadorian daily newspapers.

Informal interviews with knowledgeable informants (politicians, academic researchers and economic journalists), Quito, July 1997.

Latin American Newsletter (London), various issues, January 1985 to February 1999.

SEVEN

Neoliberal Reforms and Populist Politics: The PRI in Mexico

JOLLE DEMMERS

We have learned that populism hurts the interests of the majority and constitutes the worst enemy of our aspirations of the popular welfare. (Carlos Salinas de Gortari, campaign speech, 11 November 1987)

During the 1980s and 1990s, 'populism' became a dirty word in certain academic and political circles of Latin America. The term was associated with inefficiency, corruption and economic decline. It was widely believed that the debt crisis, the economic crisis of the early 1980s and the new wind of neoliberalism had done away with populist policies. Latin American populism was pronounced dead and buried along with the economic model of import substitution industrialization (ISI). However, as this book shows, this diagnosis proved premature. Populist parties managed to survive the turbulent years of neoliberal transformation, as did certain aspects of populism. In this chapter, the case of the Mexican Revolutionary Institutional Party (Partido Revolucionario Institucional – PRI) is analysed. The following pages show how Mexico went through the shift from ISI to neoliberalism and discusses the political consequences of this shift, focusing mostly on the Salinas years (1988–94). We will see how Mexico's neoliberal administrations of the 1990s had their 'populist side', manifested by a rise of presidentialism and a personalist and populist style of government.

The PRI Regime: Stability Explained

With the demise of the Communist Party of the Soviet Union, the Mexican PRI inherited the dubious honour of being the world's longest-ruling political party. How is it possible for a political party to govern a country for seven decades? This question has kept many journalists, social scientists and politicians busy for a considerable time. This section reviews the most well-known interpretations of Mexico's post-revolutionary past and looks at the most important theories and concepts used to explain the extraordinary stability of the Mexican regime.

MEXICO'S POST-REVOLUTIONARY PAST   In general, the PRI is seen as the key to Mexico's long-term political stability and the mechanism through which political conflict has been contained. Originally established as the Revolutionary National Party (PNR) in 1929, the PRI offered an organizational framework for the reconciliation of competing political interests in the tumultuous years following the revolution. Under President Lázaro Cárdenas, who governed the country between 1934 and 1940, the party became thoroughly restructured and institutionalized. Cárdenas' most important political achievement was to bring popular movements under state control by incorporating local peasant and worker organizations into national confederations. The incorporation of these organizations into the party was facilitated by extensive land reform and labour legislation. Although his successors abandoned most of Cárdenas' social policies, the regime retained its grip on power through the institutions he created. After 1940 political control became highly centralized: peasant and labour leadership was controlled by the president and political offices were allotted by sector to cooperative labour and peasant leaders (Teichman 1992: 89). The resulting system was built on two political structures. On the one hand, corporatist mechanisms ('worker', 'peasant' and 'popular sectors') secured the downward transmission of centralized power controlled by the president and his political offices. On the other hand, at the local level a network of patron–client relationships manipulated by *caciques* (local 'bosses') coexisted with the new system.[1] This structure is generally perceived to have maintained political stability in Mexico until the 1960s, through a combination of centralized political power, revolutionary ideology, regular elections, elite renewal, executive succession and the capacity of the PRI to please both its left and right constituencies. A crucial element in explaining Mexico's long-term political stability is what can be called the 'Mexican consensus'. For much of the period between 1929 and the 1980s, the PRI included a heterogeneous collection of sociopolitical actors who, although they fiercely disagreed on a number of points, were linked by a consensus on general political and economic objectives of development (Cornelius et al. 1989; Cook et al. 1994: 12). Among these were issues such as the need for elite circulation (no re-election), capitalist development and – perhaps most importantly – the role of the state in the economy. This was reflected in the economic policy of ISI, a deliberate strategy of production for the domestic market fostered and fomented by the state, which characterized the Mexican development model from the 1940s to the 1970s.[2] The exhaustion of this model during the 1970s is generally seen as one of the most crucial developments in Mexico's recent history (Cornelius et al. 1989: 4). The ISI policy is seen as having supported political stability in Mexico for decades by at the same time generating economic growth[3] and increasing state (economic) power.[4] Its important role in the national economy allowed the ruling party to both 'manipulate' – that is, undergird – its political legitimacy by sending a flow of material benefits to its constituencies (in the form of subsidies and social programmes) and 'repress' – that is, use its control in, for instance, state companies, the media and the bureaucracy to co-opt, exclude or repress – opposition.

This mixture of state corporatism, clientelism and import substitution – also referred to as 'classic populism' – came under pressure in the late 1960s. The student revolt of 1968 and the massacre at Tlatelolco is generally perceived as a watershed, marking the beginning of what many analysts see as 'Mexico's crisis'. Since then, economic differentiation and the call for political participation have challenged the political framework – no matter how flexible – that had guaranteed political stability in Mexico for almost four decades. Since that time, scholars have increasingly wondered where Mexico is 'going to', and have started to describe Mexico as a country 'in crisis' and 'in transition'. Although the ruling party could still depend upon a vast variety of resources, mechanisms and strategies to dominate the country, the stable structure of the 1930s–1960s and the consensus began to show serious cracks.[5] The regime responded to the demands of social groups for effective participation with gradual, carefully calculated liberalizing reforms on the one hand and repression on the other. The 1970s and 1980s are often pictured as years in which the regime tried unsuccessfully to re-establish stability. The exhaustion of the development model of ISI and the economic crisis of 1982 aggravated this situation. Before we continue this story and look at 'Mexico's neoliberal experience', we first briefly address the generally used theories and ideas explaining Mexico's regime stability.

AUTHORITARIANISM IN MEXICO: CORPORATISM AND CLIENTELISM
Analysts assessing the Mexican political system have long looked for models and theories to explain the success of the PRI. In the 1950s and 1960s, scholars depicted the regime as representative and pluralist (Cline 1963; Needler 1971). According to Cornelius et al. (1989), some analysts characterized the system as a 'one-party democracy' in the process of modernization and evolution toward 'true' (North Atlantic-style) democracy. The Mexican system was seen as representative because, despite the absence of fair elections, the various interests and demands of the population were represented through the PRI and its sectors and were reflected in government policy. This is what some analysts call 'substantial democracy' as opposed to 'formal democracy' (Bailey 1988: 64–5). In the substantive version of democracy, individuals are thought to gain a sense of efficacy from participation in groups that in turn are connected to the PRI system. Thus, for example, rural cooperativists may act through their associations to push for land or water claims, businessmen work through their chambers, workers through unions, and so forth. During

the disenchantment of the 1970s, this rather optimistic assessment of the Mexican regime made way for the characterization of Mexican politics as corporatist and authoritarian (Gonzalez Casanova 1970; Hansen 1971; Reyna 1977). Often the term authoritarianism was preceded by 'semi', 'moderate' or 'inclusionary'. Cornelius and Craig (1988: 8) provide an excellent example: 'Since 1940 Mexico has had a pragmatic and moderate authoritarian regime, not the zealously repressive kind that emerged in the southern cone in the 1960s and 1970s; an inclusionary system, given to co-optation and incorporation rather than exclusion or annihilation; an institutional system, not a personalistic instrument; and a civilian-dominated government, not a military government.'[6] Scholars emphasizing authoritarianism pointed at the many strategies the federal authorities used to repress or co-opt political opposition and control peasant and worker organizations, while promoting economic policies favouring a small elite.

Although the above descriptions of the Mexican regime clearly resemble the 'classic populism' as discussed in the introductory chapter – drawing on a heterogeneous coalition, reference to 'the people', reformist rather than revolutionary, personalistic leadership, redistribution – scholars of Mexican politics tend to use concepts such as corporatism and clientelism instead of populism. Both concepts are briefly explained below.

CORPORATISM Corporatism is generally seen as an important component in understanding Mexican authoritarianism, for it helps to explain the regime's ability to rule with a relatively low level of overt violence. For instance, Reyna (1977: 159), co-editor of the influential book *Authoritarianism in Mexico*, explains the stability of the Mexican system by the 'corporatist, nonfascist structure of the state, which has been able to regulate conflict, although sometimes through very authoritarian solutions'.[7] By incorporating strategic groups into the state apparatus, the regime is able to demobilize, 'de-radicalize' and control their demands. 'Depoliticization in the Mexican political system has allowed a sophisticated use of the bargaining process within the limits of the state' (Reyna 1977: 161). In this sense, corporatism can be seen as an 'alternative to the indiscriminate use of repressive measures' (ibid.). Of course, Reyna admits that incorporation in itself is insufficient. It has to be combined with the meeting of some demands and the granting of some concessions. 'It is necessary to give something in order to receive something. Once some benefits were given, the state received disciplined labour and peasant organizations' (ibid.). In effect, Reyna claims that there is only one real political centre in Mexico. 'The state can activate or exclude the masses according to the circumstances. In some cases, the state stimulates political mobilization to build legitimacy in a context which does not threaten any institutions. In other cases, it demobilizes through incorporation into existing organizations or those created ad hoc, in order to exclude or "de-radicalize" demands that may affect the strategic centre of the system, capital accumulation' (Reyna

1977: 162). This assessment of the Mexican political regime was very influential for a long time (and, for a large part, still is influential). The Mexican
regime is seen as a rational entity performing a balancing act between
pressures from below – to which it partly responds and that are partly
repressed – and pressures from above (the private sector, the dominant
classes), to which it generally responds. In fact, according to this view the
Mexican regime is constantly looking for the best way to legitimize the system.
Therefore, Mexican politics is seen as a careful mix of strategies to maintain
party dominance such as redistributive policies, pre-emptive reforms, co-
optation and, if necessary, repression.

CLIENTELISM Whereas corporatism is often seen as the organizing structure of authoritarianism, clientelism is understood as the key mechanism of
political integration in an authoritarian regime (Grindle 1977; Kaufman 1981;
Brachet-Márquez 1992). Corporatism provides the regime with a stable power
base; clientelism contributes to regime stability by preventing the organization
of horizontal interest groups. Clientelism can be understood as the structuring
of political power through networks of informal relations that link individuals
of unequal power in relationships of exchange (Brachet-Márquez 1992: 93–
4). When applied to Mexico, the metaphor of the pyramid is often used to
explain the working of clientelism. The pyramid is made up of a chain of
vertical, personalistic ties that originate at the top in the presidency, and
subsequently find their way down to the official party, the core of the state
apparatus, and the mass organizations. From the presidency, favours are
dispensed directly and indirectly to those below through complex patron-
client networks that link the top of the social structure to the base. This
clientelist political structure inhibits the organization of horizontal interest
groups (based on party or class). Hence civil society is seen as a fragmented
set of vertical relationships (Brachet-Márquez 1992).

The concepts of clientelism and corporatism have played an important
role in explaining authoritarianism and regime stability in Mexico. Both models
understand the Mexican political system as highly centralized and rational.[8]
The picture that is drawn is one of a highly efficient, calculating and powerful
regime, capable of manipulating and moulding any force or movement that
might threaten its dominance. Both the regime's institutional set-up (strong
presidency, party, corporatist structures) and its mode of political organization
(clientelism, elite circulation, political entrepreneurism) reinforce this notion.
Civil society, in contrast, is taken to be divided and fragmented by the vertical
relationships inherent in clientelism and corporatism. The inability of individuals to organize themselves horizontally, which this perspective takes as
axiomatic, severely limits their political strength. Of course, scholars have
admitted that the logic of these models at times conflicts with reality. And
indeed, it would be nonsense to argue that Mexico has not known organized
popular protest or opposition. There is ample proof of union activism in

the 1940s, 1950s and 1970s, the student uprising of 1968, and rural guerrilla movements in the 1970s. Moreover, political opposition has been organized in political parties such as the National Action Party (Partido de Accíon Nacional – PAN) (since 1939), Socialist Popular Party (Partido Popular Socialista – PPS) (1958) and Authentic Party of the Mexican Revolution (Partido Authéntico de la Révolucion Mexicana – PARM) (1954). However, the fact that most of these revolts and opposition movements have been either repressed, co-opted or otherwise silenced is seen to underpin the power of the regime and its capacity to maintain the status quo, and is used as an argument to defend the pyramidical, state-centred view of power. A direct consequence of the above view of the Mexican regime as highly centralized and of Mexican society as lacking the capacity of exerting pressure on the state is that the initial impetus for change – that is, any kind of policy reform – depends entirely on the personalities, values and ideas of elites and the president (Brachet-Márquez 1992: 99). Recently, this somewhat rigid, state-centred idea of Mexican politics has been criticized by authors who stress a more dynamic and dialectic understanding of Mexican politics. The critique on the idea of the 'all-powerful state' and the attribution of a greater role to civil society in contesting and constructing power in Mexico appeared in the 1980s. This caused an outpouring of studies on popular movements, NGOs and other independent organizations. A more recent critique on the idea of the centralist, hegemonic state stresses the importance of the Mexican region as political location. Although it is generally admitted that Mexico has an unusually strong and efficient state apparatus these analysts claim that the Mexican state and regime should be apprehended as 'parts of a complex and changing centre that coexists with and is constituted and embedded in the diversity of regional and cultural constructions evolving throughout Mexico since the 1930s' (Rubin 1996: 86).

In the second part of this chapter we will see how the above concepts can be of use in analysing the political impact of neoliberal reform in Mexico. First, however, we look at the nature and content of the neoliberal restructuring measures.

Neoliberalism: The New 'Normalcy'

Needless to say, Mexico's 1982 economic crisis and shift to a free market economy was not an isolated event. Nor was it an internal, national affair. In the whole of Latin America the development strategy based on private property, state intervention and import substitution, which proved to be (economically) successful during the postwar years, collapsed in the 1980s. Although the causes of the collapse of economic growth are not obvious, the response to it is easier to identify. According to Przeworski, this response is best described as 'modernisation via internationalisation': many developing countries[9] in the 1980s adopted the development strategy of the advanced capitalist world. They adopted the 'political, economic and cultural organisation already existing elsewhere: democracy, markets, and an individualistic, consumption-oriented culture that dominates the advanced capitalist world' (Przeworski 1995: 3).

Notwithstanding the role of domestic factors, four international factors can be seen as responsible for this dramatic shift in development strategy. First, the globalization of production and finance made the old style of national independence increasingly hard to defend. Second, a new political and ideological force superimposed itself on this global economic environment. Supported by the administrations of particularly Thatcher and Reagan, the 'New Right' or 'neoliberal' ideology has become hegemonic worldwide, or as Overbeek and van der Pijl have put it, neoliberalism has become 'the new normalcy' (Overbeek and van der Pijl 1993: 2). Third, this new force appeared to be reinforced by the powerful example of the 'Asian Tigers'. Fourth, with the end of the Cold War and the disintegration of the Soviet Union, an important alternative disappeared (Przeworski 1995: 4–5). Obviously, apart from these more or less general trends, the specific policies and pressures of international institutions such as the World Bank and the International Monetary Fund played an important role in directing developing nations towards the adoption of neoliberal policies.

This section presents an overview of the main economic restructuring measures taken by both the de la Madrid and the Salinas administration. I am not an economist, and it is not my intention to discuss these reforms in detail. Rather, I focus on those aspects that are of importance to the course of this chapter. Therefore, what are stressed here are the socioeconomic consequences of the neoliberal reforms as well as the reorientation of the role of the state in the economy. In the discussion on the political impact of these changes in the next section, attention is paid to the role of the various actors and interest groups involved.

DE LA MADRID: 1982–88 As stated, the crisis of 1982 is generally perceived as marking the shift to a free market economy in Mexico.[10] In response to the debt crisis, the newly installed president, de la Madrid, introduced a policy of structural adjustment, seeking first to stabilize the economy and then to restructure it by promoting economic liberalization. The austerity measures of the de la Madrid administration first and foremost focused on the reduction of the budget deficit and the stabilization of the exchange rate.[11] The stabilization plan sharply limited wage increases, cut government social spending, and reduced or eliminated a broad range of government consumption subsidies. During the first years of the austerity programme, economic recovery was seriously hampered by a number of factors. For instance, high debt service payments made it very difficult for the government to reschedule Mexico's foreign debt (Urquidi 1994). In addition, low levels of domestic and foreign investment, unstable prices for

Mexico's petroleum exports, insufficient access to foreign credit and high inflation constrained economic recovery. The endurance of the economic crisis and the new drop in oil prices in 1985 led government officials, pressured by both internal and external actors, to re-examine the country's overall strategy for economic development and especially the role of the public sector.[12] Consequently, starting in 1985, liberalization and deregulation became the key words of Mexico's economic policy. This resulted in the privatization of medium-sized and small state companies, the liberalization of the country's trade and industrial policy regime and the deregulation of foreign investment flows and domestic economic activities. Another sign of the policy shift of 1985 was Mexico's entry into the GATT in 1986, ending more than a decade of bitter debate over whether to accept the liberal trade provisions embodied in the treaty (Kaufman 1989: 118; Cypher 1990: 181). For Mexico, membership of the GATT involved the abolishing of a large number of nationalist and populist regulations. Again subsidies were eliminated and import restrictions limited, and the Bank of Mexico was given greater autonomy (Cook et al. 1994: 15; Urquidi 1994; Ros 1994; Lustig 1992; Cypher 1990).

An important incentive for the adoption of market reforms by Mexican government officials was the need to attract foreign capital. For instance, both the Baker (1985) and Brady (1989) US government plans conditioned additional foreign lending on the willingness of debtor countries to adopt neoliberal market reforms (Cook et al. 1994). Equally, the World Bank demanded economic liberalization reforms in return for loans. However, internal forces called for neoliberal reform as well. Although the importance of external pressures and 'conditional loans' made by the World Bank and US programmes should not be underestimated, a number of scholars nevertheless interpret the policy shift of 1985 as a largely internal affair. Cypher (1990: 189), for instance, argues that 'internal policy changes arising from forces internal to the Mexican social formation – above all the rising weight of the neoliberal ideology that the industrial and financial groups championed – had set the stage for this threshold step'.

Although Mexico encountered many difficulties in fighting the economic crisis and making the shift to a market economy, some authors claim that in Mexico this shift proceeded much more rapidly and smoothly than in a number of other Latin American countries (Ros 1994; Centeno 1994). The reasons for this were said to be the economic policy makers' relative decision-making autonomy in a strong presidentialist system, Mexico's importance to the USA and its traditionally low degree of indexation in the wage-price system, and the flexibility that the system of state–labour relations gave economic policy-makers in setting wages. In his last year in office, with the upcoming presidential elections and the threat of a general strike, de la Madrid decided to attack the (still) high inflation rate by means of 'shock therapy'.[13] This was done through the implementation of a 'pact' between government, labour unions and business, the so-called Pacto de Solidaridad.[14]

Put simply, in the pact unions agreed to wage controls in exchange for price curbs (Cypher calls this the constitution of a 'no-strike pledge' by labour (1990: 196)). Agreement was reached on a policy of wage lags, the regulation of prices of basic consumer goods, the raising of public sector rates, the reduction of subsidies, and the stabilization of the exchange rate.[15] The pact had both economic and political consequences. Economically, the rate of inflation indeed decreased: by mid-1988 the monthly rate was down to 'only' 52 per cent (Cypher 1990: 196). In addition, real wages fell another 29 per cent in the course of the first year of the pact, and the exchange rate was stabilized. This ended, at least temporarily, the cycle of massive devaluation that had characterized de la Madrid's term. By the time Salinas had taken office, the stabilization policy adopted under the pact proved to be instrumental in achieving the successful renegotiation of the external debt in 1989 within the terms of the Brady Initiative (Urquidi 1994: 57).

The political meaning of the pact can be assessed in various ways. According to Cypher (1990: 196), 'the Pacto showed that de la Madrid and Salinas were willing to put the entire corporatist apparatus of the state into play in order to ensure that profit margins could be restored by way of further cuts in the real wage'. The political effect of the pact, according to this view, was the restoration of confidence of important business associations in the PRI. The subsequent shift (or return) to the PRI of business sectors that had previously supported the right-wing PAN was not unimportant considering the upcoming presidential elections in 1988. In partial contrast, however, Centeno (1994: 195–6) holds that the pact demonstrated 'the willingness and ability of the regime to control various social actors'. Although he admits that the costs of adjustment were borne mainly by the bottom two-thirds of the population, Centeno here refers to both the labour unions and private industry:

> As in the cases of the East Asian economies, the state demanded discipline not only from labour but also from capital ... The key to the success of the Pacto ... was the enforced cooperation of private industry. When the government did not receive the required cooperation from producers and retailers, it reportedly threatened major business leaders with sanctions, audits, and loss of government contracts.

SALINAS DE GORTARI: 1988–94 Whereas de la Madrid had at times been hesitant or reluctant to carry through restructuring policies, Salinas was much more straightforward. Under his administration, neoliberal reforms were extended and deepened, he introduced sweeping industrial and trade deregulation and stimulated foreign investment. Clearly, Salinas was more explicit in his choice of a free market economy, something that was reflected both in his political discourse and new-found 'ideology' of *liberalismo social* and in his actions, such as the large-scale privatization of state companies, the reform of Constitutional Article 27 and his negotiations for a free trade agreement with Canada and the USA (NAFTA). Obviously, the restructuring policy of de la Madrid had paved the way for such measures. Under Salinas, the trade liberalization programme, initiated under de la Madrid in 1985 was taken a step further. This was reflected in NAFTA, which after four years of negoti-ations came into effect on 1 January 1994. The treaty's main feature was the gradual removal of trade barriers and tariffs between the USA, Canada and Mexico. The barriers were not taken down instantly, since certain restrictions on intra-NAFTA trade remained. For instance, trade in agriculture, auto-mobiles, textiles and clothing was to be phased out over a period of 15 years (Weiss 1996: 65). For Mexico, an important aim of the free trade agreement was to attract further foreign investment. The objective was to modernize the productive assets of the Mexican economy by making use of the finance, technology and management skills of foreign investors. Foreign capital was needed to cover the growing trade imbalance (Weiss 1996). In return, foreign investors could benefit from Mexico's low labour costs and access to its domestic market. In 1992, for instance, average wages in the *maquiladora* (assembly plants) industry were only 15 per cent of those in US manufacturing (Hufbauer and Schott 1993).

Another important and controversial policy change initiated under Salinas was the opening of the agricultural sector to foreign competition. By re-forming Article 27 of the Mexican Constitution, the Salinas administration broke with the taboo – in political discourse at least – of not protecting the institution of the *ejido* enshrined in the 1917 Constitution. The key provisions of the reform were the ending of the land reform and land redistribution programme; the right of *ejiditarios* to sell, rent, sharecrop or mortgage their parcels (before these were inalienable) and the possibility for private capital to purchase former *ejido* holdings (Austin 1994: 327).[16]

The privatization of state companies was another important strand of the neoliberal experiment. Under Salinas large public enterprises were sold; these included the telecommunications company (TELMEX), two airlines (Aero-méxico, Mexicana), the large steel, fertilizer and sugar companies as well the commercial banks.[17] Whereas in 1982 there were 1,155 state-owned enterprises, in 1993 this number had dropped to little more than two hundred. According to Weiss (1996), the privatization experiment has a wider interpretation than simply the sale of public sector assets. In this wider context it refers to an opening up of new investment opportunities for the private sector in areas previously reserved for the state. Examples of this include the operation of toll roads by private firms and private investment in electricity generation (Weiss 1996: 68).

The economic crisis and the restructuring measures of the 1980s affected Mexicans from all walks of life. In 1989, GDP per capita was 9 per cent below its 1980 level, average real wages in manufacturing were down 24 per cent, and real minimum wages were down 49 per cent (Sheahan 1991). Between 1982 and 1994, real wages declined by 40.8 per cent. During the

1980s, according to official figures, extreme poverty increased by 4.4 per cent and overall poverty by 5.5 per cent (PRONASOL 1990).[18] Ironically, the number of billionaires in Mexico rose from two to 24 during the Salinas administration, and the assets of the richest Mexican came to total more than the combined annual income of the poorest 17 million. The share of national income corresponding to the richest 20 per cent of the population grew from 48.4 per cent to 54.2 per cent between 1984 and 1992. The poorest 20 per cent, in contrast, saw their share fall from 5 per cent to 4.3 per cent (Development Gap 1994).

As can be seen from the above, the restructuring measures and neoliberal reforms of the de la Madrid and Salinas administrations entailed a reorientation of the role of the state in the economy as well as a shift in perceptions on government responsibility. Both presidents, in their State of the Nation speeches, stressed the need for efficiency and individual responsibility. In his campaign speech in 1987, Salinas attacked what he called populism by stating: 'We have learned that populism hurts the interests of the majority and constitutes the worst enemy of our aspirations of the popular welfare.'[19] Although direct state intervention in the economy declined, the government's capacity to enforce new policies should not be underestimated. This is reflected in the role the government played in the pacts of 1987 and under the Salinas administration. How this new economic role of· the government affected the political position of the ruling party, the internal relations of the state elite, and state–society relations is discussed in the section below.

Political Consequences

The discussion on the political impact of the transition from an import substitution model of economic development to one focused on export promotion and free trade is complex. As we have seen, Mexico experienced numerous economic changes during the 1980s and 1990s. On the political level, shifts occurred as well. Contrasting developments can be perceived, combining a heightened prominence of opposition parties, popular mobilization, and greater electoral competitiveness, with strong presidentialism, (political) violence, and abuse of executive authority.[20] Identifying these economic and political shifts is not so difficult; linking them, however, is more tricky. A key issue, for instance, is whether certain political changes can be seen as the product of neoliberal reforms, or whether they derive from social or political developments that follow a logic distinct from transformations in the economic sphere. To put it boldly, should the electoral victories of the PAN on the state and municipal levels be attributed to the decline in state power, the crisis of the PRI, resulting from the 'neoliberal revolution' (declining state capacity)? Or are they the outcome of a long-term process of increased levels of urbanization, education and literacy, which now manifests itself in the ballot-box (citizenship, pluralism)? Obviously, the most sensible answer to this question would be 'both'. However, if we want to understand how neoliberalism affected Mexican politics, it is important to distinguish these kind of processes. A second problem in studying the relation between economic liberalism and political change is how to make a distinction between the effect of the economic crisis of the 1980s and that of the neoliberal reform policy. In this respect, it is often stated that it was the economic crisis of the 1980s more than any government effort to redefine the state's role in the economy and its interaction with society that shaped the actions of various elements of Mexican society (Brachet-Márquez 1992; Cook et al. 1994; Haber 1994).[21]

Generally, as a method for dealing with this problem, participants in the discussion on neoliberal reform and political change in Mexico apply an actor-oriented approach. For instance, Cook et al. (1994: 7–8) suggest an analytical approach that is focused on 'the shifts in state–society relations that have occurred in the context of economic restructuring and the redefinition of Mexico's long-term development strategy'. They hold, as do many others, that the post-1982 economic crisis and the ongoing process of economic restructuring eroded the regime's traditional bases of support and threatened the interests of key social actors. Further, the Salinas administration in particular is seen as having marked an important transition, in that it both implemented major economic changes and oversaw the initial transformation of the political coalition that had long supported post-revolutionary author-itarian rule. Hence the authors suggest examining both the pressures that gave rise to these coalitional changes and their political implications. Such an actor-oriented approach to the study of political change in an authoritarian regime would then permit 'a disaggregated examination of the intersection between economic and political opening, without assuming that democratisa-tion is necessarily the outcome'. So, in fact, the 'impact' of economic restructuring is assessed through the analysis of shifting patterns of interaction and political relationships, and the possible political repercussions of these shifts. These political (coalition) shifts are most often studied on two levels. First, studies are made of the growing disunity of Mexico's post-revolutionary governing coalition in the context of neoliberal reforms. Second, analysis focuses on the relation between neoliberal reform and the changing balance of state–society relations.

NEOLIBERALISM AND SHIFTS IN THE RULING COALITION The study of coalition shifts and conflicts in Mexico's governing elite can be useful in many respects. First of all, it helps to understand how we can account for the transition to neoliberalism. How is it possible that the same political party that since the 1930s had propagated a policy of 'revolutionary national-ism', a protected market and import substitution, in the 1980s suddenly made the shift to the celebration of the free market, competition and international integration? How can we account for such a process, how does it work? Is this the outcome of a battle of ideas, or is it the product of the rise of a group of new actors? Although it is clear that pressure exerted by both domestic capital and the international economy helped determine the Mexican government's policies, it would be too simple to reduce the state's role to nothing more than an instrument of a dominant capital group or given class. Or as Centeno (1994: 191) puts it: 'The important question is not whether capital forced the regime in a particular direction but why the government was willing to acquiesce.'

In most countries the adoption of neoliberal policy was identified with the rise of a certain political party, which often fiercely rejected (aspects of) the social democratic and Keynesian policies of the past. In Mexico, this shift took place within one and the same party, the PRI. Therefore, a study of coalition shifts and elite dynamics within the ruling party can provide insight into both the process of the 'rise of neoliberalism' and, consequently, the political implications of this policy shift.

In popular Mexican usage, the neoliberal reforms of the 1980s and 1990s are said to have increased the tensions between the (almost archetypal) *políticos* and *técnicos* within the state apparatus and the ruling party.[22] The *político*, or 'dinosaur' is generally portrayed as a bossy, pompous, often corrupt member of the party's old guard, who is terrified of losing his economic privileges. His counterpart, the *técnico*, is pictured as a young, pragmatic, US-educated politician eager for change and reform.[23] Recent studies on elite dynamics in Mexico by Camp (1990), Centeno and Maxfield (1992) and Centeno (1994) show the decline in the fortunes of the more traditional *políticos* and the rise of a new group of *técnicos* within the Mexican elite, marked by the selection of de la Madrid in 1982 and Salinas in 1988 and their subsequent personnel appointments. Centeno's analysis of the Mexican ruling elite based on social origins, education, political activity and professional experience shows the rise of a new technocratic elite.[24] This group consists mainly of second-generation PRI politicians, with fathers in the political and economic elite. Many members of the new elite have studied economics in UNAM or at private universities (especially ITAM and Colegio de México) and obtained postgraduate degrees from elite schools in the USA. They have been politically active in the national level of the PRI, but mostly in the 'technical' branch (the Institute of Political, Economic and Social Studies: IEPES) or shadow cabinet around the president elect. Their career patterns are characterized by entry into the bureaucracy at high levels, allowing them to skip long in-stitutional apprenticeships. They are concentrated in those organizations in charge of planning, particularly the Ministry of Planning and Budget (SPP) (before 1992). Despite the smaller number of professional years (the result of their relative youth), they exhibit more institutional mobility and are less bound to specific bureaucratic territories (Centeno 1994: 107). Technocrats clearly dominated the de la Madrid administration, and again in the Salinas cabinet comprised the largest group.

In general, the rise of this new elite – the technocrats – is closely related to three processes. First, it can be related to the increasing complexity of the modern economy and the need for technical experts. This is not a new idea. As early as 1964, Schmitter and Haas underlined the link between the rise of *técnicos* and Mexico's integration in the Latin American economy. However, the nature of the economic crisis that Mexico faced in the 1980s and the importance of managing the debt significantly increased the power of financial experts. 'Mexico's planners and financiers were able to provide (or appeared to provide) a solution to the two central problems facing the regime: the legitimacy crisis originating in the exhaustion of the import substitution industrialisation and the financial pressures brought about by the debt crisis after 1982' (Centeno and Maxfield 1992: 78). Apart from this economic variable, political factors played an important role in the rise of the new group of policy-makers.

The rise of the technocratic elite is closely linked to the growing power of the Presidential Office, the SPP, and the party think-tank IEPES.[25] Over the past decades, an institutional change has taken place in Mexico in favour of these agencies and away from the Ministry of the Interior and the PRI. Those individuals who are now being referred to as technocrats have profited most from this power shift, often through careful political calculation and loyalty to the 'right' – that is, the successful – *camarilla*.[26] This institutional change is generally traced back to the Echeverría administration (1970–76). Echeverría is seen to have initiated the modern-day version of presidentialism in Mexico, characterized by the centralization of power in the executive office, and away from the party.[27] Until the Díaz Ordáz administration (1964–70) there had always been a close relationship between the president and the party. Mexican presidents generally started their political careers in the PRI and served in a variety of political/administrative posts before they reached the highest position as head of the executive. Under Echeverría this close relationship began to weaken. During his term of office Echeverría was in conflict with both the political and the technical sector of the bureaucracy. On the one hand he wanted to distance himself as much as possible from the repression of 1968 (the Tlatelolco massacre) and therefore replaced many of the traditional *políticos* with a younger generation of men. On the other hand, officials (or *técnicos*) from the Bank of Mexico and the Treasury (SHCP) opposed the president's plans for increased state intervention. As a result. Echeverría declared that from that time on 'economic policy is made at Los Pinos' (the presidential palace). Consequently, during his administration Echeverría successfully managed partially to move power over finances to the presidency and the newly created SPP.[28] In addition, bureaucrats within the SPP used their control over the federal budget to take over many functions of the Ministry of the Interior. In sum, Echeverría remoulded the civil service to fit his own needs and aspirations. In addition, he brought in a new generation of bureaucrats, giving impetus to the rise of a new ruling elite. The SPP became the nursery for the future elite. For instance, both de la Madrid and Salinas came from the SPP, and half of Salinas' cabinet previously worked there. Echeverría, in fact, initiated a new trend: '(I)n economic crisis the president would bypass the party and establish a direct, personal relationship with the corporatist structure itself. In troubled times, the president could go beyond the party and exercise a "personal style of government"' (Dresser 1994: 136). It is often claimed that Salinas, in particular, followed the same strategy. When in the late 1980s and early 1990s the PRI failed as a political legitimator, Salinas placed the responsibility for generating consensus on the presidency itself (Dresser 1994). Like Echeverría, he cultivated the image of a 'man of the people', placing all hope and attention on the president, away from the (troubled) party. Due to this rise of the power of the presidency, since Echeverría, finding access to the presidential *camarilla* has become an extremely important criterion for political success.

What now can be seen as the main political implications of the rise of this new group within Mexico's governing elite during the 1980s and 1990s? First, among the issues mentioned by Centeno and Maxfield, ideological homogeneity is pointed out as an important political implication and characteristic of the new governing elite. Free markets and international integration are seen as the most important ingredients for Mexico's development.

Another important implication of the rise of the neoliberal faction in the governing coalition was the split-off movement within the PRI, named the Democratic Current (CD). Important members of this group were Cuauhtémoc Cárdenas (son of the former president Cárdenas) and Porfirio Muñoz Ledo, who later became central figures in the left-wing opposition party, the Party of the Democratic Revolution (PRD). At first, the CD pleaded for internal party reform and a more equitable model of economic development, and presented itself as a critical, democratic current within the party. However, when Cárdenas was excluded from participation in the race for nomination as presidential candidate, and de la Madrid picked Salinas as his successor, Cárdenas, Muñoz Ledo and other members of the CD broke with the PRI and founded the PRD. Many observers saw this alienation of traditional PRI supporters and the split in the governing elite as an important reason for the PRI's electoral débâcle in 1988. Not surprisingly, the PRD was quick to capitalize on the PRI's retreat from its earlier promises of social justice and redistribution. In his 1988 campaign, Cárdenas defended state intervention, fiercely criticized government austerity measures and extensively claimed his personal identification with revolutionary nationalist policy positions (Dresser 1994; Cook et al. 1994: 21). In fact, in the long term, one could claim that the rise of the technocratic elite and the consequent coalition shifts within Mexico's ruling elite led to increased electoral competition, caused by the establishment of a split-off movement.

A third consequence of the rise of the neoliberal faction within the ruling elite and the top level of the PRI was the splintering of the PRI itself. In this respect, the 1988 elections are often seen as the PRI's 'wake-up call' (Dresser 1994). The outcome of the elections and the strength of the opposition painfully revealed the incapacity of the party (and its corporatist machine) to deliver votes, particularly in the urban areas. As a result, Salinas, soon after taking office, initiated a 'modernization' of the party, starting with the designating of Luis Donaldo Colosio as PRI president. Colosio and his group of 'neo-priístas'[29] had to renovate the party, starting with the reform of the candidate selection process and the creation of a new electoral base, as a way to 'open up the party'. Though many of the 'modernization reforms' proved to be largely symbolic and often 'neo-priístas' merely donned modernizing masks because they believed it may help their political careers, it did create severe tensions within the party (see Dresser 1994). Often conflicts flared up within the party between the pro- and anti-reform groups, between the renovators and the party's old guard. The latter felt they were being attacked on two fronts: by the government's neoliberal reforms (wage austerity, privatizations, declining state resources) and by the modernization of the party (sectoral leaders had to give up their monopoly on interest representation).[30]

Two other issues need mentioning here. Rather than political implications of the technocratization of Mexico's political elite these are processes that were closely related to the rise of the new elite. The first issue concerns the growing rift between the administrative spheres of government, that is, the economic cabinet and the PRI. As we have seen, the centre of political decision-making shifted from the political areas of government (Ministry of the Interior, the PRI) to the financial and planning areas (Finance, Budget and Planning, IEPES). This institutional shift away from the party is often interpreted as having seriously undermined the 'historic alliance' between the executive and the official party.

The second phenomenon, which is closely related to the one above, is the connection of the rise of the technocratic elite with the growth of the power of the presidency. Both processes generally are traced back to the Echeverría administration during the 1970s. Generally, it is claimed that although presidentialism has always been an important characteristic of post-revolutionary Mexico, it became much more pronounced after 1970. Under de la Madrid, and even more so under Salinas, presidentialism flourished.

In conclusion, during the past two decades Mexico has seen the rise of a new technocratic elite that supports a neoliberal view of development, a strengthening of the presidency and the financial sectors of the bureaucracy, and a growing rift between the party and the executive. The traditional sectors in the bureaucracy have been weakened. The analysis of shifts within Mexico's elite coalition helps us to understand both how the transition to a neoliberal model of development came about and what the political implications of this shift are. However, the above discussion is limited to internal political changes within the top level. Clearly, the shift to neoliberalism had an effect on the relations between the ruling elite and its constituency, and, in a broader context, between state and society, an issue to which I now turn my attention.

NEOLIBERALISM AND THE TRANSFORMATION OF STATE–SOCIETY RELATIONS Generally, scholars agree on the idea that the transition from an import-substitution model of development to a neoliberal model implied a reordering of the coalition of social actors supporting the Mexican regime. However, opinions differ on what exactly are and will be the political implications of this change. Both the economic crisis and neoliberal reforms are thought to have 'eroded the regime's traditional bases of support' (Cook et al. 1994); 'strained the legitimacy of the ruling elite' (Klesner 1994); made the 'PRI lose ground as a legitimator of the regime' (Dresser 1994); 'created a series of ideological problems for the regime' (Whitehead 1994) and led to 'the decline of corporatism as a system of support' (Morris 1993). However, it is important to note the 'time factor' as an element shaping the above discussion. Theoretical interpretations of Mexican politics were often heavily influenced by the 'politics of the moment'. For instance, in the late 1980s, the academic discussion on Mexico's political future was dominated by the idea that the PRI would not survive its severe crisis of legitimacy and representation. Hence ideas emerged on the relationship between economic liberalization and the formation of democracy. In contrast, throughout the Salinas administration it became apparent that, in part, the regime was able to come up with solutions, or, at least, responses to this crisis. By that time, ideas had emerged on the 'transformation of state–society relations' and on neocorporatism and neoclientelism. In this section we look at a number of issues that are repeatedly stressed in the discussion on neoliberalism and state–society relations in Mexico: i.e. corporatism, clientelism and political liberalization. Here these earlier-discussed aspects of Mexican authoritarianism are viewed in the light of neoliberal transformation.

NEOLIBERALISM AND CORPORATISM The economic restructuring of the Mexican economy, the harsh austerity measures and the public spending cuts of the 1980s are thought to have seriously damaged the system of authoritarian-corporatism as it had operated in Mexico for decades. The de la Madrid attempt to restore the troubled economy depended on such measures as wage controls, a reduced budget for social programmes, the elimination and reduction of subsidies, and the stifling of labour demands. Many of these policies, focused on reducing the state's presence in key areas of the economy, cut to the core of Mexico's redistributive coalitions and system of corporatism. As mentioned before, the success of Mexican corporatism heavily depended on the 'give and take' principle. The corporate structures granted control to the state but also gave tangible benefits to the sectors. Due to economic growth and plentiful resources there was always the possibility that every group would have (part of) its demands met. However, with the economic crisis and the shift from a state-led to a private-led economy, state resources declined and important segments within the PRI coalition – such as organized labour and bureaucrats – stopped receiving their usual shares of the economic pie. The impact of these changes is assessed in various ways. A number of authors claim that the adoption of a market economy is fundamentally incompatible with corporatism. They hold that neoliberalism will force the political system to democratize (Roett 1993; Rubio 1993; Delal Baer 1993). Others perceive, rather than the emerging of a more democratic system, the establishment of neocorporatist and neoclientelist forms of state–society relations (De la Garza Toledo 1994; Harvey 1993; Bízberg 1993).

Both Rubio and Delal Baer believe that Mexico will embrace democracy in the not too distant future. Both hold the shift to a free market economy as being largely responsible for democratization. Although they admit the capacity of the bureaucracy and the sectors to postpone the democratization of Mexico's political system, they see plenty of reasons for this eventually to happen: the evolution of civil society, the modernization of the PRI and the skills of both the de la Madrid and Salinas administrations. Their basic argument is as follows. Economic liberalization reduces the role of government in the economy. The Mexican economic reform is decentralizing decision-making and gradually decoupling the economy from single-party control by the PRI. Political diversity has emerged as a result of the decline of corporatist organizations, the displacement of party apparatchiks, privatization, deregulation, and trade liberalization. Mexican society finds itself less dependent on a state-driven economy, and, as a result, less beholden to political authorities (Delal Baer 1993: 51). Rubio stresses how economic reform and a free market economy stimulate political participation and create a democratic political culture. As an example, he points at the impact of neoliberalism on consumers and the workplace. In contrast to a closed, protectionist economy, a free economy is characterized by a greater supply of (consumer) goods and services. The possibility to choose from a variety of brands of the same article gives the consumer a feeling of freedom and independence. According to Rubio, the growth of consumer options has a political significance. For why participate in decisions at the shop level but not at the city, state or national levels? Freedom of choice in the supermarket is only a small step away from freedom at the ballot-box. 'Intentionally or not, economic liberalisation brings a transformation of the entire political structure of the country. The relationship between economic liberalisation and the formation of democracy is not direct, immediate, or automatic, but it is absolute' (Rubio 1993: 41). Accordingly, it is pointed out how economic reforms eroded important characteristics of the traditional political system, such as corporatism and clientelism. For instance, fiscal austerity and privatization were not compatible with the demands for patronage and special favours from certain politicians and bureaucrats. 'The introduction of market forces and privatisation interfered with the lucrative manipulation of the Mexican economy for personal ends' (Delal Baer 1993: 54). With the benefit of hindsight, this very optimistic reading of the influence of neoliberal reform seems rather naive: by the mid-1990s the Salinas family, for instance, had become widely know for its involvement in corruption and drugs trafficking. The positive interpretation of developments in Mexican politics was most probably coloured by the years following the 1991 elections: Salinas' prestige was rising, the NAFTA negotiations would soon be concluded, and the promising Luis Donaldo Colosio was picked as the new candidate for president. Salinas was praised for his efforts to engage the PRI in 'a self-restructuring tailored to the realities of a market economy' (Delal Baer 1993: 56). According to this interpretation of Mexican politics, the party embraced the objective of winning votes and electoral competition, making a shift away from corporatism and toward the linking with grassroots organization (concertación). Next, it was claimed that under Salinas a new legitimating doctrine was formulated, one compatible with a market economy, and the relationship with business was restored (privatization of the banks, NAFTA). Furthermore, anti-corruption acts such as the arrest of La Quina, the leader of the oil workers' union, were valued as restoring relations with the alienated middle classes. Through the social self-help programme PRONASOL, Salinas made social policy 'compatible' with economic reform. So, according to Delal Baer (1993: 60), the PRI had transformed itself from a corporatist party entrenched in a government-owned economy to a geographically based party focused on electoral turnout in an open economy. Economic reform, efficiency and market forces had replaced patronage and corporatism. Only because the PRI engaged in a process of self-demolition and self-reconstruction was it able to withstand the corrosive effects of economic market reform. Because of this success, especially if it was to be accompanied by economic growth, Delal Baer mentions the possibility that the PRI will continue to govern Mexico in the future, but always in a more open and democratic context.

The idea that neoliberalism has seriously eroded the old power structures such as corporatism and clientelism is widely shared among Mexicanists. However, opinions differ on whether these structures have been replaced by more competitive and democratic forms of state–society relations. In particular, presidentialism and neocorporatism are seen as new mechanisms of control. Dresser (1994: 136), for instance, claims that the neoliberal policies seriously undermined the PRI's corporatist structure and hegemonic status. The dismantling process that was begun by de la Madrid harmed the party in several ways: it became unable to meet the demands of its corporate sectors, which were accustomed to a flow of material benefits, and, powerless to guarantee electoral victories, the PRI lost ground as a legitimator of the regime. However, other phenomena, which are overlooked by both Rubio and Delal Baer, took place simultaneously, that is, the growth of the power of the presidency and the rise of neocorporatism. With the party failing as a legitimator, Salinas placed the responsibility for generating consensus on the presidency itself. Examples of this are both the Economic Solidarity Pacts (PSE/PECE) and the PRONASOL programme. Although the pacts initially were set up as a concerted effort of productive sectors to reduce high inflation rates and stabilize the Mexican economy, they soon became political instruments for governance in the hands of the president. 'Under the pact, the president and his economic team map out goals, negotiate their timing and implementation with representatives of business associations, and then use the institutional arena provided by the pact to inform labour of agreed-upon decisions' (Dresser 1994: 138). This new kind of 'elite corporatism' eroded the power and influence of sectoral leaders: it took away their power to negotiate wage increases and placed it in the hands of the executive branch. In effect, Dresser concludes, the president and his economic team have taken over the alliances previously forged by the PRI.

De la Garza Toledo (1994) claims something similar. He states that Mexico made the transition from a 'social authoritarian' style of development to a 'neoliberal authoritarian' style. Although the 1980s are often pictured as a period in which Mexico experienced the transition from a social-corporatist state to a neoliberal state, De la Garza Toledo points out that, as in most other countries, the 'neoliberal consensus is not fully formed'. Although the state is less proprietary, it has remained strong. The state deregulates and privatizes, but not totally. From the perspective of Salinas' ideology of social liberalism, democracy is not limited to the individual, but it includes space for corporatist organizations (as in Salinas' 1992 statement that 'the PRI is a party of citizens and of organisations and sectors') (de la Garza Toledo 1994: 200).[31] Although unions are included in the decision-making process, their influence has declined substantially.[32] The state's relationship with unions has become more authoritarian, with less negotiation than before.[33] In addition, a shift took place in the character of union–state relations: away from the PRI and various state institutions toward a more direct relationship with the presidency. De la Garza Todelo concludes that Mexican corporatism has changed, not disappeared. For most 'official' labour organizations, this change included a loss of influence in politics, economic and social security policy-making, conflict management, and industrial relations, all areas in which they were once prominent.

NEOLIBERALISM AND CLIENTELISM In the discussion on neoliberalism and the transformation of state–society relations in Mexico, the issue of clientelism is repeatedly stressed. On the one hand, it is claimed that neoliberal reforms, free markets, competition and efficiency seriously limited the room for patronage and ended clientelist relationships. On the other hand, authors claim that increased presidentialism, increased income inequality and the loss of certain social rights have provided a fertile environment for personalism and unstable bargaining relationships.

As mentioned above, from the moment Salinas took office, he actively attempted to transform state–society relations in Mexico. The efforts of the Salinas administration to reduce state regulation and change the social and economic role of the state were interpreted by many observers as necessary steps towards modernizing the country and bringing the state apparatus into line with the neoliberal development model (Delal Baer 1993). However, other, more critical, observers saw the government's policy changes and state reforms as driven by political interests and partisan electoral considerations (Bailey 1994; Dresser 1991; Cook et al. 1994). Clearly, Salinas came to office at a particularly difficult time: the 1988 election results showed both the public's serious dissatisfaction with the PRI and the threat of the leftist PRD, a party that had successfully taken over important parts of the PRI's traditional constituency among workers and the urban poor. The 1988 elections also revealed other issues. It became clear that the party's corporatist machine had proved incapable of delivering votes, especially in the urban areas. The political framework of corporatism could no longer cover the increasingly heterogeneous Mexican society, consisting of a great diversity of groups such as slum-dwellers, informal sector workers, yuppies, urban middle classes and migrants. Further, as in the case of the oil workers' union, conflicts between union bosses and government technocrats over economic restructuring came to a point that the former withdrew their support for the PRI in the 1988 elections.[34]

In sum, in order to regain political legitimacy and continue the neoliberal restructuring programme, new relations with groups in society had to be created. Two of the most well-known examples of Salinas' attempt to renew state–society relations – apart from his restoration of relations with the Catholic Church and the 'modernization' of the PRI – were his *concertación social* and the PRONASOL programme. The strategy of *concertación* was especially focused on, and relations were established between independent peasant and urban popular movements and the Salinas administration. *Concertación* was to represent a new form of state–society relations in which the state established problem-solving partnerships with social organizations (Cook et al. 1994: 30). By advocating *concertación*, Salinas tried to stress the government's willingness to open a dialogue with groups that had previously been excluded from policy circles. A critical assessment of the *concertación* policy stresses that it was also used as a strategy to isolate popular movements from the PRD, as demands were negotiated through the direct intervention of the president (as happened with the Popular Defense Committee (CDP) in Durango). Another critique is that the policy was used to create a form of neo-corporatism. For instance, in the labour sector *concertación social* was used to support the leader of the Mexican Telephone Workers' Union (STRM) in his desire to form a new labour federation that was equipped to compete with the long-dominant CTM (see Harvey 1993; Cook et al. 1994; Haber 1994; Demmers and Hogenboom 1992).

The National Solidarity Programme (PRONASOL) is by far Salinas' most discussed attempt to transform state–society relations in Mexico. The official description of PRONASOL presents it as an efficient poverty-alleviation programme that sought to transform state–society relations by encouraging citizens to design and implement community development and public works projects. The programme was set up to support those groups and individuals that had been the most hurt by the harsh austerity measures of the 1980s and the shift in development strategy, such as small farmers, workers and the urban poor. In contrast to traditional corporatist relations, PRONASOL embodied a 'new' relationship with society, emphasizing self-help, community participation and limited bureaucracy. Instead of establishing top-down bureaucratic structures, the programme aimed to build on representative local organizations in both urban and rural areas (see Dresser 1991; Cook et al. 1994: 30). However, critics of the programme point out how PRONASOL funds were used for political purposes. They emphasize the unequal amount of funds that Salinas channelled to areas where voters had supported Cárdenas in 1988, undermining the opposition (Molinar Horcasitas 1994). Further, in some areas programme administrators imposed political conditions on PRONASOL funding, thus continuing old forms of clientelism and repression (Haber 1994). In addition, PRONASOL is said to have had a depoliticizing and demobilizing effect: 'PRONASOL provided incentives for autonomous organisations to focus on local community development projects, rather than on national political demands or the construction of independent political alliances' (Cook et al. 1994: 31). As with the *concertación* policy, negotiations with the government were limited to strictly 'technical', not political, issues. Moreover, PRONASOL reinforced presidentialism. The close personal identification of Salinas with the programme led many critics to accuse the president of trying to create his own political party outside the PRI. Indeed, the programme was set up in such a way that requests for funding were to be directed to the president's office, circumventing both the state bureaucracy and local *priístas*. Salinas' personalistic style of governing and his use of executive powers to reshape relations with society is claimed to have encouraged leaders of (mass) organizations and union leaders to develop relations with the president rather than with the PRI (Haber 1994; Cook et al. 1994: 33). In general, social actors' increased dependence upon personalized relations with the president for organizational gains and survival indicates a serious weakening of key political institutions, especially the ruling party. Rather than reflecting a broad commitment to political beliefs such as those embodied in revolutionary nationalism or a pragmatic set of calculations regarding long-term political inclusion (such as state-subsidized organizations; claims of a 'right' to political representation in the PRI), such ties to the federal executive increasingly reflect momentary, highly pragmatic, inherently unstable 'alliances' based on specific bargaining relationships. This causes many critics to conclude that, in fact, with the implementation of PRO-NASOL the state moved from constitutional guarantees to labour (Article

123) and the poor (Article 3, 27) to vague promises of 'solidarity' (Cook et al. 1994: 33; Bailey 1994).

POLITICAL LIBERALIZATION   As mentioned at various points in the above discussion, one of the effects of the neoliberal reforms was that the PRI had to compete with other political parties in a more open political arena. Political and electoral reforms, both implemented under de la Madrid and Salinas, made it possible for opposition parties to win elections on municipal and even on state levels. For instance, in 1989 the PAN broke the PRI's monopoly on state governments by winning the elections in Baja California, and later the party won control over the state governments of Chihuahua and Guanajuato and a number of important cities, including Mexicali, Oaxaca, Zamora, Hermosillo, Ciudad Juárez and the capital of Yucatán, Mérida. Importantly, the PRD won the mayoral elections of Mexico City in 1997. Traditionally, the PRI drew electoral support from the Mexican countryside, unionized urban and industrial workers, public employees and sections of the urban middle classes. However, after the early 1970s, the transformation of Mexican society, which had grown increasingly complex due to increasing urbanization and rising educational levels, slowly eroded the PRI's traditional bases of electoral support and the party's capacity to attract urban middle-class voters. Besides, the political reform of 1977 made competition from opposition parties possible.[35] However, authors generally agree that it was the massive popular discontent with the government's economic austerity measures and the social costs of the neoliberal reforms of the 1980s and 1990s that produced heightened support for the opposition and that can be seen as the starting-point of anti-authoritarian mobilization (Klesner 1994; Cook et al. 1994; Loaeza 1994).

Both the de la Madrid and Salinas administrations responded to the increased electoral mobilization with a series of fragmentary political liberalization reforms. For instance, the de la Madrid administration resorted to a regulated political opening, which produced the 1986 Federal Electoral Code. Subsequent openings in the form of electoral reforms (in 1989, 1990, 1993, 1994 and 1996) gradually expanded the channels for independent participation and representation. Whereas certain scholars and Mexicanists see in these political liberalization reforms (and in the growing electoral successes of the opposition, particularly the PAN) a clear sign that Mexico is on its way towards democracy, others warn that political liberalization should not be mistaken for democratization. They claim that in Mexico, instead of a transitional formula, political liberalization has been a means of restoring political balance (Loaeza 1994: 106; Molinar Horcasitas 1994).[36] The strategy of granting limited liberalizing reforms in response to the demands of independent or opposition groups was applied by the Mexican government as early as the 1960s. 'If democratisation were the result of a cumulative process of liberalising measures, Mexican authoritarianism would have been dismantled long ago,' Loaeza (1994: 107) remarks with some irony. In contrast to democratization, political liberalization is a reversible process: the governing elite maintains control over the process of change. In this case, although changes may occur in response to demands from below, it remains a project directed from above. It is marked by a low degree of institutionalization (see Loaeza 1994: 107–10). The political liberalization reforms of the past decade have had a clear impact on Mexican politics. Electoral outcomes on the state and municipal levels have become less predictable. Whereas in the past nomination by the PRI was a certain route to power, in most regions in Mexico this is no longer the case. However, although political participation and competition have increased, forces and tactics that are not part of the formal process can still determine outcomes (Loaeza 1994: 106). This is reflected in, for instance, the way the government treats opposition parties. The Salinas administration was much more willing to accept electoral victories by the conservative PAN than by the leftist PRD. Moreover, the concentrated power of the federal executive and the persistence of close links between the state apparatus and the PRI continue to limit fair political competition. In addition, the low degree of institutionalization made it possible for the regime to apply different rules and strategies to different groups. This arbitrary attitude was reflected in that under Salinas a relatively open relationship between state elites and urban popular movements contrasted with a more closed environment for labour unions; electoral competitiveness was combined with increased repression of leftist opposition; and the improved interaction between the state and independent social actors contrasted with the limited tolerance for militant political activity (Cook et al. 1994).

Continuity and Change

Mexico's neoliberal restructuring has been accompanied by substantial shifts and changes in the country's political system. Among the most important are the rise of a new technocratic governing elite, more vigorous party competition, a growing rift between the executive and the PRI, and the strengthening of presidentialism. Moreover, opposition parties have developed a stronger organizational presence in many regions, the traditional corporatist structures have been eroded, and the private sector has gained political weight, whereas the unions' negotiation capacity declined. The regime attempted to create a new 'modernized' relationship with the increasingly pluralistic Mexican society with the help of *concertación social* and the PRONASOL programme.

Although a number of scholars see in these political shifts and changes proof of fundamental regime change and the democratization of Mexico's political system, the majority of Mexicanists discussed in this chapter reject this idea. Their cases illustrate how traditional clientelist and corporatist mechanisms of control were reproduced and modernized under the Salinas administration. Very much in line with what happened in the rest of Latin

America, populist policies were replaced by neopopulist ones, or, as is discussed in this chapter, clientelist and corporatist relations made way for neoclientelism and neocorporatism. What conclusions can we draw from this? Apparently, the shift from a model of development based on ISI to a neoliberal model did not involve a fundamental change in political style: in the way of doing politics. Populism in Mexico was stripped of its socio-economic characteristics of the 1930s–1970s period: 'populism' even became a dirty word in the 1990s. Nevertheless, the political characteristics of populism lived on, and even flourished in the neoliberal era: the personalist charismatic leadership, the seemingly direct, quasi-personal way of reaching the masses, the bypassing of established intermediary organizations, they were all (still) there. In many ways, Salinas was the quintessential 'populist leader'. Casually dressed in leather jacket, he toured the country, promoting his 'Solidarity' programme, visiting remote areas, being 'a man of the people', very much in the footsteps of his (classic) populist predecessors Lázaro Cárdenas and Echeverría. Salinas strengthened the power of the executive and presidentialism. Playing 'political hardball' he arrested powerful union leaders, removed state governors, and became closely associated with the poverty-alleviation programme PRONASOL. And, despite repeated critiques, Salinas' 'neopopulist' strategy was successful. Although he is now one of the most mocked Mexican politicians, at the time he was popular, as was his 'hope-generating' Solidarity programme. Whereas the 1988 presidential elections had been highly contentious, in the mid-term elections of 1991 the PRI showed much better results, and in 1994 Ernesto Zedillo managed to win the election with (presumably) low levels of fraud.

After Salinas' dramatic downfall and the severe economic crises of the late 1990s, neopopulism lives on in Mexico. Capitalizing on the PRI's 'betrayal of the people', opposition parties such as the Christian Democratic PAN are now flirting with populism (Knight 1998: 247; Demmers 1998). Meanwhile, Cuauthémoc Cárdenas, the embodiment of Mexican populism, after a serious defeat in the 1994 elections, managed to win the mayorship of Mexico City in 1997. Clearly, populism – that is, populism as a political style – is not dead and buried along with ISI. Instead, as is shown in this book, both in practice and in theory, Latin American populism is still full of vitality.

Notes

1. In general terms, the *cacique* can be seen as a local (male) leader linked to political patrons at a higher level, who maintains his own power by winning resources from above for the communities he represents (Gledhill 1994: 109).

2. This period is often divided into two development models. First, Mexico's public policy was characterized by the model of Stabilizing Development (1940s–1960s), in which private capital played a leading role in generating economic growth, and the government's economic role was limited to assuring a stable exchange rate, a favourable fiscal climate and protectionism. A crucial element of Stabilizing Development was the idea of trickle-

down growth. Under Echeverría, and after the political crisis of 1968, this model was replaced by a new one called Shared Development. Echeverría rapidly enlarged the scope of government activity and increased the size of the bureaucracy. During this *sexenio* (1970–76), the state almost replaced the private sector as the major economic investor. Under López Portillo (1976–82), a return was made to a more orthodox economic policy. However, due to the oil boom and the related possibilities to obtain unprecedented foreign credits, the late 1970s were marked by the expansion of the state's role in the economy and an increase in public sector participation (Centeno 1994: 177–89).

3. For years, the ISI model was very successful. Between 1940 and 1960, the GDP more than tripled. During the 1960s, Mexico achieved a per capita growth rate of 3.3 per cent per year. By the late 1970s, manufacturing had come to represent nearly 40 per cent of national output. This became known as the 'Mexican miracle', a combination of both political stability and economic progress, exemplary in the developing world (Cornelius et al. 1989: 4).

4. Since the 1930s, no economic, social or political field in Mexico has been free of state intervention. Important sectors under direct control of the Mexican state were tele-communications, petroleum, energy and the railroads. On the eve of the 1982 economic crisis, there were 1,155 state-owned enterprises (Romero and Méndez 1990: 193). The state mediated relations between labour and capital, provided health care for over 50 per cent of the population, and controlled half of the arable land through the *ejido* system. By 1982, government expenditure represented 46.1 per cent of GDP (Dresser 1994: 126–7).

5. For instance, conflicts flared up in the Economic Cabinet between structuralists, who wanted to stimulate production and reorganize consumption and distribution through state action, and monetarists, who were primarily interested in monetary controls and who opposed increased state intervention in the economy. The two groups especially disagreed on the size of the government deficits that were being financed with new foreign loans (Centeno 1994: 187).

6. Centeno (1994: 32) describes the Mexican regime as an 'electoral-bureaucratic authoritarian regime'.

7. Reyna argues that there is no single model, or pure type, of corporatism. He defines corporatism as 'the "nuclearization" of politically significant groups in society through a complex network of political organizations relating those groups to the decision-making process. A corporatist political structure tends to eliminate competition for power and emphasize conciliation among different societal groups through the vertical or subordinated relationship to the state apparatus' (Reyna 1977: 155–6).

8. Of course, other interpretations are available on corporatism and clientelism in Mexico. However, I consider the assessments of Reyna and Kaufman to be rather commendable.

9. Przeworski refers here both to the 'capitalist South' and to the former communist countries in the East.

10. See on the origins of the Mexican debt crisis and the role of various interest groups Urquidi 1994: 56; Cypher 1990: 171–4.

11. The two policy instruments that are generally used to stabilize an economy in crisis are 1) the level of the government budget deficit and 2) the exchange rate. Both these mechanisms are central to policy in Mexico. At the beginning of the 1980s government deficits were too high, and this stimulated inflation, depressed private investment and created unsustainable external debts. Also, the exchange rate had become significantly overvalued (see Weiss 1996: 59–64).

12. See on external pressures (World Bank) and internal pressures (industrial and financial groups in Mexico) Cypher 1990: 188–9.

13. Despite high interest rates, the inflation rate averaged 88 per cent per year between 1982 and 1988 (calculated from data presented in Lustig 1992, table 2.4 in Cook et al. 1994: 15). In 1987, inflation stood at roughly 159 per cent, even higher than that achieved in the tumultuous days of 1982 (Cypher 1990: 195).

14. The two supporting pillars of the Economic Solidarity Pact (PSE) were the new external loans recently accumulated under the Baker plan (about US$13 billion gross) and the rigorous contraction of public sector spending up to the point where an actual primary fiscal surplus would be generated equal to about 8 per cent of GDP.

15. Under Salinas the PSE was replaced by the basically similar Pact for Stability and Economic Growth, the PECE.

16. See on the Article 27 reforms Gledhill 1996; Jones 1996.

17. The selling off of commercial banks, which had been nationalized in 1982, was of special importance for (international) confidence-building, since it completed the series of policy reversals since the crisis years of the early 1980s (Weiss 1996: 67).

18. In 1979, 7.7 per cent of children between the ages of one and four in rural areas suffered from severe malnutrition. The figure today is more than double that, while between 1982 and 1990 the number dying of malnutrition rose by 220 per cent (INEGI, Secretaría de Salud, Sexto Informe, Salinas de Gortari, 1994).

19. Campaign Speech, 11 November 1987. Quoted in Salinas de Gortari, *Tesis de Campaña: Ideas y Compromisos*, Mexico, PRI, 1988.

20. For instance, in the first two years under Salinas more state governors were removed than in any administration since that of Miguel Alemán (1946–52) (Camp 1993: 27).

21. Haber (1994), for instance, shows how the economic crisis of the 1980s and the de la Madrid administration's disregard of the housing needs, particularly after the 1985 Mexico City earthquake, gave a strong impulse to the formation of some of Mexico's strongest urban popular movements.

22. The division of the Mexican ruling elite into *técnicos* and *políticos* stems from the 1960s.

23. In academic literature, the *político–técnico* division is often used to distinguish differences in career patterns and ideological guidelines. In this usage, the *político* is characterized by loyalty to the PRI and political experience (elections), whereas the *técnico* is valued for (technical) expertise and bureaucratic experience. Ideologically, they are different in that *políticos* cling to the ideals of the revolution as a means to maintain government legitimacy, whereas *técnicos* believe legitimacy is served best through professional administration and the use of technical – as opposed to political – guidelines for decision-making.

24. Centeno's analysis is based on samples of government officials made up of all those at the director-general level or above, in 1983, 1986 and 1989. Additional information is taken from Roderic Camp, *Mexican Political Biographies, 1935–1981* (1982), Tucson: University of Arizona Press.

25. See for information on IEPES (later Cambio XXI) Centeno and Maxfield 1992: 69.

26. The *camarilla* is a political clique, largely formed on the basis of personal contact or friendship (see Camp 1990).

27. Before that time, to put it simply, Mexico had been run by, on the one hand the president, representing the *políticos* and serving as a 'minister of politics' and, on the other hand the secretary of the treasury, representing the *técnicos* and serving as 'minister of economics' (Kaufman, 1979; Centeno and Maxfield 1992). These two sectors, political and technical, within the bureaucracy were each responsible for their own aspect of governance and respected the other's domain. 'This balance of power was disrupted during the Echeverría administration, which led to a loss of influence by both the political and technical wings of the bureaucracy and their replacement by a critical third group of political

technocrats which grew along with the power of the presidency' (Centeno and Maxfield 1992: 79).

28. The SPP combined the old Office of the Presidency with the programming and expenditure budgeting functions of the SHCP. It was meant to replace a more centralized, presidentially controlled form of decision-making for the inter-ministerial coordination between Commerce, the SHCP and SEMIP. The creation of the SPP was seen as an assault on the power and autonomy of other ministries since it gave the SPP centralized control over all expenditures. The SPP's increasingly important political role has earned it unofficial status as the fourth sector of the PRI, in addition to the CNC, the CTM and the CNOP (Centeno and Maxfield 1992: 83; Bailey 1988).

29. Dresser (1994: 134) describes 'neo-priístas' as being based on the assumption that the PRI of the past is dead. The party's corporatist structure no longer works as a mechanism of political support. The PRI needs to construct a new electoral base within a participatory society, and this depends on a reform of the candidate selection process that would promote the election of local, more representative leaders.

30. The Colosio murder is often interpreted as an example of the fierce rivalry within the PRI: rumours suggested that Colosio was murdered because he was considered too progressive, pro-democratic and a threat to the privileges of the PRI 'dinosaurs'.

31. This statement of Salinas is often used to illustrate the change in political discourse. It was actually at the PRI's Fourteenth National Assembly in September 1990 that the party statute was changed. Previously the PRI defined itself as a party of 'sectors and citizens'; the new statute changed the preferential order and placed the citizenry first (see Dresser 1994: 135).

32. This conclusion is based on research on union power concerning the regulation of wages, union control over employment, union management of industrial relations, and worker-employer conflicts (1994: 201–13).

33. In general, where unions opposed economic restructuring the regime sought to replace existing leaders with more amenable ones, as in the case of the oil workers' and teachers' unions. Where union bosses supported the introduction of neoliberal policies, the regime backed them, regardless of the rank-and-file members, as happened with the Ford workers at the Cuautitlán plant in 1990 (see Harvey 1993: 20–3).

34. As a result, many oil workers voted for the PRD instead. This was one of the reasons why Salinas arrested the union's secretary of social works and its moral leader, Joaquín Hernández Galicia (*La Quina*) in 1989 (Harvey 1993: 20).

35. In 1977, a new Federal Law on Political Organizations and Electoral Processes came into being. This law provided a range of administrative changes that improved possibilities for opposition parties, like the facilitation of registration of these parties and the increase of the size of the Chamber of Deputies. Although the law seemed promising, critics noted that it contributed to the PRI's political legitimacy by incorporating the majority of the opposition into the party system according to the regime's own rules (Hellman 1983: 129–35).

36. Both Przeworski (1991) and O'Donnell and Schmitter (1986) claim that political liberalization within an authoritarian regime is a temporary, intermediate state, resulting either in democratization or in the hardening of authoritarianism.

References

AUSTIN (1994) 'The reform of Article 27 and urbanisation of the Ejido in Mexico', *Bulletin of Latin American Research*, 13 (3): 327–35.

Bailey, John (1988) *Governing Mexico: The Statecraft of Crisis Management*, New York: St. Martin's Press.

Bailey, John (1994) 'Centralism and political change in Mexico: the case of national solidarity', in Wayne A. Cornelius, Ann L. Craig and Jonathan Fox (eds), *Transforming State–Society Relations in Mexico: The National Solidarity Strategy*, La Jolla: Center for U.S.–Mexican Studies, University of California, San Diego.

Bízberg, Iván (1993) 'Modernisation and corporatism in government–labour relations', in Neil Harvey (ed.), *Mexico: Dilemmas of Transition*, London: British Academic Press and Institute of Latin American Studies.

Brachet-Márquez, Viviane (1992) 'Explaining sociopolitical change in Latin America: the case of Mexico', *Latin American Research Review*, 27 (3): 91–121.

Camp, Roderic A. (1990) 'Camarillas in Mexican politics: the case of the Salinas cabinet', *Mexican Studies/Estudios Mexicanos* 6 (1), Winter: 85–107.

— (1993) 'Political liberalization: the last key to economic modernization in Mexico?', in Riordan Roett (ed.), *Political and Economic Liberalization in Mexico: At a Critical Juncture?*, Boulder, CO and London: Lynne Rienner.

Centeno, Miguel Angel (1994) *Democracy within Reason: Technocratic Revolution in Mexico*, Pennsylvania: Pennsylvania State University Press.

Centeno, Miguel Angel and Sylvia Maxfield (1992) 'The marriage of finance and order: changes in the Mexican political elite', *Journal of Latin American Studies*, 24 (1): 57–85.

Cline, Howard F. (1963) *Mexico: Revolution to Evolution, 1940–1960*, New York: Oxford University Press.

Cook, Lorena Maria, Kevin J. Middlebrook and Juan Molinar Horcasitas (1994) 'The politics of economic restructuring in Mexico: actors, sequencing, and coalition change', in Lorena Maria Cook, Kevin J. Middlebrook and Juan Molinar Horcasitas (eds), *The Politics of Economic Restructuring: State–Society Relations and Regime Change in Mexico*, La Jolla: Center for U.S.–Mexican Studies, University of California, San Diego.

Cornelius, Wayne A. and Ann L. Craig (1988) *Politics in Mexico: An Introduction and Overview*, La Jolla: Center for U.S.–Mexican Studies, University of California, San Diego.

Cornelius, Wayne A., Judith Gentleman and Peter H. Smith (eds) (1989) *Mexico's Alternative Political Futures*, La Jolla: Center for U.S.–Mexican Studies, University of California, San Diego.

Cornelius, Wayne A., Ann L. Craig and Jonathan Fox (eds) (1994) *Transforming State–Society Relations in Mexico: The National Solidarity Strategy*, La Jolla: Center for U.S.–Mexican Studies, University of California, San Diego.

Cypher, James M. (1990) *State and Capital in Mexico: Development Policy Since 1940*, Boulder, CO and Oxford: Westview Press.

Davis, Diane E. (1989) 'Divided over democracy: the embeddedness of state and class conflicts in contemporary Mexico', *Politics and Society*, 17 (3): 247–79.

De la Garza Toledo, Enrique (1994) 'The restructuring of state–labor relations in Mexico', in Lorena Maria Cook, Kevin J. Middlebrook and Juan Molinar Horcasitas (eds), *The Politics of Economic Restructuring: State–Society Relations and Regime Change in Mexico*, La Jolla: Center for U.S.–Mexican Studies, University of California, San Diego.

Delal Baer, M. (1993) 'Mexico's second revolution: pathways to liberalization', in Riordan Roett (ed.), *Political and Economic Liberalization in Mexico: At a Critical Juncture?*, Boulder, CO and London: Lynne Rienner.

Demmers, Jolle (1998) *Friends and bitter enemies: politics and neoliberal reform in Yucatán, Mexico*, Amsterdam: Thela Thesis.

Demmers, Jolle and Barbara Hogenboom (1992) 'Popular organization and party domin-ance: the political role of environmental NGOs in Mexico', Amsterdam: Universiteit van Amsterdam, MA thesis.

Development Gap (1994) *The Polarization of Mexican Society: a Grassroots View of World Bank Adjustment Policies*, Washington, DC: Development Gap.

Dresser, Denise (1991) *Neopopulist Solutions to Neoliberal Problems: Mexico's National Solidarity Program*, La Jolla: Center for U.S.–Mexican Studies, University of California, San Diego.

— (1994) 'Embellishment, empowerment, or euthanasia of the PRI? Neoliberalism and party reform in Mexico', in Lorena Maria Cook, Kevin J. Middlebrook and Juan Molinar Horcasitas (eds), *The Politics of Economic Restructuring: State–Society Relations and Regime Change in Mexico*, La Jolla: Center for U.S.–Mexican Studies, University of California, San Diego.

Foweraker, Joe and Ann L. Craig (eds) (1990) *Popular Movements and Political Change in Mexico*, Boulder, CO and London: Lynne Rienner.

Foweraker, Joe (1993) *Popular Mobilization in Mexico: The Teachers' Movement 1977–87*, Cambridge: Cambridge University Press.

Fox, Jonathan (1994) 'The difficult transition from clientelism to citizenship: lesson from Mexico', *World Politics*, 46 (2): 151–84.

Gledhill, John (1995) *Neoliberalism, Transnationalization and Rural Poverty: A Case Study of Michoacán, Mexico*, Boulder, CO: Westview Press.

— (1996) 'The state, the countryside ... and capitalism', in R. Aitken, N. Craske, G. Jones and D. Stansfield (eds), *Dismantling the Mexican State?*, London: Macmillan.

González Casanova, Pablo (1970) *Democracy in Mexico*, Oxford: Oxford University Press.

Grindle, M. (1977) *Bureaucrats, Politicians, and Peasants in Mexico*, Berkeley and Los Angeles: University of California Press.

Haber, Paul Lawrence (1994) 'The art and implications of political restructuring in Mexico: the case of urban popular movements', in Lorena Maria Cook, Kevin J. Middlebrook and Juan Molinar Horcasitas (eds), *The Politics of Economic Restructuring: State–Society Relations and Regime Change in Mexico*, La Jolla: Center for U.S.–Mexican Studies, University of California, San Diego.

Hansen, Roger (1971) *The Politics of Mexican Development*, Baltimore, MD: Johns Hopkins University Press.

Harvey, Neil (1993) 'The difficult transition: neoliberalism and neocorporatism in Mexico', in Neil Harvey (ed.), *Mexico: Dilemmas of Transition*, London: Institute of Latin American Studies and British Academic Press.

Hellman, Judith Adler (1991) 'Mexican popular movements, clientelism, and the process of democratization', paper presented at the CEDLA/CERLAC joint workshop on Social Movements and Power Relations: The Latin American Experience, 13–15 November 1991, Amsterdam.

Hufbauer, G. and J. Schott (1993) *NAFTA: An Assessment*, Washington, DC: Institute for International Economics.

Jones, Gareth A. (1996) 'Dismantling the Ejido: a lesson in controlled pluralism', in R. Aitken, N. Craske, G. Jones and D. Stansfield (eds), *Dismantling the Mexican State?*, London: Macmillan.

Kaufman, Purcell S. (1981) 'Mexico: clientelism, corporatism and political stability', in S. N. Eisenstadt and R. Lemarchand (eds) *Political Clientelism, Patronage and Development*, Beverly Hills and London: Sage.

Kaufman, Robert (1989) 'Economic orthodoxy and political change in Mexico: the stabil-ization and adjustment policies of the de la Madrid administration', in Barbara Stallings and Robert Kaufman (eds), *Debt and Democracy in Latin America*, Boulder, CO, San Francisco and London: Westview Press.

— (1990) 'Stabilization and adjustment in Argentina, Brazil, and Mexico', in Joan M. Nelson (ed.), *Economic Crisis and Policy Choice: The Politics of Adjustment in the Third World*, Princeton, NJ: Princeton University Press.

Kaufman, Susan (1977) 'Decision making in an authoritarian regime: theoretical implications from a case study', in José Luis Reyna and Richard S. Weinert (eds), *Authoritarianism in Mexico*, Philadelphia: Institute for the Study of Human Issues.

Klesner, Joseph L. (1994) 'Realignment or dealignment? Consequences of economic crisis and restructuring for the Mexican party system', in Lorena Maria Cook, Kevin J. Middlebrook and Juan Molinar Horcasitas (eds), *The Politics of Economic Restructuring: State–Society Relations and Regime Change in Mexico*, La Jolla: Center for U.S.–Mexican Studies, University of California, San Diego.

Knight, Alan (1998) 'Populism and neo-populism in Latin America, especially Mexico', *Journal of Latin American Studies*, 30: 223–48.

Loaeza, Soledad (1994) 'Political liberalization and uncertainty in Mexico', in Lorena Maria Cook, Kevin J. Middlebrook and Juan Molinar Horcasitas (eds), *The Politics of Economic Restructuring: State–Society Relations and Regime Change in Mexico*, La Jolla: Center for U.S.– Mexican Studies, University of California, San Diego.

Lustig, Nora (1992) *Mexico: The Remaking of an Economy*, Washington, DC: Brookings Institution.

Meyer, Lorenzo (1989) 'Democratization of the PRI: mission impossible?', in Wayne A. Cornelius, Judith Gentleman and Peter H. Smith (eds), *Mexico's Alternative Political Futures*, La Jolla: Center for U.S.–Mexican Studies, University of California, San Diego.

Molinar Horcasitas, Juan (1994) 'Changing the balance of power in a hegemonic party system', in Arend Lijphart and Carlos Waisman (eds), *Institutional Design and Democratization*, Boulder, CO: Westview Press.

Morris, Stephen D. (1992) 'Political reformism in Mexico: Salinas at the brink', *Journal of InterAmerican Studies and World Affairs*, 34 (1), Spring: 27–57.

— (1993) 'Political reformism in Mexico: past and present', *Latin American Research Review*, 28 (2): 191–205.

Needler, Martin C. (1971) *Politics and Society in Mexico*, Alburquerque: University of New Mexico Press.

O'Donnell, G. and P. C. Schmitter (1986) *Tentative Conclusion about Uncertain Democracies*, Baltimore: Johns Hopkins University Press.

Overbeek, Henk and Kees van der Pijl (1993) 'Restructuring capital and restructuring hegemony: neo-liberalism and the unmaking of the post-war order', in Henk Overbeek (ed.), *Restructuring Hegemony in the Global Political Economy: The Rise of Transnational Neoliberalism in the 1980s*, London and New York: Routledge.

Philip, George (1992) *The Presidency in Mexican Politics*, New York: St. Martin's Press.

PRONASOL (1990) *Secretaría de Desarrollo Urbano y Ecología*, Mexico, DF.

Przeworski, Adam (1991) *Democracy and the Market: Political and Economic Reforms in Eastern Europe and Latin America*, Cambridge: Cambridge University Press.

— (1995) *Sustainable Democracy*, Cambridge: Cambridge University Press.

Reding, Andrew (1991) 'Mexico: the crumbling of the "perfect dictatorship"', *World Policy Journal*, 3 (2), Spring: 255–82.

Reyna, José Luis (1977) 'Redefining the authoritarian regime', in José Luis Reyna and Richard S. Weinert (eds), *Authoritarianism in Mexico*, Philadelphia: Institute for the Study of Human Issues.

Roberts, Bryan. (1992) 'The place of regions in Mexico', in Eric Van Young (ed.), *Mexico's Regions: Comparative History and Development*, La Jolla: Center of U.S.-Mexican Studies, University of California, San Diego.

Roett, Riordan (1993) 'At the crossroads: liberalism in Mexico', in Riordan Roett (ed.) *Political and Economic Liberalization in Mexico: At a Critical Juncture?*, Boulder, CO and London: Lynne Rienner.

Romero, Miguel A. and Luis Méndez (1990) 'La reestructuración de la industria paraestatal', in Augusto Bolívar and Rosa Albina Garavito (eds), *México en la Década de los Ochentas: La Modernización en Cifras*, Mexico, DF: UAMA.

Ros, Jaime (1994) 'Mexico in the 1990s: a new economic miracle? Some notes on the economic and policy legacy of the 1980s', in Lorena Maria Cook, Kevin J. Middlebrook and Juan Molinar Horcasitas (eds), *The Politics of Economic Restructuring: State–Society Relations and Regime Change in Mexico*, La Jolla: Center for U.S.–Mexican Studies, University of California, San Diego.

Rubio, Luis (1993) 'Economic reform and political change in Mexico', in Riordan Roett (ed.), *Political and Economic Liberalization in Mexico: At a Critical Juncture?*, Boulder, CO and London: Lynne Rienner.

Rubin, Jeffrey W. (1996) 'Decentering the regime: culture and regional politics in Mexico', *Latin American Research Review*, 31 (3): 85–126.

Sheahan, John (1991) *Conflict and Change in Mexican Economic Strategy: Implications for Mexico and for Latin America*, Monograph Series, no. 34, La Jolla: Center for U.S.–Mexican Studies, University of California, San Diego.

Story, Dale (1986) *Industry, the State, and Public Policy in Mexico*, Austin: University of Texas Press.

Teichman, Judith (1992) 'The Mexican state and the political implications of economic restructuring', *Latin American Perspectives Issue 73*, 19 (2) Spring: 88–104.

Urquidi, Víctor L. (1994) 'The outlook for Mexican development in the 1990s', in Lorena Maria Cook, Kevin J. Middlebrook and Juan Molinar Horcasitas (eds), *The Politics of Economic Restructuring: State–Society Relations and Regime Change in Mexico*, La Jolla: Center for U.S.–Mexican Studies, University of California, San Diego.

Weiss, John (1996) 'Economic policy reform in Mexico: the liberalism experiment', in R. Aitken, N. Craske, G. Jones and D. Stansfield (eds), *Dismantling the Mexican State?*, London: Macmillan.

Whitehead, Laurence (1994) 'Prospects for a "transition" from authoritarian rule in Mexico', in Lorena Maria Cook, Kevin J. Middlebrook and Juan Molinar Horcasitas (eds), *The Politics of Economic Restructuring: State–Society Relations and Regime Change in Mexico*, La Jolla: Center for U.S.–Mexican Studies, University of California, San Diego.

EIGHT

The Double Defeat of the Revolutionary Left in Central America

KEES BIEKART

Twenty years after the Sandinista revolutionary victory in Nicaragua, the Central American left finds itself in an uneasy situation; not to speak of a serious identity crisis. In two countries it constitutes the largest opposition force, in the other three it is virtually marginalized. In Nicaragua, the Sandinista Liberation Front became an opposition party in the 1990s and lost not only two presidential elections but also much of its popular credibility. This was largely due to internal rivalry and scandals caused by Sandinista leaders. A tactical pact between the FSLN and right-wing president Arnoldo Alemán further undermined popular support for the Sandinista party. In El Salvador, the guerrilla movement FMLN faced similar criticism. After negotiating an end to the civil war of the 1980s, the party became the largest opposition party. But internal struggles surfaced, leading to a split in 1994. Despite good election results during municipal elections, the party was unable to unite itself behind a strong presidential candidate for the 1999 elections. Although traditionally weaker compared to Nicaragua and El Salvador, the left in the other Central American countries also experienced disappointing electoral outcomes and internal party rivalry.

Performing an oppositional role in postwar democratic transitions was not exactly the aspiration of these left-wing parties, most of them emerging out of armed revolutionary struggles. The transformation from a guerrilla force to a political party required other organizational structures and new relationships with traditional constituencies. It also demanded the development of new strategic visions about how to counter neoliberal adjustment policies. These new visions were generally absent or weakened by a lack of consensus. On several occasions the legalized left even sided with those parties whose policies were most strongly opposed. This chapter will examine this apparent contradiction.

Reformism During the Early Cold War

It would of course be incorrect to speak of the Central American left, as Torres Rivas (1996) and others have pointed out. There was never a united movement, nor have political parties of the left demonstrated a common strategy or longer-term vision. This diversity of expressions by the left has to be examined first in order to understand their current identity crisis. Although with its roots in the early decades of the twentieth century, the growing strength of the left (and the development of its various expressions) in Central America can be understood as part of a long process of demanding participation in the political system. The incorporation of oppositional forces into the political arena had been systematically denied by the military governments for several decades, which shaped much of its organizational development and political programmes.[1]

The first coherent call for opening up the political arena to (left-wing) opposition parties in Central America dates back to the 1940s. Military *caudillos* had been governing all over the region for a decade, with Anastasio Somoza Garcia in Nicaragua and Jorge Ubico in Guatemala as the most notorious examples. Their dominance was being questioned by the end of the Second World War: newly emerging opposition movements of progressive parties and unions challenged the traditional two-party systems and demanded an end to authoritarian rule. These opposition movements were not extremely radical, although their reformist demands did encounter a radical response by the military rulers. In El Salvador a coup was staged by young reformist military officers in April 1944. It was a first sign that the unity of the ruling bloc was vulnerable to the reformist movement. However, the Salvadorean coup soon was aborted, unleashing a wave of political repression and triggering a counter-coup by conservative officers. But the wave of political mobilization was not stopped and would spill over to other countries in Central America. The authoritarian regimes in Honduras and Nicaragua managed to contain the unrest, but in Guatemala and Costa Rica the traditional political system started to crack (Bulmer-Thomas 1987).

The so-called Guatemalan 'revolution' of 1944–54 was in many aspects quite different from the Costa Rican process following the 1948 civil war. In Guatemala a general strike in 1944 made an end to the rule of General Ubico. Although parliament tried to appoint a successor to prolong authoritarian rule, a broad opposition movement forged an alliance with reformist officers. They staged a coup a few months later and called for presidential elections, which were won by opposition leader Arévalo. This was the start of a decade in which political democracy suddenly flourished (Dunkerly 1988). A new Labour Code contributed to increased unionization and social mobilization. Although many coup attempts were staged to remove Arévalo, the armed forces were unable to regain power. Arévalo's minister of defence, Jacobo Arbenz, carefully managed to frustrate these attempts. It was the same Arbenz who succeeded

Arévalo in the 1951 presidential elections, leading to a more radical course of the Guatemalan reform process. A land reform programme was launched, among other reforms, generating great concern of US companies for their properties and finally leading to the counter-revolutionary (US-backed) coup in 1954. The reform programme was reversed and the opposition would be excluded from the political arena for another three decades.

In Costa Rica, the process of social modernization and political reform was far more gradual. It started during the administration of 'civilian *caudillo*' Calderón Guardia in 1942, who introduced a number of social reforms such as a social security system and a Labour Code. These measures responded to demands that had been forwarded by the opposition, despite strong resistance from the traditional coffee growers. Calderón's efforts to improve the conditions for workers and the urban poor were rewarded with broad support from intellectuals and the Catholic Church. His social policies contributed to another election victory of his alliance in 1944 and would lay the basis for Costa Rica's social welfare system. The policies also generated political unrest, eventually erupting into a short period of civil war in 1948 when electoral fraud prevented a victory of the opposition. Led by the charismatic José Figueres, the opposition overthrew the government with support from a small guerrilla army and restored stability, in which the army was abolished and Calderón's social reform programme was formally incorporated into the new constitution. Unlike the temporary 'spring' in Guatemala, the Costa Rican reform process proved to be viable and contributed to social stability up to the current period.

A common characteristic of the early democratic reform processes in these two countries was the remarkable role of communist parties. It was the first time that left-wing parties were playing a prominent role in forging political change in Central America, although in quite different ways. The Costa Rican Communist Party, founded in 1931 and actively organizing the 1934 general strike in the banana plantations, managed to get 10 per cent of the parliamentary seats in the early 1940s. Although they initially opposed President Calderón's policies, the strong reaction of the oligarchy to the new reform programme prompted the communists (who changed their name into the Popular Vanguard Party – PVP) to support Calderón. A unique alliance was the result, in which the communist PVP worked together with the Catholic Church and the National Republican Party (PRN) of Calderón. It was a remarkable alliance, in which banana workers and part of the prominent oligarchic families formed a bloc against those forces opposing social change (Rojas 1993). One of these opponents was José Figueres, who represented a social democratic movement that demanded more profound reforms of the state and the productive system. Figueres was a dedicated anti-communist, which helped him on his road to power at the start of the Cold War. In the early 1950s he outlawed the Communist Party and its unions, while continuing the social reform programme that these groups previously had set in motion.

The Communist Party in Guatemala (the Guatemalan Workers' Party – PGT) played no role in the initial phase of the Guatemalan revolution, and was not founded until 1948. President Arévalo opposed communism and opted for a reformist policy that in many aspects was equal to the programme of Calderón in Costa Rica a few years earlier. After Arbenz had taken over as president in 1951, the communist PGT gradually gained force and was legalized, incorporating many young followers of Arévalo. The revolutionary ideas of the PGT influenced Arbenz's government, especially his thinking about the need for a land reform programme. This programme generated unrest among the large landowners and eventually led to the fall of Arbenz and the start of the counter-revolution. But as Dunkerly (1988: 147) has commented, the influence of the Guatemalan communists has often been overstated. They had no followers in the armed forces and their main support base was in the relatively weak industrial manufacturing sector. The US government gratefully made use of the radical language of the young communist cadre amidst the Cold War to prepare for a coup and to restore the traditional power elite.

Both communist parties had pursued strategies of strategic alliances with middle-class parties to confront the oligarchy and to facilitate capitalist modernization. This would, it was believed, eventually generate counter-forces that would undermine capitalism itself. The purpose was clearly not to seize state power. For that reason the two main programmatic communist issues of that period were the demand for political participation of the excluded (in order to forge alliances with the bourgeoisie) and agrarian reform, necessary to confront the oligarchy. But unlike in Europe of the late nineteenth century, an independent middle class was virtually absent in Central America. The Guatemalan land reform programme was indeed implemented, but also generated a strong counter-force that would later wipe out the Communist Party structure for several decades. It marked the start of a growing anti-communist tradition throughout the region that can be traced up to the present day.

Many similarities can be drawn between the Guatemalan and the Costa Rican process of social modernization. For the first time in the history of Central America the traditional liberal establishment, characterized by a ruling oligarchy protected by the armed forces and a politically and socially excluded majority, was effectively challenged. A series of social and political reforms restricted the traditional rulers and opened the door for political democracy and social justice. In both processes left-wing parties played a stimulating role, eventually also leading to their political marginalization. But the big differences were related to the contexts in which these efforts for reform took place. Costa Rica's society was less polarized compared to Guatemala, where the backward social conditions of the Indian majority sharply contrasted with the concentration of power and wealth of a small ruling class. These extreme circumstances in Guatemala also contributed to more radical approaches for reform, which proved also to generate more radical responses.

Another way to approach these different experiences is to counterpose revolution and reform, as Torres Rivas (1993) has suggested. In this view, the personalities of Arbenz and Figueres represent the two extremes of progressive thinking in postwar Central America, with Arbenz as a promotor of a nationalist-revolutionary project with a radical approach to agrarian reform, although within the boundaries of a capitalist development model. Arbenz believed that his policies contributed to transform Guatemala from a colonial and dependent into a modern capitalist society with social justice. Figueres, on the other hand, was more moderate and pragmatic. He took more time to introduce reforms and gave priority to the development of a strong public sector. Dunkerly (1988), however, points out that the reform programmes in both countries were not essentially opposed to each other. What seem to have differed decisively were two elements. One was the ideologically more radical discourse of Arbenz, strongly opposing US interference in the region, which made his government rather vulnerable in a hardening Cold War climate. Figueres's anti-communism and pro-US attitude certainly gave him a lot more breathing space. The second element was directly related to this: the Costa Rican reform process was slow and gradual and not as hastily implemented as Arbenz's programme. Arbenz probably enjoyed broader popular support, but he also made more enemies than he was able to confront. Therefore, Central America's early progressive democratic experiences were more than just a choice for revolution or reformism: when societies are more socially polarized, any attempt towards political or social reform tends to provoke radicalism, automatically deepening social polarization.

The Revolutionary Movements of the 1970s

The 1944–54 period was a lost opportunity for political reform in Central America that would have bitter consequences a few decades later. The violent crisis of the late 1970s and early 1980s was rooted in the persistence of authoritarian rule by the dominant classes (with an increasingly military component) over a long period of time, combined with the failure to introduce reforms to tackle the problems of social and political exclusion. Only Costa Rica, and to a certain extent Honduras, managed to escape the wave of political escalation starting in the late 1970s. What these 'postponed democratic transitions' in Guatemala, El Salvador and Nicaragua had in common was a 'double denial' of the dominant classes. On the one hand, they refused to introduce a series of social reforms necessary to confront growing social inequalities. On the other hand, they were unwilling to open up the political arena for new reformist political parties led by the urban middle sectors. The result was that social discontent and political exclusion in the 25 years between the violent end of the 'Guatemalan revolution' and the start of the Sandinista revolution had to be contained by state-led repression. Three additional factors that facilitated the postponement of democratic transitions and gradually aggravated its consequences became visible in the late 1970s: economic expansion, ambiguous policies of US governments and anti-communism fuelled by the Cold War.

The first element was the recovery of the Central American economies in the 1950s, which suggests that the export-led growth model was not yet exhausted. Rising coffee prices and a diversification of export crops (cotton, beef and sugar) contributed to a sharp increase in exports. This economic expansion facilitated a transformation in the export sector and contributed to an expanding and modernizing state apparatus. The traditional member of the oligarchy also underwent a gradual transformation from a 'landlord-capitalist into a capitalist-landlord' who could prosper thanks to the over exploitation of rural labour (Torres Rivas 1989: 49–50). That is, the expanding modern export economy also contributed to a semi-proletarianization of *campesinos*, the small agricultural producers of basic grains for local consumption. Rapid population growth (100 per cent increase in 20 years) and uneven land distribution dramatically increased rural unemployment and contributed to both rural and urban impoverishment. This in turn would create a breeding-ground for radical protest and social mobilization in the 1970s.

A second factor influencing the outcome of these postponed transitions was the ambiguity of US foreign policy. Although US governments were aware of the need to introduce social reforms and to contribute to political liberalization in Central America, these 'good intentions' (as President Kennedy called them) were overshadowed by Cold War imperatives. Two examples illustrate this ambiguity. One was the active US role in removing the Arbenz government in Guatemala, which had been labelled as a communist threat to the hemisphere. But most reforms introduced during the Guatemalan revolution were quite moderate and would have been perfectly in line with the reform policies promoted by the USA in the early 1960s (Dunkerly 1988). Another example was Kennedy's Alliance for Progress, a US aid programme intended to stimulate social reforms in Latin America in reaction to the 1959 Cuban revolution. However, this programme soon became a tool for counter-insurgency operations in which Central American armed forces received modern weapons and training to combat emerging guerrilla activity. Even if it is argued that US policy was ambiguous only on paper and that in practice it deliberately supported authoritarian regimes in their efforts to resist popular pressures, the outcome is the same: the USA was a key factor in postponing democratic transitions in Central America up to the 1980s.

A third factor that furthered the practice of social and political exclusion was ideological: a primitive and belligerent anti-communist culture that had been flourishing in the region since the 1930s. It was not simply Cold War anti-communism, stimulated by the USA and cultivated by the Catholic hierarchy and the armed forces that had taken root in Central America; especially after the removal of Arbenz (1954) and the Cuban revolution (1959), anti-communism became the leading ideology of Central America's dominant sectors against the advocates of social and political change. Torres Rivas (1996: 26) observes that it was more than just a political ideology, 'as it also contained religious values, affirming the family, private property, tradition, a sense of obedience, authority, hierarchy, and therefore did not identify opponents but enemies, political enemies'. In the name of this right-wing nationalist ideology, the worst crimes against human rights were justified against leaders of popular organizations, progressive intellectuals and any other opponent of the authoritarian system.

Within this setting a new generation of the Central American left emerged, dedicated to armed revolutionary struggle. The evolution of these revolutionary movements actually comprised two subsequent generations. The first consisted of tiny political parties, inspired by the Cuban revolution, trying to set up foci of resistance in rural areas. In Guatemala these groups were initially formed by progressive military officers, who rebelled against government corruption and the absence of democratic liberties. This was, for example, the case with the Revolutionary Movement of 13 November (MR-13), founded in 1960. In the same year, the communist PGT also had decided to support 'all forms of struggle'. Two years later the Rebellious Armed Forces (FAR) was formed, which (despite being defeated twice by the armed forces) later became part of the Guatemalan National Revolutionary Party (URNG). Throughout the 1960s, the Guatemalan revolutionaries effectively managed to stage protracted guerrilla warfare, which was not paralleled in neighbouring countries, even in Nicaragua, where the Sandinista National Liberation Front (FSLN) undertook several abortive attempts to start an armed struggle against the Somoza regime (Rojas 1993).

However, well-organized counter-insurgency operations by the US-trained security forces managed to defeat all these revolutionary guerrilla groups by the late 1960s, thereby unleashing a widespread campaign of terror that would continue for another decade. Dunkerly (1988) points at the different origins and tactics of the early guerrilla struggles in Guatemala and Nicaragua. The former was rooted in the overthrow of the Arbenz government and had closer relations with the Cubans. Moreover, the FAR and MR-13 really were a challenge to the state and suffered (just as their successors after their defeat in 1971) from more sustained repression in several waves, ending in the massacres among the indigenous communities in the early 1980s. Although the early FSLN in Nicaragua also was seriously weakened by repression by Somoza's National Guard, its rural guerrilla strategy until 1971 had been a failure due to a lack of political and military infrastructure.

The second generation of political-military organizations emerged in the early 1970s in Guatemala, Nicaragua and El Salvador. They had learned their lessons from the earlier defeats and had therefore improved their organizational structures and acquired popular support in both rural and urban areas. In Guatemala, new guerrilla organizations EGP (Guerrilla Army of the Poor) and ORPA (Organization of the People in Arms) started to build up popular support in the Indian highlands. The FSLN in Nicaragua, after going through a serious internal crisis, was slow in building up popular support and expanded only after 1977. The five small revolutionary groups in El Salvador, all emerging in the 1970s, would gain strength after the exposure of extensive electoral fraud, also in 1977. The Communist Party, which had been established in 1930, turned to armed struggle in the 1970s even though its secretary-general, Cayetano Carpio, had left the party in 1970 to form the Popular Liberation Forces (FPL).[2]

The political programmes of these revolutionary movements were a combination of old and new demands, mixed with local and imported elements. The old demands of political participation and agrarian reform still dominated as central objectives to realize democracy with social justice. But unlike in the 1950s this 'real democracy' was no longer viewed to be possible within the framework of capitalist development. In the 1970s, the revolutionary aspect was not to realize participatory democracy as such, but to realize this within a new socioeconomic setting in which the traditional power-holders had been defeated. Although this was sometimes termed 'socialism', a coherent vision of the Central American left on a socialist future was not really developed. More prominent was a strong rejection of the dominant role of the USA in the region in its support of authoritarianism (expressed as anti-imperialism) and the right of the small Central American nation-states to pursue more independent foreign policies. Liberation theology also clearly influenced the revolutionary parties in their decision to side with the poor. A common denominator was an overriding emphasis on the way the revolution had to be achieved: by popular armed struggle.

Many different views existed about how this struggle was to be most effectively put in practice. For example, the FSLN was divided into three different 'tendencies', preferring a central role for the workers (proletarian faction), a (Maoist) 'protracted people's war', or mass insurrection by multi-class coalitions (*tercerista* faction). Similar differences of tactics existed among the other revolutionary organizations in the region and were often more important than debates about the eventual outcome of the struggle. This was understandable given the tense political situation in Central America in the late 1970s. The escalation of the political crisis suddenly gave a momentum to revolutionary movements, in which unity and the formation of fronts moved the discussion towards tactical issues. It was in this period that the term 'political-military organizations' emerged, illustrating an ambiguity in which revolution was understood as armed struggle, transforming political dimensions into military considerations and internal democracy into vertical hierarchy (Torres Rivas 1996: 46).

Without getting into a detailed analysis of the nature of the political crisis of the late 1970s, it is important to note that it was essentially a crisis of authoritarian rule. It also showed that reformist options were no longer viable, especially after moderate reformist parties were unable to take power as a result of manipulated elections. The constituencies of these parties started to realize the limits of electoral politics, and mistrust arose about the viability of a 'third option' between authoritarianism and revolution. Electoral fraud in El Salvador (in 1972 and 1977) prevented the victory of the Christian Democrats, producing a wave of popular protest. It ushered in a period of repression against progressive forces, causing the Christian Democrats and other moderate forces to openly conclude that the legal (electoral) path had been exhausted. In Guatemala this turning point came in 1974, when the electoral victory of a broad opposition coalition led by the Christian Democrats was nullified by the military regime, again leading to popular protest. In Nicaragua, the impossibility of opening up the political arena was confirmed in the 1974 elections, leading to the formation of a moderate anti-Somoza front headed by Pedro Joaquín Chamorro. However, Chamorro was assassinated and his movement merged with a larger (FSLN-dominated) alliance. In the process this moderate opposition force lost control over a radicalizing opposition and was condemned to play a secondary role after Somoza's defeat.

As a result, political-military organizations rapidly expanded their popular base by incorporating radicalizing urban and rural popular sectors, leading to the formation of well-organized unified revolutionary movements: the URNG in Guatemala, the FMLN in El Salvador and the FSLN in Nicaragua. The Guatemalan revolutionary organizations drew their popular support mainly from the rural (Indian) population, who had been the victims of an intensive campaign of state terror by the military regime of Lucas García, which came to power in 1978. The new rural and urban organization structure of the Guerrilla Army of the Poor (EGP) coincided with the emergence of the Committee of Workers' Unity (CUC), a new radical peasant organization founded by Indian *campesinos* from the highlands. While military repression had seriously weakened the urban labour movement, the CUC managed to organize large demonstrations and a successful strike in the southern sugar and cotton plantations in early 1980, in which migrant workers and poor Ladinos also took part. Continued repression on a large scale contributed to the unification of the revolutionary movement within the URNG in 1982 (Jonas 1991; Le Bot 1992).

In El Salvador, popular support for guerrilla organizations increased in both rural and urban areas. Broad popular fronts of mass organizations emerged, such as the United Popular Action Front (FAPU) and the Revolutionary Popular Bloc (BPR). Their incorporation of strong labour unions such as ANDES and FECCAS typified a radicalization of the Salvadorean popular movement. These popular fronts were either set up (BPR) or taken over (FAPU) by the five political-military organizations.[3] Although primarily starting in urban areas, increased repression after the assassination of Archbishop Romero in 1980 forced these popular fronts to go underground and to shift their emphasis towards rural areas, where the Farabundo Martí National Liberation Front (FMLN) was formed in 1981 to coordinate armed struggle.

In Nicaragua, the incorporation of popular organizations into a combined rural and urban revolutionary struggle started later but advanced most rapidly, leading to the popular insurrection of 1979. The level of popular mobilization was still low in late 1977 and accelerated only after the assassination of opposition leader Pedro Joaquín Chamorro in January 1978. By that time the FSLN was becoming united and had moral support from a group of prominent middle-class individuals (Los Doce), which later merged into a broader opposition coalition. The FSLN increased its popularity after demonstrations during Chamorro's funeral were called off by the moderate opposition to prevent escalation, and after successful attacks on army barracks and a spectacular raid on the National Palace in August 1978. Within a year, the FSLN had gained control of the rural and urban unions and formed the United Popular Movement (MPU), demanding a series of social and political reforms. This programme was effectively implemented by the new Sandinista government after the FSLN defeated the National Guard in the large-scale offensive of 1979.

Revolution and Counter-revolution in the 1980s

By late 1979, the Central American left was experiencing a period of euphoria. In Nicaragua, the authoritarian regime of Somoza had been eliminated and the entire National Guard was expelled to neighbouring countries, where some of them would later start the US-financed counter-revolution. The new Sandinista government enjoyed international support for its basic principles (political pluralism, a mixed economy and non-alignment) and introduced fundamental political and social reforms, among them a land redistribution programme. In El Salvador, a group of young military officers ended the Romero regime in October 1979. The military coup was welcomed by popular organizations and the entire opposition, whose leaders accepted several cabinet posts in the new junta. In Honduras, a number of small political-military organizations emerged, inspired by the Sandinista revolution and actively supporting the struggle of the FMLN in El Salvador.

But the euphoria did not last very long. In El Salvador, conservative army officers refused to be placed under civilian control. The reformist programme of the new military junta – including agrarian reform and the nationalization of banks and foreign trade – was sabotaged by the oligarchy and only contributed to further escalation towards civil war, after Archbishop Romero and the entire leadership of the moderate left-wing opposition were assassinated in 1980. In Guatemala, a military coup was staged by young officers in 1982, led by former presidential candidate General Ríos Montt. It was a protest against electoral fraud by the Lucas García regime and because of discontent inside the army over the failure to defeat the guerrilla movement. The new junta ruled for just over a year, in which the bloodiest counter-insurgency campaign of modern Central American history was waged before it was replaced by the old military hierarchy. The Guatemalan revolutionary movement was severely weakened and would never regain its strength of the late 1970s. Only Costa Rica and Honduras managed to avoid the escalation of political polarization into civil wars. However, increased US military aid to destabilize the Sandinista government and to support the counter-revolutionary offensive in El Salvador did affect the internal politics of Costa Rica and Honduras, particularly after the contras started operations from their territories. Especially in Honduras, the small revolutionary parties were seriously weakened by large counter-insurgency campaigns between 1982 and 1984.

This is not to say that the revolutionary left was quickly and instantly defeated. To the contrary: the decade of the 1980s was for many in Central America a decade of revolution. Throughout these years the Sandinistas remained in power and mobilized popular energies to realize the ideals of a more just and participatory society. They could count on generous support from the international aid community and thousands of solidarity groups throughout the world. In El Salvador, the FMLN was able to resist large US-financed counter-offensives by special army battalions. By the mid-1980s it controlled extensive areas of the Salvadorean countryside. In Guatemala the guerrilla movement had been severely weakened, but a revival of the popular movement in the late 1980s was a sign that hopes for social change were not yet exhausted. Incipient processes of democratic transition were starting throughout Central America: after several decades of authoritarian rule something seemed to be changing fundamentally in the 1980s.

But by the early 1990s this triumphalist mood was over. The FSLN had lost the February 1990 elections to the oppostion and in El Salvador and Guatemala the revolutionary movements had entered negotiations with their governments, making an end to decades of armed struggle. The hopes of realizing revolutionary changes with popular struggles in the Central American region were suddenly over. Although it can be questioned whether it really was that sudden, with hindsight it can be argued that a number of developments already pointed in the direction of a defeat of the revolutionary aspirations. The end of the Cold War, generating a worldwide crisis of the left, was certainly a factor. Another important factor was the huge US counter-offensive in the region. US support to the contras undermined the Nicaraguan revolution, and the multi-billion dollar arms supplies to the Salvadorean armed forces contributed to a stalemate in the Salvadorean civil war. But probably more important was the silent revolution that accompanied the counter-revolutionary offensive of the 1980s led by the USA: the modernization of the right. It was this new generation of modern business leaders that managed to take control of the major right-wing parties and the governments in the region, starting with Alfredo Cristiani in El Salvador.[4]

The victory of this new right was directly related to the political defeat of the oligarchy during the crisis of the late 1970s and the neoliberal transformations of the Central American economies in the 1980s.[5] The so-called modernization of the economic model was enhanced by a range of structural adjustment programmes, which were demanded by the international financial institutions in order to qualify for new loans. The new measures required, among other things, a number of reforms in the financial system, a reduction of the fiscal deficit, privatization of public companies and new capital incentives to promote non-traditional exports (Timossi 1989). Complementary to economic stabilization a US-financed programme of political modernization was launched, promoting democratic elections and a number of reforms of the state apparatus. Initially, the purpose was to legitimize the governments the USA was supporting amidst 'low-intensity warfare', notably the José Napoleón Duarte government in El Salvador. But it was in later stages also meant to offer large segments of the middle classes renewed access to the political arena (Vilas 1995).

The modernization of the right, the end of the Cold War, the US-financed low-intensity warfare and the gradual opening of the political arena in the 1980s are all elements that cannot be easily separated, as they mutually reinforced each other. But they all, directly or indirectly, contributed to the downfall of the 'revolutionary project' in Central America. This happened most dramatically in Nicaragua, where the Sandinista government was pressured by the USA to convene general elections after the Sandinista armed forces had managed to defeat the contras militarily. The elections were held in 1990 and won by the opposition, basically because the Nicaraguan people did not want the war to continue. In El Salvador the FMLN was not militarily defeated, but forced to start negotiations with the right-wing government of Cristiani. The origins of the civil war were only a marginal issue of the negotiation process. In accepting the framework of dialogue and electoral competition, the central goal of the revolutionary struggle – to conquer state power and change society – was given up.

But the left actually had no alternative by the late 1980s. During the Central American presidential summits following the Esquipulas agreement of August 1987, Nicaraguan President Daniel Ortega was faced with united pressure from his colleagues to follow a path that was inevitably leading to a political defeat of the Sandinista revolution. The FMLN experienced a similar dilemma: it could not reject Cristiani's offer to resume peace negotiations, although it knew it was part of his election campaign. Moreover, the FMLN was convinced that Cristiani would never seriously enter peace talks, so it accepted the offer. The alternative would have been to continue a war for which it was increasingly losing popular support. By accepting the conversion from a guerrilla army into a legal political party (in the case of the FMLN) and by accepting the rules of the electoral game (in the case of the FSLN) the revolutionary project in Central America had *de facto* surrendered.

Splits and Alliances in the 1990s

Political confusion was reigning amongst the Central American left by the early 1990s. This was fuelled by a gradual alienation of revolutionary leaders from their most stalwart followers. Soon after their electoral defeat, for example, the Sandinista leaders were involved in a scandal about expropriating former government properties. In El Salvador former FMLN commanders publicly stated a preference for a social democratic course of their newly legalized political party. The right was able to take advantage of this confusion and during elections easily defeated the left-wing parties of the opposition that had recently entered the political arena. This was in a sense remarkable: these parties, which had championed a range of neoliberal adjustment packages, leading to a deeper poverty gap, increased direct taxing, a decline of public services and a collapse of the peasant economy, received a majority vote from the population. How was this possible? After all, it was the left that with its surrender had contributed to furthering democratic transition, providing credibility to a new and more inclusive political system.

This 'double defeat' of the left requires closer examination, as it would have fundamental consequences for its strategies in the late 1990s. In Nicaragua the 'double defeat' was probably most spectacular. After all, the FSLN had been victorious in overthrowing the Somoza dictatorship after a fierce popular struggle, followed by a decade of revolutionary government. But it turned out to be rather difficult to change an impoverished society, even more because the achievements of the Sandinistas were daily challenged by one of the world's superpowers. The euphoria about revolutionary changes would gradually vanish: the Nicaraguan people were no longer prepared to sacrifice their children for a war that seemed to be endless. Inevitable macroeconomic adjustments in the late 1980s contributed to further social impoverishment and eroded popular support for a continuation of the Sandinista presidency. But it was not just the acceptance of electoral participation by the US-supported opposition that ended the revolution. As Carlos Vilas (1990: 18) commented: 'We have to recognize that the revolutionary process got stuck in its own internal tensions and ambiguities long before the Sandinistas were defeated in the polls.'

This was the case with the so-called 'piñata', in which shortly after the elections many Sandinista officials enriched themselves by expropriating houses, vehicles and other government properties. Although they justified it by claiming the right to compensation for their active contribution to the public cause, it illustrated the difficulty to eliminate traditional corrupt practices in an impoverished society. As a party of the opposition, the FSLN proclaimed to continue the revolution by 'governing from below', giving priority to strong linkages with mass organizations. Indeed, the party continued to be the strongest popular party in the region, forging alliances with the new government of Chamorro against the more reactionary right-wing opposition. But at the same time, the FSLN witnessed how the achievements of the revolutionary period were gradually torn down, including purges in the army and the police, which had been previously run by Sandinista officers.

The FSLN party structure also started to crack during the oppositional era. Initiatives to democratize the internal structure and to replace several of the traditional nine commanders generated heated discussions about the future of the FSLN. With the presidential elections approaching in 1996 it even led to a split in the party when Sergio Ramirez (the ex-vice president during the 1980s) decided to leave the party. He considered that the FSLN was unable to adapt to the new circumstances and that its resistance to pursue a more social democratic line would inevitably lead to a new electoral defeat. Ramirez founded the Renovated Sandinista Movement (MRS) but did not manage to take many followers with him. As a result of the party split the FSLN was further weakened, also because the Sandinista constituency rejected the *caudillo* behaviour of many of their leaders (Carrión 1994). Nobody was surprised that eventually the right-wing Liberal Party of Alemán, which was associated with the Somoza era, easily won the 1996 presidential elections.

After two years of opposition to Alemán's government, however, former Sandinista President Daniel Ortega started secret talks with Alemán about constitutional reforms. Ortega, who had been publicly damaged by a sex scandal, wanted to make sure that the FSLN was not going to lose the next presidential elections. The constitutional reforms were aimed at limiting electoral coalitions and minimizing the number of parties, all measures that would contribute to strengthen the bipartisan system of Liberals and Sandinistas. Ortega believed that this would give the FSLN a better chance of returning to power in the next elections. When the Ortega–Alemán pact became public (in June 1999) the reaction of FSLN followers was furious: it was considered to be a 'pact with the devil' and an acceptance of the corrupt practices of the Alemán government. Obviously, Alemán was pleased with this pact, as the FSLN had been the main opposition to his neoliberal programme. But local observers raised a fundamental question: is the FSLN with this pact preparing to win the next elections, or, on the contrary, to lose them again? (Equipo Nitlapán-Envío 1999).

The double defeat of the FMLN in El Salvador came in 1994, when it was beaten by the neoliberals of the National Republican Alliance (ARENA) during the so-called 'elections of the century', in which for the first time all opposition parties were participating. The presidential candidate of the united left-wing opposition was Rubén Zamora, a representative of the moderate left-wing Social Christian Party (PSC) who was considered to be a reasonable alternative to the conservative *caudillo* Calderón Sol. But the left-wing alliance lost the presidency by a vast margin, although the FMLN became the largest opposition party in parliament. The right-wing ARENA was far better prepared for the electoral contest and played the same card that Chamorro had used in the Nicaraguan elections: a victory of the left could mean a return to civil war and misery. But the difference with Nicaragua was that the FMLN did not perceive the start of negotiations in 1990 as a defeat. On the contrary, it entered these talks as part of a new strategy in the late 1980s to conquer state power by peaceful means. It was rather the outcome of the negotiations, with its emphasis on demilitarization and its meagre impact on socioeconomic issues, that with hindsight can be considered as a political defeat.[6] But the FMLN presented the 1992 peace agreement as a victory to its combatants, who would be granted access to a land transfer programme and other facilities to enable them to reintegrate into civilian life. However, the ARENA governments of Christiani and Calderón Sol managed to jeopardize many of the agreements and even contributed to a remilitarization of Salvadorean society by incorporating the armed forces into a campaign to diminish the wave of criminal violence that struck the country in the mid-1990s.

The parallel with Nicaragua was the split in the FMLN, occurring not long after the 1994 elections were lost. During a vote in parliament about the election of the executive commission, part of the FMLN parliamentarians supported the right-wing ARENA candidate. The split was provoked by the ERP and RN tendencies of the FMLN under the leadership of former commander Joaquín Villalobos. Although the FMLN always had been a coordination of five different ideological tendencies, rather than a united front, it was the first time that dissidents had openly put a bomb under the party. Villalobos and his followers founded the Democratic Party (PD), in which next to the ERP and the RN also the small social democratic National Revolutionary Movement (MNR) participated.[7] The PD openly declared its adherence to a social democratic programme and explained its move by pointing at the implementation of the peace agreement. With the end of the war, it was argued, the FMLN had lost not only its military role but also its political function (Guido Béjar 1994).

Villalobos was accused by his former comrades of having become an ordinary bourgeois politician, searching for personal glamour and pronouncing political ideas that were contrary to his practice of a former revolutionary front commander. But it should not be forgotten that differences about strategy and political vision always had been present in the ranks of the FMLN, only the end of the war made these differences surface. In 1995 the PD of Villalobos even decided to forge an alliance with the governing ARENA party, which was ratified in the San Andrés pact. This open support for a neoliberal programme by former FMLN combatants proved that the left, as soon as it had entered the political arena, had made a rather smooth shift from revolutionary struggle to political opportunism.

At the municipal level, the FMLN was more successful. Although it won only a disappointing 15 municipalities in the 1994 elections, a more solid election campaign in 1997 resulted in success in 48 municipalities (including the metropolitan government of the capital). But the FMLN was internally divided about the 1999 presidential election strategy. Comparable to the Nicaraguan FSLN, the FMLN could not reach a consensus about the way to beat the ARENA party in order to seize government power. Rivalry emerged between an orthodox and a renovating tendency at a party convention in 1998, leading to chaos and a loss of support from its traditional constituency. Many FMLN members even abstained from voting in the 1999 presidential elections, which were easily won by ARENA candidate Francisco Flores. Voter turn-out during these elections experienced a record low of 39 per cent, illustrating the loss of confidence of many Salvadoreans in the newly democratized political system.

In the other three Central American countries the left continues to be in a marginal position. In Guatemala, the URNG signed a peace agreement in late 1996 with the government of the neoliberal Alvaro Arzú. The Guatemalan guerrilla movement had been defeated militarily already in the early 1980s, but continued its operations on a small scale up to the mid-1990s. The URNG had long before given up hope of a revolutionary victory and decided to enter the electoral path in 1995 under the banner of the Guatemalan National Democratic Front (FDNG). Although it won only a few parliamentary seats, this was seen as a first step towards broadening its presence in the political arena (Biekart 1999). In Honduras the former revolutionary groups decided to end their struggle in the early 1990s. The rigid bipartisan political system of Liberals and Nationalists has up to now not provided any space for a third, more progressive, political force.

Only Costa Rica, with its longer existence of the social democratic National Liberation Party (PLN), founded by José Figueres, has managed to become a constant political factor among the left in the Central American region. In the 1980s the PLN started to follow a more pragmatic course, particularly under the presidency of Nobel Peace Prize laureate Oscar Arias. During his government neoliberal structural adjustment policies were introduced and the party gradually started to move to a more conservative position. Currently the PLN is going through a period of crisis, especially because its traditional social base no longer accepts the erosion of Costa Rica's welfare system. The social consensus model that was the basis for several decades of social modernization has been exhausted. Although not defeated as in neighbouring countries, the Costa Rican left is struggling with the question that Torres Rivas (1996: 96) has posed as 'how to be social democratic in a neoliberal climate'.

Conclusions

The experience of the Central American left over the past decades has had an enormous impact throughout Latin America. The diversity of movements and tactical shifts is rich and not yet very well documented. This chapter has tried to explain a peculiar paradox of the Central American left: in its effort to seize state power it finally ended up supporting those political forces that are held responsible for a growing poverty gap and for obstructing democratic transitions in the region. The shift from reformism in the 1950s to revolutionary struggles in the 1970s was explained as a product of a sustained process by the dominant classes to keep the political arena closed to oppositional forces. Reformist parties that were claiming a third way between reformism and revolution were crushed by the magnitude of the crisis, finally also ending many decades of authoritarian rule by the oligarchy.

The struggle for revolutionary changes in the impoverished Central American societies was eventually lost. A number of reasons have been provided for this defeat, in which the end of the Cold War and the emergence of a new modernized right stand out. By accepting the rules of the electoral game, the left had to alter its revolutionary goals and all political-military organizations were converted into political parties. However, by openly participating in electoral politics it eventually legitimized the new neoliberal order, even more because it turned out to be impossible to defeat this neoliberal right at the ballot-box. To overcome this trauma of a double defeat, some left-wing parties have chosen in recent years to forge alliances with their opponents to strengthen their position in the political arena. Others have warned that this will further increase the distance with those marginalized forces that the left claims to represent, inevitably leading to new defeats in the future.

This dramatic situation cannot be attributed solely to external circumstances. The large-scale US 'low-intensity warfare' of the 1980s effectively frustrated the Sandinista revolution and contributed to a stalemate in the Salvadorean civil war. But it would be too easy to argue that the revolutionary left was defeated only by US counter-insurgency. The end of the Cold War certainly generated a crisis of left-wing strategizing and definitely contributed to an end of the revolutionary perspective. But the main cause for the current stalemate of the left seems to be its difficulty to perform a central role in a democratized political setting. Whether it is unwillingness or incompetence can be debated, but somehow the former revolutionary leaders cannot see why those social forces that are mostly suffering from current neoliberal policies have lost their faith in the left.

Notes

1. For a more detailed analysis of democratic transition in Central America up to the late 1990s, see Biekart 1999.

2. Other emerging political-military organizations were the People's Revolutionary Army (ERP, founded in 1972), from which the Armed Forces for National Resistance (RN) split off in 1975, and the Central American Revolutionary Workers' Party (PRTC, founded as a regional party in 1976) (Montgomery 1995: 101–9).

3. Five alliances of military and popular fronts were formed, prior to the foundation of the FMLN from previously existing organizations (dates refer to the year of foundation): FPL (1970) and BPR (1975); RN (1975) and FAPU (1974); ERP (1972) and LP-28 (1978); PCS (1930) and UDN (1967); PRTC (1976) and MLP (1979). In 1980 the popular fronts were dissolved and only the military organizations continued (Montgomery 1995).

4. The sequence of electoral victories by the new 'modern' right in Central America actually was amazing. Cristiani became president in 1989. One year later Callejas of the National Party became president in Honduras, just like Calderón of the Social Christian Party in Costa Rica. Serrano won the presidency in Guatemala in 1991. Chamorro (1990 president of Nicaragua) was not really a representative of this new right, but many of her cabinet members were. The chain of right-wing electoral victories continued in the mid-1990s with Calderón Sol in El Salvador, Alvaro Arzú in Guatemala and Arnoldo Alemán in Nicaragua.

5. Structural adjustment policies were first introduced in Costa Rica (1982), followed by Guatemala (1986), El Salvador (1987), Nicaragua (1988) and Honduras (1988). See Menjívar (1992).

6. Even the negotiator for the government admitted that the peace agreement of 1992 was essentially about demilitarizing the country and that the socioeconomic paragraphs (such as the land transfer programme or the socioeconomic forum) were only formally accepted to please the FMLN constituency. The government was well aware that as soon as the FMLN was demobilized these issues could be easily downplayed (author's interview with David Escobar Galindo, 20 September 1996).

7. The FMLN continued with the tendencies of the PCS, FPL and PRTC and minor factions of the RN and ERP. For a detailed analysis of the FMLN split see Guido Béjar (1994).

References

Biekart, Kees (1999) *The Politics of Civil Society Building: European Private Aid Agencies and Democratic Transitions in Central America*, Utrecht: International Books.

Bulmer-Thomas, Victor (1987) *The Political Economy of Central America Since 1920*, Cambridge: Cambridge University Press.

Carr, Barry and Steve Ellner (eds) (1993) *The Latin American Left: From the Fall of Allende to Perestroika*, Boulder, CO: Westview Press.

Carrión, Luís (1994) 'Sandinismo: renovación o retórica', *Espacios*, 2, October–December: 39–43.

Castañeda, Jorge G. (1993) *Utopia Unarmed: The Latin American Left after the Cold War*, New York: Vintage Books.

Dunkerly, James (1988) *Power in the Isthmus: A Political History of Modern Central America*, London: Verso.

— (1994) *The Pacification of Central America: Political Change in the Isthmus, 1987–1993*, London: Verso.

Equipo Nitlapán-Envío (1999) 'Pacto: frutos amargos y hondas raíces', *Envío*, 208, Julio: 3–11.

Guido Béjar, Rafael (1992) 'El tiempo de adios: La izquierda y el cambio social en El Salvador', *Polémica*, 16, January–April: 3–12.

— (1994) 'Crísis y renovación en la izquierda salvadoreña', *Espacios*, 2, October–December: 24–32.

Jonas, Susanne (1991) *The Battle for Guatemala: Rebels, Death Squads, and US Power*, Boulder, CO: Westview Press.

Le Bot, Yvon (1992) *La Guerre en terre maya: Communauté, violence et modernité au Guatemala*, Paris: Editions Karthala.

Menjívar, Rafael (1992) 'La concertación en la estratégia de desarrollo de Centroamérica', in Eduardo Stein and Salvador Arias (eds), *Democracia sin Pobreza*, San José: DEI–CADESCA, pp. 305–46.

Montgomery, T. S. (1995) *Revolution in El Salvador: From Civil Strife to Civil Peace*, Boulder, CO: Westview Press.

Petras, James (1997) 'Latin America: the resurgence of the left', *New Left Review*, 223: 17–68.

Rojas, Manuel (1993) 'De la Posguerra a la Crísis (1945–1979): La política', in Hector Pérez-Brignoli (ed.), *Historia general de Centroamérica* (Vol. V), Madrid and San José: CEE–FLACSO, pp. 85–163.

— (1995) 'Consolidar la Democracia en Centroamérica: Una Ardua Tarea', in Klaus-Dieter Tangermann (ed.), *Ilusiones y Dilemas*, San José: FLACSO, pp. 99–155.

Timossi, Gerardo (1989) *Centroamérica, Deuda Externa y Ajuste Estructural: Las Transformaciones Económicas de la Crisis*, Managua: CRIES–DEI.

Torres Rivas, Edelberto (1989) *Repression and Resistance: The Struggle for Democracy in Central America*, Boulder, CO: Westview Press.

— (1993) 'Personalities, ideologies and circumstances: social democracy in Central America', in Menno Vellinga (ed.), *Social Democracy in Latin America*, Boulder, CO: Westview Press, pp. 240–51.

— (1996) *Encrucijadas e incertezas en la izquierda centroamericana: Ensayo preliminar de interpretación*, Guatemala: FLACSO.

Vilas, Carlos (1990) 'What went wrong?', *Nacla Report on the Americas*, 24 (1): 10–18.

— (1995) *Between Earthquakes and Volcanoes: Market, State, and the Revolutions in Central America*, New York: Monthly Review Press.

Index

Acción Democrática (Venezuela), 6
Afghanistan, invaded by USSR, 84
AFL-CIO, 67
Agrario Nacional (Argentina), 36
Agreement for Democracy (CD – Chile), 85
Agricultural Boards (Argentina), abolition of, 48
Alarcon, Fabio, 143
Alemán, Arnaldo, 182, 195
Alessandri, Jorge, 65, 71, 73
Alfonsín, Raúl, 5, 23, 43, 45, 46
Allende, Salvador, 7, 8, 66, 69, 71, 73, 78, 79, 81; collapse of government, 82
Alliance for Progress, 187
Almeyda, Clodomiro, 83
Alsogaray, Alvaro, 39
Altamirano, Carlos, 83
Amin, Samir, 42
Ampuero, Radl, 68
Andean Group, 15
anti-communism, 43, 60, 185, 186, 187, 188
anti-imperialism, 63, 68, 79, 189; abandonment of, 10
Aramburu, Eugenio, 38
Arbenz, Jacobo, 183, 185, 186, 187, 188
Arévalo, Juan José, 183, 184, 185
Argentina, xii, 4, 5, 11, 15, 18, 73, 146; agro-export economy of, 24–9; as trader in world economy, 26; dependence on British Empire, 26, 28–9, 32; exports and imports of, 52, 55; Five Year Plan, 35; growth of, 25, 27, 42, 50; military coups in, 29, 38, 43, 55; neutrality of, 33; shift to open economy, 22–59; transnationalization of economy, 52
Arias, Oscar, 197
Arzú, Alvaro, 197
Asian Socialist Conference, 70
Asian Tigers, 156

austerity, 133, 143, 145–6, 156, 165; programmes, 120
Austral Plan (Argentina), 44
Australia, 31
Authentic Party of the Mexican Revolution (PARM), 155
authoritarianism, 169; crisis of, 190; in Mexico, 152–3, 172

Baker Plan, 157
balance of payments deficits, 145; in Argentina, 52, 53, 55
banking system in Argentina, 51–2
banks, surplus capital of, 137, 139
Barrantes, Alfonso, 113, 114, 118, 119, 120, 127
Berlinguer, Enrico, 84
Blanco, Hugo, 112
Bolivia, 4, 15, 123
Borja, Rodrigo, 146
bourgeoisie, 79; industrial, 28; national, 24, 42, 43, 49, 75, 77, 125
Brady Plan, 47, 157
Brandt, Willy, 8
Braun, Oscar, 41, 42
Brazil, xii, 4, 5, 15, 52, 53, 56, 73, 89–107, 124; economic crisis in, xii, 13, 14, 89, 148; economic stabilization in, 98–9; economic transformation in, 18; federalism in, 92–3; political party system in, 93–4; *Real* plan, 18, 89, 90, 96, 99–101; rescue package for, 100
British Empire: Argentina's dependence on, 28–9, 32; decline of, 26
Bucaram, Abdala, 143, 145, 146
Bucaram, Assad, 135
Buenos Aires, growth of, 28
Bunge, Alejandro, 29
bureaucracy, 97, 117, 165, 167; as clientelist mechanism, 6

Mexican Telephone Workers' Union
(STRM), 170
Mexico, xii, 4, 5, 6, 8, 11, 12, 15, 17, 18, 49,
137; authoritarianism in, 152–3;
clientelism in, 154–5, 169–72;
corporatism in, 153–4, 166–9; entry into
GATT, 157; populism in, 150–81
Mexico City, mayoral elections in, 172, 174
migration, 27; in Argentina, 25, 28, 32, 33;
to Santiago, 69
Miller, Hurtado, 122
Mitterrand, François, 84
modernization, 16, 94, 152, 155, 165, 170,
185, 192, 193, 198
Movement of the Revolutionary Left (MIR
– Chile), 75
Movimiento Libertad (ML – Peru), 117
MRTA guerrilla movement (Peru), 116
Muñoz Ledo, Porfirio, 164

National Action Party (PAN – Mexico),
155, 158, 160, 172, 173
National Confederation of Industry (CNI
– Brazil), 91
National Confederation of Commerce
(CNC – Brazil), 91
National Confederation of Workers in
Agriculture (CNTAG – Brazil), 91
National Liberation Front (FLN – Algeria),
73
National Liberation Front (FNL – Chile), 71
National Liberation Party (Costa Rica), 197
National Republican Alliance (ARENA –
El Salvador), 195, 196, 197
National Republican Party (Costa Rica),
184
National Society of Agriculture (SNA –
Chile), 64
National Solidarity Programme
(PRONASOL – Mexico), 168, 169, 170,
171, 173
nationalization, 36, 81, 191; in Chile (of
copper industry, 74; of export sector, 4,
62; of US mining companies, 79); in
Peru, 115, 125 (of banks, 117); of
Argentine Central Bank, 35; of
Argentinian debt, 45, 46; neo-liberalism,
xi, 2, 9–12, 22, 47, 89, 96, 108, 119,
132–49; fascist core of, 148; in Brazil,
98; in Ecuador, 141–3; in Mexico,
150–81; in Peru, 122–6; rejected in Peru,
126; shift to, 1, 2, 5, 165

neo-populism, 11; emergence of, 2;
marriage with neo-liberalism, 12
Neves, Tancredo, 96
New International Economic Order, 8
Nicaragua, 183, 186, 188, 189, 190, 191,
193, 196
El Niño, 144
Noboa, Gustavo, 133
North American Free Trade Agreement
(NAFTA), xii, 15, 159, 168

oil crisis, 136
oligarchy, 109; emergence of, 28
oligarquía terrateniente, 27
Onganía, Juan Carlos, 41
open economy, 18, 143; in Argentina, 22–59
Organization of Non-Aligned Nations, 8
Organization of the People in Arms
(ORPA – Guatemala), 189
Ortega, Daniel, 193, 195
Ortiz, Roberto, 33
Ottawa Conference, 30
Overbeek, Henk, 156

Pacto de Solidaridad (Mexico), 157
Palme, Olof, 9
pampas: crop production in, 30; drought
in, 37
Papandreou, Andreas, 84
Paraguay, 15
Party of the Democratic Revolution (PRD
– Mexico), 164, 170, 172, 173
'paternal strike' (Chile), 81
Patria Roja (Peru), 124
Pax Americana, 7
Paz Estenssoro, Victor, 4, 123
Pease, Henry, 120
People's Revolutionary Army (ERP – El
Salvador), 196
Pérez de Cuéllar, Javier, 125
Perón, Eva, 35
Perón, Isabel, 23
Perón, Juan Domingo, 4, 33, 34, 37, 42, 134
Peronism, 18, 34–8, 39, 49, 67, 68, 69, 146;
and structural adjustment, 43–53; rise
of, role of, 22–59; seen as revolutionary
movement, 40
Peru, xii, 4, 5, 6, 11, 12, 18, 65, 146; as
exporter of raw materials, 123; Peruvian
Revolution, 109, 110; populism in, 108–
31; split of left movement in, 109, 124
peso: Argentinian (convertibility of, 46–7;